Antitrust Law and Local Government

Recent Titles from QUORUM BOOKS

Payments in the Financial Services Industry of the 1980s: Conference Proceedings
Federal Reserve Bank of Atlanta, Sponsor

Japanese Business Law and the Legal System
Elliott J. Hahn

YOUTHJOBS: Toward a Private/Public Partnership
David Bresnick

State Government Export Promotion: An Exporter's Guide
Alan R. Posner

Principles for Electric Power Policy
Technology Futures, Inc., and Scientific Foresight, Inc.

The Debt Dilemma of Developing Nations: Issues and Cases
Chris C. Carvounis

Business and Technological Dynamics in Newly Industrializing Asia
Wenlee Ting

Employee Development Programs: An Organizational Approach
Bobby C. Vaught, Frank Hoy, and W. Wray Buchanan

International Accounting: Issues and Solutions
Ahmed Belkaoui

Witness Intimidation: The Law's Response
Michael H. Graham

Transatlantic Trends in Retailing: Takeovers and Flow of Know-How
Madhav P. Kacker

Technology Transfer: Geographic, Economic, Cultural, and Technical Dimensions
A. Coskun Samli, Editor

The Prospects of American Industrial Recovery
John E. Ullmann

Antitrust Law and Local Government

Mark R. Lee

Q
Quorum Books
Westport, Connecticut • London, England

Library of Congress Cataloging in Publication Data

Lee, Mark R., 1949-
Antitrust law and local government.

Bibliography: p.
Includes index.
1. Local government—Law and legislation—United States. 2. Antitrust law—United States. 3. Government liability—United States. I. Title.
KF5300.L43 1985 343.73′072 84-23722
ISBN 0-89930-090-1 (lib. bdg.) 347.30372

Library of Congress Catalog Card Number: 84-23722
ISBN: 0-89930-090-1

First published in 1985 by Quorum Books

Greenwood Press
A division of Congressional Information Service, Inc.
88 Post Road West
Westport, Connecticut 06881

Printed in the United States of America

10 9 8 7 6 5 4 3 2 1

This book is for my Dad and for Shira,
he who could have only imagined her
and she who will only remember him,
and it is for my Mom and for Laney,
who, with love, create that which is imagined and
preserve that which must be remembered.

CONTENTS

FIGURES

ACKNOWLEDGMENTS

It is a pleasure to acknowledge the debts I owe in connection with the publication of this book: to Professor Robert C. Means, now a vice president of Swanson Energy Group in Washington, D.C., whose powerful mind and outstanding teaching sparked my interest in law and economics and established a standard of rigorous analysis to which I have aspired in writing this book; to James V. O'Brien, now of the St. Louis firm of Lewis & Rice, Jeffrey Hine, now of the Cape Girardeau, Missouri, firm of Oliver, Oliver, Waltz & Cook, and Michael Upperman of the class of 1985, Southern Illinois University School of Law, who assisted me so very well with the research required for this book; and to Vera Felts of the Southern Illinois University School of Law, who prepared the entire manuscript (making a word processor perform feats of which even its manufacturer did not think it capable), much of it while I was abroad and thus unavailable for consultation, and still found time to relieve me of many of the burdens routinely borne by authors and provide me with much-needed encouragement.

Antitrust Law and Local Government

INTRODUCTION: IMMOVABLE OBJECT VERSUS IRRESISTIBLE FORCE

In *City of Lafayette v. Louisiana Power & Light*[1] and more recently in *Community Communications Co. v. City of Boulder*[2] cities argued that they were immune from antitrust suits by virtue of their status as political subdivisions of a state.[3] The Supreme Court rejected their argument and effectively relegated them to the same treatment on the merits[4] accorded private enterprises under the Sherman and Clayton Acts.[5] Relegating them to that treatment practically requires sweeping change of some kind because almost all local governments engage in a host of practices which, if engaged in by private enterprises, would be subject to expensive scrutiny and quite possibly condemnation under those statutes as they are now interpreted. Local government and antitrust law, as we now know them, cannot coexist comfortably.

Congress probably lessened the change-causing power of the Court's decisions when it passed the Local Government Antitrust Act of 1984.[6] That Act bars treble damage seeking claimants, except those who filed their claims before September 24, 1984, from obtaining any monetary relief from local governments if the perpetrators of the offenses acted "in an official capacity." This bar will reduce the gain that some potential claimants will expect to realize from the antitrust claims that they might make against local governments,[7] and it will therefore result in the filing of fewer such claims. The fewer the claims that are filed, the less the power of the Court's decisions.

But many claims will still be filed. Obviously, the Local Government Antitrust Act of 1984 will not deter the Federal Trade Commission and the Department of Justice from filing claims in the course of their enforcement work. Nor will it deter many private enterprises from filing claims. Even before the passage of the act, quite a few antitrust claimants against local governments sought only equitable relief, and many of the others must have known that it was unlikely that they would obtain anything else. The plaintiffs in the *Boulder* case were such claimants. The Act creates no bar for them; they may still obtain equitable relief along with "the cost of suit, including a reasonable attorney's fee." In fact, the Act may increase the chances that such claimants will obtain that relief since it renders the remedy at law—monetary damages—inadequate. In any event, it should not reduce the number of claims that these potential claimants file. Nor should it reduce the number filed by those becoming involved in disputes with local governments who, at a rather small incremental cost, could press antitrust claims against them. This group includes anyone who could plausibly challenge the behavior by which they were aggrieved as not only an antitrust offense but also as a deprivation of constitutional rights, a breach of contract, a tort, or the like.

Apparently, there are many who could mount such a challenge; in the reported cases dealing with antitrust claims against local governments, almost all of the claimants did just that. Certainly the antitrust claimants in the *Boulder* and *Lafayette* cases did. This group also includes anyone sued by a local government who could file a colorable antitrust counterclaim attacking behavior intimately connected with the subject matter of the local government's suit. The antitrust claimants in *Lafayette* were such defendants. Even those who would find it expensive to press antitrust claims against local governments will do so if they perceive a reasonable chance of persuading a fact finder that the perpetrators of the offense did not act "in an official capacity."[8] As long as a sizeable number of antitrust claims continue to be made against local governments, the Court's decisions will pack considerable change-causing power—albeit somewhat lessened by the Local Government Antitrust Act of 1984. The Act will probably do no more than slow the pace of sweeping change.

Before the passage of the Local Government Antitrust Act of

1984, it was widely feared that the Court's decisions would transform local government.[9] The Act may ameliorate, but it will hardly eliminate that fear. In an effort to comply with antitrust law, or to avoid the extraordinary expense of antitrust litigation, local governments may choose to pursue fewer ends and pursue them with less effective means. Those that choose to do otherwise may find that they must use their revenues to pay attorneys' fees and discovery costs rather than to support their customary activities. Cassandras have predicted that in some instances, local governments may be unable to effectively protect the health, safety, and welfare of their citizens.[10] It is the novel thesis of this book, however, that when antitrust is "brought to mainstreet,"[11] it will more likely be the interpretation of the antitrust statutes—the common law of antitrust—rather than local government that will be transformed.

Ironically, it is the threat to local government posed by the common law of antitrust that would trigger the transformation. Courts will likely be reluctant to hold local governments liable for practices that they would routinely condemn as anti-competitive if engaged in by a private enterprise. That reluctance could well prompt courts to reexamine the rationale for condemnation to determine whether it applies to the practice when engaged in by a local government and whether it is consistent with the purpose of the antitrust statutes. In almost every case that reexamination would reveal that condemnation can be justified, if at all, only on the basis of either a preference for "smaller," "less advantaged" firms over "larger," "more advantaged" ones or the pursuit of enterprise egalitarianism.[12] Those populist policies, whatever their merit, do not even speak to disputes between local governments, which are populist-preferred institutions, and private enterprises, so courts undertaking the reexamination would presumably find the challenged practices lawful. Local governments would thus emerge unscathed, but not so antitrust law. Courts that had found the practices lawful when engaged in by local governments would be practically bound, under *City of Lafayette* and *City of Boulder*, to disregard the status of the defendant and find them lawful even when engaged in by private enterprises.[13] Several such findings would work a major retrenchment in antitrust doctrine.

Retrenchment, in turn, could and certainly should give way to wholesale reform. Once populist policies were discarded as unhelpful or misleading in determining the legality of some practices, antitrust courts could well begin to doubt their utility in determining the legality of others. It would appear thoughtless or unprincipled to ignore populist policies or bow to them, depending solely upon whether challenged practices had been, or might be, engaged in by local governments. Indeed, the Supreme Court's decisions in the city-immunity cases seemingly bar such a course. So courts might be moved to reject populist policies entirely as a touchstone in interpreting the Sherman and Clayton Acts, and to replace them with the only competing policy, the maximization of consumer welfare.[14] In that event the antitrust juggernaut which the Court unleashed in *City of Lafayette* and *City of Boulder* would not smash local government but instead be redirected by it.

NOTES

1. 435 U.S. 389 (1978).

2. 455 U.S. 40 (1982).

3. They claimed immunity under the general rubric of the "state action exemption," first recognized by the Supreme Court in Parker v. Brown, 317 U.S. 341 (1943). The cities' argument is analyzed in some detail in Chapter 1.

4. As a practical matter, the Court may have also limited the state action antitrust immunity of local governments to about that enjoyed by private enterprises acting at the behest of the state. The only advantage that local governments would appear to have in this respect is that they may be able to substitute their status as political subdivisions of a state for "active state supervision," a requisite for private enterprises claiming state action immunity. Areeda, *Antitrust Immunity for "State Action" after Lafayette*, 95 Harv. L. Rev. 435 (1981).

5. Sherman Act, 15 U.S.C. §§ 1-7 (1976); Clayton Act, Public Law No. 63-212, 38 Stat. 730 (1914) (codified as amended in scattered sections of 15 U.S.C., 28 U.S.C., and 29 U.S.C.).

6. Act of October 24, 1984, Public Law 98-544 (both houses of Congress passed H.R. 6027 on August 8, 1984, and President Reagan signed it on Oct. 24, 1984).

7. For some of those potential claimants, the reduction in expected gain will be small. Many of them will have little hope of proving that

they suffered any damages as a result of a local government's alleged misbehavior and even less hope of proving that whatever damages they did suffer stemmed from an "antitrust injury." *See* Brunswick Corp. v. Pueblo Bowl-O-Mat, Inc., 429 U.S. 477 (1977). These claimants can reasonably expect to obtain "monetary relief" equal only to "the cost of suit, including a reasonable attorney's fee," discounted by the probability of prevailing, and the Local Government Antitrust Act of 1984 will not change that at all. *See* text immediately following.

Of course, claimants who filed before September 24, 1984 (who number "in the hundreds" according to the National Law Journal; *New Antitrust Act May do Little to Stem Suits,* National Law Journal, Dec. 3, 1984, Vol. 7, No. 13, p. 1, col. 4), might still reasonably expect to obtain that relief, and perhaps more. The Act provides that the bar on obtaining monetary relief "shall not apply to cases commenced before the effective date of [the] Act unless the defendant establishes and the court determines in light of all the circumstances, including the stage of litigation and the availability of alternative relief under the Clayton Act, that it would be inequitable not to apply this subsection to a pending case."

8. This group will consist largely of those who can show that the perpetrators failed to discharge their responsibilities to constituents or otherwise breached duties imposed by non-antitrust law. The plaintiffs in Affiliated Capital Corp. v. City of Houston, 519 F. Supp. 991 (S.D. Tex. 1981) *rev'd* 700 F.2d 226 (5th Cir. 1983), *vacated* 714 F.2d 25 (5th Cir. 1984), *rev'd on reh'g (en banc)* 735 F.2d 1555 (5th Cir.), would have belonged to this group. For an analysis of the relationship between such misbehavior and antitrust law see Chapter 8.

9. City of Lafayette v. Louisiana Power & Light Co., 435 U.S. 389, 438-440 (Stewart dissenting). Civiletti, *The Fallout from Community Communications Co. v. City of Boulder: Prospects for a Legislative Solution,* 32 Cath. U.L. Rev. 379, 385-86, 388 (1983); Areeda, *supra* note 4, at 439; Note, *Community Communications Co. v. City of Boulder: The Emasculation of Municipal Immunity from Sherman Act Liability,* 32 Cath. U.L. Rev. 413, 432 (1983). It was also argued that the Court's decisions would dramatically alter the relationships between states and local government, in general, and the "home rule" movement, in particular. 435 U.S. at 434-438 (Stewart dissenting). Civiletti, at 387-89. Bangasser, *Exposure of Municipal Corporations to Liability for Violations of the Antitrust Laws: Antitrust Immunity after the City of Lafayette Decision,* 11 Urb. L. Rev. vii (1979); Comment, *City of Lafayette v. Louisiana Power & Light Co.: Will Municipal Antitrust Liability Doom Effective State-Local Government Relations?,* 36 Wash. & Lee L. Rev. 129 (1979); Note, 32 Cath. U.L. Rev., at 431.

10. Among the better known ones are Justice Rehnquist ("The Court's decision in this case is flawed in two serious respects, and will thereby impede, if not paralyze, local governments' efforts to enact ordinances and regulations aimed at protecting public health, safety, and welfare." 455 U.S. 40, 60 [Rehnquist, J., dissenting]), retired Justice Stewart (435 U.S. 426 [Stewart, J. dissenting]), and former Attorney General Civiletti. Civiletti, *supra* note 9, at 387.

11. The phrase was first used in a speech by former Deputy Assistant Attorney General Joe Sims at the 72d annual conference of the Municipal Finance Officers Association (May 15, 1978). *See also* Sims, *Antitrust Comes to City Hall*, 3 Regulation 35 (1979).

12. In some cases even those inapplicable populist policies would not justify condemnation. *See, e.g.*, Ladue Local Lines, Inc. v. Bi-State Development Agency, 433 F.2d 131 (8th Cir. 1970); Heille v. City of St. Paul, 512 F. Supp. 810 (D. Minn. 1981), *aff'd*, 671 F.2d 1134 (8th Cir. 1982). They are discussed in Chapter 7.

13. The practices include "tying," resale price maintenance, restricting distributors' territories, exclusive dealing, and almost all other refusals to deal, among others.

14. *See* R. Bork, The Antitrust Paradox: A Policy at War with Itself p. 7 and generally (1978).

PART I

LOCAL GOVERNMENT LIABILITY AND ITS IMPACT ON ANTITRUST DOCTRINE

1

THE SEMINAL CASES AND THEIR TEACHING: "SAME TREATMENT"

CITY OF LAFAYETTE

City of Lafayette v. Louisiana Power & Light apparently arose out of a prosaic, albeit rancorous, economic battle between, on the one hand, two municipalities which operated their own utility systems and, on the other, three integrated electric power companies which both supplied them with electricity at wholesale and competed with them for customers at retail. The municipalities brought the battle to court. Pursuing an all-too-common plan of attack,[1] they filed a complaint in which they accused the power companies of violating the federal antitrust statutes.[2] One of the power companies, Louisiana Power & Light (LP&L), responded with what was then a somewhat unusual counterattack. It filed a counterclaim in which it levelled the same accusation against the municipalities. LP&L alleged that the municipalities had violated the antitrust statutes by (1) placing covenants in debentures forbidding utility competition within their boundaries; (2) conspiring with an electric power cooperative to engage in sham litigation designed to forestall the building of a nuclear powered generating plant; and (3) conspiring with that cooperative and a private company to provide electric power for a period longer than permitted under Louisiana law. LP&L also alleged that one of the municipalities, the City of Plaquemine, had violated the federal antitrust statutes by refusing to provide gas and water to customers who resided outside the city limits unless they purchased all of their electricity from it.

The municipalities moved to dismiss the counterclaim on the ground that even if LP&L proved its allegations, it would still not be entitled to any relief since the antitrust statutes are inapplicable to subdivisions of a state. The district court reluctantly agreed, so it granted the motion.[3] On appeal, the Fifth Circuit Court of Appeals reversed the district court, holding that a "subordinate state governmental body is not *ipso facto* exempt from the operation of the antitrust laws."[4] Rather, suggested the court, the conduct of such a governmental body is exempt if it is the type of anticompetitive restraint "contemplated" by the state legislature. The Fifth Circuit ordered a remand for the purpose of determining whether the Louisiana legislature had contemplated the sort of transgressions that the municipalities had allegedly committed.

On writ of certiorari, the Supreme Court affirmed the Fifth Circuit's order. It began its reasoning by invoking the rebuttable presumption that the federal antitrust statutes apply to local governments since local governments are nowhere expressly exempted from their reach. The Court then tested three arguments advanced by the municipalities to determine whether the presumption had been rebutted. The arguments were based upon (1) the predicted consequences of a contrary interpretation for local governments; (2) the purported general purpose of antitrust law; and (3) the *Parker*[5] state action doctrine. The Court's analysis of these arguments is especially important for present purposes because it practically dictates that practices challenged as antitrust offenses be treated the same on the merits regardless of whether local governments or private enterprises use them.

The first argument considered by the Court was that the statutes must not apply to local governments because using, or threatening to use, antitrust sanctions against them would disrupt their essential operations, a result which those statutes were not designed to achieve. The Court treated the argument as if it were addressed solely to the availability of antitrust remedies separate and apart from adverse antitrust judgments[6] and so had no difficulty disposing of it.[7] The Court observed that no general principle suggested that local governments should be relieved of the remedies provided in federal statutes. Whether local governments should be relieved of particular remedies provided by the federal antitrust statutes, said the Court, was not an issue ripe for resolution, since a judgment on the merits had not been entered, much less a remedy imposed.

The second argument considered by the Court was that it would be inconsistent with the general purpose of the federal antitrust statutes to apply them to local governments.[8] The municipalities, who relied upon oft-cited rhetoric in the Court's opinions, asserted that that purpose was a populist one. The statutes, they claimed, were designed to check "private power derived from amassed capital or shrewd business practice," thus providing protection against "abuses" of that power.[9] So understood, the statutes had no role to play in limiting the conduct of local governments since they are charged with the responsibility of serving their citizenry, not earning profits for their shareholders, and they are controlled by officials elected by that citizenry.[10] The Court was unpersuaded. It implicitly recognized that the primary purpose of the federal antitrust statutes was to maximize consumer welfare when it asserted that the harm which those statutes were designed to prevent was the "distortion of the rational and efficient allocation of resources and the efficiency of free markets which the regime of competition . . . is thought to engender." The Court maintained that local governments, like private enterprises, could cause that harm because in discharging their responsibilities, different though they might be from those of private enterprises, local governments might seek to benefit at the expense of the welfare of others and succeed in doing so. It doubted that those adversely affected would generally be able to subject the officials of local governments to electoral discipline or to secure relief from a state legislature. In any event, their ability to do so was irrelevant to the application of the antitrust statutes. "In enacting the Sherman Act," stated the Court, ". . . Congress mandated competition as the polestar by which all must be guided in ordering their business affairs. It did not leave this fundamental national policy to the vagaries of the political process, but . . . to be administered by neutral courts . . . without regard to the amount of influence [an enterprise] might have with local or state legislatures."[11] Thus, the Court concluded, it would be consistent with the purpose of the federal antitrust statutes to apply them to local governments.[12]

The third and final argument considered by the Court was that the federal antitrust statutes are inapplicable to local governments under the *Parker* state action doctrine since local governments are merely subdivisions of a state and exercise only those powers granted by it.[13] The Court was largely unpersuaded because it did not believe that the principles of federalism underlying *Parker* required that all the deference accorded sovereign states also be accorded non-sovereign local governments. The Court did not reject the argument in its entirety, however, for it recognized that local governments might take allegedly anticompetitive action on behalf of the state. Some deference was therefore required, but only when local governments engaged in certain conduct.

No one test for identifying exempt conduct commanded the support of a majority of the Court. Four justices subscribed to a local-conduct/state-policy test, a test that they seemed to think was embodied in *Goldfarb v. Virginia State Bar Ass'n.*[14] In *Goldfarb* the Court held that the enforcement of a lawyers' minimum fee schedule by the Virginia State Bar Association could be scrutinized under the federal antitrust statutes. It could be scrutinized even though the Bar Association was a state agency because it was not directed or authorized by the Virginia legislature or supreme court, and was therefore not undertaken by the State as sovereign. The plurality adopted the view that the conduct of local government should be considered as undertaken by the State as sovereign, and therefore shielded under *Parker,* if engaged in "pursuant to state policy to displace competition with regulation or monopoly public service."[15] According to them, an inquiry had to be made in connection with any challenged conduct to determine whether it was authorized or directed by the State. That inquiry had to be made, at least initially, by the trial judge, so the plurality ordered a remand. They advised the judge, however, that he should respond to the inquiry with a yes if he found "from the authority given a governmental entity to operate in a particular area, that the legislature contemplated the kind of action complained of."[16]

Chief Justice Burger supplied the fifth vote for affirmance, but he subscribed to a "governmental"/"proprietary" test for identifying exempt conduct.[17] Under that test, "governmental" conduct was always exempt, but the "proprietary" kind was so only if it were undertaken pursuant to a state policy to displace competition with regulation or monopoly public service and was no more restrictive of competition than necessary to effectuate that policy. Since he believed that the conduct challenged by LP&L was unquestionably "proprietary," he concurred in the remand.

CITY OF BOULDER

In *Community Communications Co. v. City of Boulder* the Court made it clear to all doubters that it meant what the plurality had said in *City of Lafayette*. The case arose out of a power struggle between an established cable television company, Community Communications Company (CCC), and a municipality, the City of Boulder, over entry into that portion of the Boulder market which had not been wired for service. In 1964 the Boulder City Council had granted CCC's predecessor in interest a non-exclusive, revocable twenty-year permit to provide cable television service within the city limits. Since then, CCC, or its predecessor, had provided that service to the University Hill area of Boulder, where 20 percent of the city's population resided, and where, for geographical reasons, broadcast signals cannot be received. Until 1979, CCC made no effort to materially enlarge its service area. Then, wishing to take advantage of recently developed technology, and perhaps fearing loss of potential business to new entrants, CCC notified the Council that it planned to do just that.

The Council was alarmed. It believed that once a cablecaster wired an area, other cablecasters would most likely refrain from offering their services there. Cablecasters would compete, it thought, only for the permit to wire. Accordingly, the Council feared that if CCC executed its plan, the people of Boulder would be denied the benefits of competition. Therefore, the Council moved to block CCC while it created a mechanism through which cablecasters could compete for permits to wire one or more portions of Boulder. It enacted an "emergency" ordinance which prohibited CCC from enlarging its service area for three months.

Boulder claimed that it was simply exercising the plenary home rule powers it had long enjoyed under the Home Rule Amendment to the Colorado Constitution. Under that amendment, Boulder's charter and ordinances supercede conflicting state statutes insofar as they bear on local matters.[18] For the purpose of the appeal, the Supreme Court assumed that the Colorado courts had held that cable television service is one of those local matters.[19]

CCC challenged the ordinance under the federal antitrust statutes. It persuaded the district court that it would likely prove, at a trial on the merits, that the city had committed an offense, so the district court preliminarily enjoined the enforcement of the ordinance.[20] The Tenth Circuit Court of Appeals, however, lifted the preliminary injunction.[21] It held that the ordinance could not be scrutinized under the federal antitrust statutes since it furthered no proprietary interest of Boulder's and since it was the sole expression of state policy on the subject matter. The Supreme Court reversed.

The Court began its analysis by reaffirming that the applicability of the federal antitrust statutes does not turn simply on the status of the defendant, but rather on the nature of the challenged conduct. Embracing the plurality's position in *City of Lafayette*, it ruled that the statutes are applicable to local governments except insofar as *Parker* shields their conduct. According to the Court, *Parker* shields only that conduct engaged in by local governments pursuant to a clearly articulated and affirmatively expressed state policy to displace competition with regulation or public-service monopoly. *Parker* shields no other conduct, not even the conduct of a municipality, like Boulder, which exercises all of the legislature's power and exercises it to the exclusion of the legislature.

The Court next considered whether Boulder had established an adequate state mandate for its conduct, an issue on which it bore the burden of persuasion. Boulder acknowledged that it had to show that Colorado, as a State, had "contemplated" its moratorium on wiring. It argued that the Court could infer that contemplation from the authority given the city under the Home Rule Amendment to regulate the local cable television market. The Court was unpersuaded. Boulder's test was right, but its application of the test was wrong. To permit a municipality to do whatever it wished, which is what Colorado had done for Boulder, was not, according to the Court, to "contemplate" a particular kind of conduct. The Court perceived that Colorado had no discernible policy with respect to cable television but rather was decidedly neutral. In making a general grant of power, Colorado had not authorized or directed Boulder to prohibit CCC from expanding its business.

THE MAJOR AND MINOR LESSONS OF *CITY OF LAFAYETTE* AND *CITY OF BOULDER*

Under *City of Lafayette* and *City of Boulder* most actions taken by local governments may be scrutinized under the federal antitrust statutes. Those decisions expressly "exempt" only actions "contemplated" by the relevant state legislature, and that exemption will likely be unavailable to, or unavailing for, most defendant local governments. It will likely be unavailable because in most cases the relevant state legislature will not have contemplated the challenged actions.[22] Legislative contemplation is a scarce resource.[23] Lawmakers can consider only a limited number of problems and devote only limited attention to each one. Until *City of Lafayette* was decided, it would have been impolitic, and perhaps improvident, for lawmakers to allocate much, if any, contemplation to the myriad ways in which local governments might use the powers delegated to them to cope with the prosaic problems that they routinely confront. It is improbable that any well-organized group demanded such contemplation; in fact, representatives of local governments probably discouraged such contemplation when seeking broad grants of power. Even where the exemption ought to be available, it will likely be unavailing due to lack of proof. Local governments, who will bear the burden of persuading courts that their actions were contemplated by the superior state legislature, will almost always have to rely on either the imprecise language of pre-*City of Lafayette* enabling statutes or constitutional provisions like Colorado's Home Rule Amendment, unaccompanied by any legislative history.[24] It is doubtful that courts, at least those lacking a preconceived determination to find immunity,[25] will be easily persuaded by such meager evidence, particularly when plaintiffs' counsel will have painted the challenged actions as pernicious efforts to restrain trade or to monopolize.[26] The Supreme Court was certainly not persuaded in *City of Boulder*.

"Limited immunity" is, however, only the minor lesson of these seminal cases. The practical importance of limited immunity largely depends upon how the conduct of local governments is treated on the merits. Although they contain some feeble disclaimers,[27] the opinions speak, albeit implicitly, to that treatment.[28] The results reached, the language employed, and the reasoning used all suggest that the principles to be used in evaluating the conduct of local governments shall be the same ones used to evaluate the conduct of private enterprises. That is the major lesson of *City of Lafayette* and *City of Boulder*.

In both cases local governments were relegated to the same treatment accorded private enterprises. Apparently, the Court reached those results purposefully. In *City of Lafayette* the Court explained, "[Our decision] means . . . that when the State itself has not directed or authorized an anticompetitive practice, the State's subdivisions in exercising their delegated power must obey the antitrust laws."[29] Unless the Court was employing doublespeak, its language, quoted with approval in *City of Boulder*,[30] must mean that substantive antitrust principles apply with equal force to non-immune local governments and private enterprises. Any other reading of that language would be inconsistent with the Court's rejection of the proposition that the applicability of the federal antitrust statutes turns on the status of the defendant.

The Court's analysis of the municipalities' arguments in *City of Lafayette* also reinforces the major lesson of the seminal cases. In rejecting their first argument, the unintended dire consequences argument, the Court seemed to recognize that pursuant to its decision trial judges would be bound to apply the same substantive antitrust principles to all defendants. Only the application of those principles could lead to unintended dire consequences. The Court merely suggested that these consequences could be avoided by limiting the remedies available to prevailing plaintiffs. In rejecting the municipalities' second argument, the populist purpose argument, the Court observed that local governments, like private enterprises, could bring about the precise harm that the federal antitrust statutes were designed to prevent.

Presumably, conduct that causes such harm should be considered a violation no matter who engages in it. That could happen only if the same substantive antitrust principles were applied to all defendants. Finally, in accepting only an attenuated version of the municipalities' third argument, the *Parker* argument, the Court ruled that local governments are entitled to no more immunity than that enjoyed by state agencies under *Goldfarb v. Virginia State Bar Ass'n*. Surely, they are entitled to no more lenient treatment on the merits. On that point *Goldfarb* is instructive. There the conduct of the defendant bar association was adjudged illegal *per se* under the same principles that would have been used to evaluate the conduct of a private enterprise.

Applying different substantive antitrust principles to local government defendants would mean, in effect, assessing the legality of challenged practices on the basis of not only the goal of the Sherman and Clayton Acts, as ordinarily conceived, but also the conflicting goals purportedly being pursued by those defendants. It is difficult to believe that the Court intended that judges do any such thing. In the first place, in *National Society of Professional Engineers v. United States*[31] the Court explicitly rejected such multiple goal analysis as improper under the antitrust statutes. That opinion was rendered subsequent to *City of Lafayette*, and it seems unlikely that the Court intended to overrule it in *City of Boulder*, a case in which the question of proper antitrust analysis was never raised.[32] In the second place, if judges were to engage in such analysis, they would be put to the task of balancing non-comparable goals. They would find that task intellectually problematic at best, and since it could not be subject to systematic review, a large number of judges might very well shirk it. Balancing goals might degenerate into giving decisive weight to one of them. Then, either local governments would be subject to the same substantive principles as private enterprises or local governments would enjoy functional, although not nominal, immunity, contrary to decisions of the Court. To reduce the risk of such degeneration, judges would have to evaluate both the wisdom of the conflicting goals purportedly being pursued by the local government defendants and the efficacy of the challenged practice in achieving them. The "reasonableness" of the conduct of local governments would then be judged much like the "reasonableness" of the conduct of state governments was judged during the heyday of substantive due process.[33] It is quite unlikely that in deciding *City of Lafayette* and *City of Boulder* the Supreme Court intended to resurrect *Lochner*[34] and like decisions from that era, and it is even less likely that lower courts will so interpret them.

NOTES

1. Municipalities in Indiana, New Jersey, Pennsylvania, and Connecticut, for example, have all employed similar tactics in their battles with private utility companies. *See* City of Mishawaka, Ind. v. American Electric Power Co., Inc., 465 F. Supp. 1320 (N.D. Ind. 1979), *aff'd in part and rev'd in part*, 616 F.2d 976 (7th Cir. 1980), *cert. denied*, 449 U.S. 1096 (1980); City of Newark v. Delmarva Power & Light Co., 467 F. Supp. 763 (D. Del. 1979); Borough of Ellwood City, Pa. v. Pennsylvania Power Co., 462 F. Supp. 1343 (W.D. Penn. 1979); City of Groton v. Connecticut Light & Power Co., 456 F. Supp. 360 (D. Conn. 1978). *See also* Indiana & Michigan Elec. Co. v. City of Anderson, 376 N.E.2d 114 (Ind. Ct. App. 1978). They were no doubt encouraged to do so by the Supreme Court's decision in Otter Tail Power Co. v. United States, 410 U.S. 366 (1973). *Otter Tail* arose out of a similar battle, but the cities involved in it somehow managed to persuade the Antitrust Division of the Department of Justice to employ these tactics on their behalf.

2. The City of Lafayette charged that the power companies monopolized and conspired to restrain trade in the generation, transmission, and distribution of electric power by preventing the construction and operation of competing utility systems. Specifically, the municipality claimed that the power companies were committing antitrust violations "by improperly refusing to wheel power, by foreclosing supplies from markets served by defendants, by engaging in boycotts against petitioners, and by utilizing sham litigation and other improper means to prevent the financing of construction of electrical generation facilities beneficial to petitioners." 435 U.S. 389, 392 n.5 (1977).

3. 1975-1 Trade Cases ¶ 65,948 (E.D. La. 1975).

4. 532 F.2d 431, 434 (5th Cir. 1976).

5. Parker v. Brown, 317 U.S. 341 (1943).

6. In fact, the Court misconstrued the cities' first argument. "Regardless of whether their defense may ultimately succeed at trial", asserted the cities, "merely exposing city governments to injunctions, treble damage liability, and perhaps criminal prosecution under the federal antitrust statutes will produce enormous uncertainty and hes-

itancy among public officials and disserve the public interest. . . . Elected officials may be unwilling to accept the economic and political risks created by the Fifth Circuit's decision." Brief for Petitioners at 20-21, City of Lafayette v. Louisiana Power & Light, 435 U.S. 389 (1978).

7. 435 U.S. 389, 400-02 (1978). The Court's disposition of the cities' unintended-dire-consequences argument, however, is less than completely convincing. It is not altogether clear how the Court could have justified a ruling that prevailing plaintiffs could not recover hitherto mandatory treble damages from local government defendants. *See* 435 U.S. at 442-443 (Blackmun, J., dissenting). Perhaps it would have argued that if liability can be limited on policy grounds not expressed in the antitrust statutes, as it was in Parker v. Brown, 317 U.S. 341 (1943), and Eastern Railroad Presidents Conference v. Noerr Freight, Inc., 365 U.S. 127 (1961), then the availability of a specific remedy could be likewise limited. Rose, *Municipal Activities and the Antitrust Laws after City of Lafayette,* 57 Univ. Det. J. Urb. L. 483, 519 (1979). Even if the Court could have justified such a ruling, it is certainly not clear what antitrust remedies could be accorded those plaintiffs that would not have "dire consequences" for local governments.

8. 435 U.S. 389, 403-08 (1978).

9. Brief for Petitioners at 22, 24, City of Lafayette v. Louisiana Power & Light Co., 435 U.S. 389 (1978).

10. 435 U.S. at 403-06. *See* Brief for Petitioners at 24, City of Lafayette v. Louisiana Power & Light Co., 435 U.S. 389 (1978).

11. 435 U.S. at 406-07.

12. 435 U.S. at 408.

13. *Id.* at 408-13.

14. 421 U.S. 773 (1975).

15. 435 U.S. 389, 413 (1975).

16. 435 U.S. 389, 415 (1975) (quoting the decision of the court of appeals, 532 F.2d 431, 434 [5th Cir. 1976]).

17. 435 U.S. 389, 418-26 (1978) (Burger, J., concurring).

18. Colo. Const. art. XX, § 6.

19. 455 U.S. 40, 53 n.16 (1982). There is no Colorado case which expressly so holds. In Manor Vail Condominium Ass'n v. Vail, 199 Colo. 62, 604 P.2d 1168 (1980), the principal case upon which Boulder relied in this regard, the Colorado supreme court considered an equal protection challenge to a cable television rate regulation. The state court upheld the regulation and merely assumed that the Town of Vail had complete authority to regulate rates without mentioning "home rule" authority.

20. 485 F. Supp. 1035 (D. Colo. 1980).

21. 630 F.2d 704 (10th Cir. 1980).

22. *Cf.* Bangasser, *Exposure of Municipal Corporations to Liability for Violations of the Antitrust Laws: Antitrust Immunity after the City of Lafayette Decision,* 11 Urb. L. Rev. vii, xxxiii (1979) ("States may also be forced, at substantial public expense, to create legislative histories from which the requisite intent can be established.").

23. *See* Williamson, *Assessing Vertical Market Restrictions: Antitrust Ramifications of the Transaction Cost Approach,* 127 U. Pa. L. Rev. 953, 956 (1979); Simon, *Rationality as Process and as Product of Thought,* 68 Am. Econ. Rev. 1 (1978).

24. Bangasser, *supra* note 22, at xxxii. After the *Boulder* opinion was published, representatives of city mayors, county councils and the like, descended upon state capitols to lobby for bills that would purportedly insulate at least some of the conduct of some local governments from antitrust scrutiny. As of November, 1984, the legislatures of Georgia, Illinois, Louisiana, Maryland, North Dakota, Tennessee, Virginia, and Washington had responded by enacting such bills into law. *See* Ga. Code Ann. §§ 23-3701 to -3705 and 69-1617 & -1618 (Cum. Supp. 1984); Illinois Antitrust Act, Ill. Rev. Stat. ch. 38, ¶ 60-12 (1983); 1984 La. Sess. Law Serv. 518 (West); La. Rev. Stat. Ann. § 4791(B) (West Supp. 1983); Md. Ann. Code art. 23A, § 2A; art. 25, § 3D; and art. 25A, § 5A (Cum. Supp. 1983); Md. Ann. Code art. 25B, § 13B (Cum. Supp. 1983); N.D. Cent. Code §§ 40-01-22 & 40-05-02; Tenn. Code Ann. §§ 7-54-101 to -110 (Supp. 1984); Va. Code §§ 56-291.3:7 & 15.1-23.1 (Cum. Supp. 1984); 1984 Wash. Legis. Serv. 126-1 to -4 (West).

Some of these statutes are rather broad. For example, the North Dakota statute simply provides that "All immunity of the state from the provisions of the Sherman . . . Act . . . is hereby extended to any city . . . acting within the scope of the grants of authority contained in [the general enabling laws]. When acting within the scope of the grants of authority contained in [those laws], a city . . . shall be presumed to be acting in furtherance of state policy." It seems rather unlikely that any court would infer from statutes like this one the kind of contemplation required by *Boulder* for local government immunity.

That inference might be drawn, however, from the more narrowly drawn statutes. For example, it might be drawn from the Louisiana statute which authorizes the parishes of Caddo and Bossier to grant exclusive franchises to providers of emergency ambulance service as long as (1) the franchises are granted pursuant to a public auction; (2) the franchises expire in no more than five years, and (3) the franchisees promise to serve all eligible medicare and medicaid recipients. La. Rev. Stat. Ann. § 4791(B) (West Supp. 1983). But, of course, statutes like that one would insulate only a fraction of the conduct of a small number of local governments from antitrust scrutiny.

25. Some courts have evidenced such determination by inferring "contemplation" from nothing more than a statute that happens to deal with the same service in connection with which a local government defendant used a challenged practice. *See* Chapter 2, n.16 and accompanying text.

26. *See, e.g.*, Campbell v. City of Chicago, 1983-2 Trade Cases ¶ 65,684 at 62, 99-196 (N.D. Ill. 1983); Central Iowa Refuse Systems, Inc. v. Des Moines Metropolitan Solid Waste Agency, 715 F.2d 419, 427 (8th Cir. 1983); Springs Ambulance Service, Inc. v. City of Rancho Mirage, Cal., 1983-2 Trade Cases ¶ 65,646 (C.D. Cal. 1983).

27. *See* 455 U.S. at 56 n.20.

28. Cirace, *An Economic Analysis of the "State-Municipal Action" Antitrust Cases*, 61 Tex. L. Rev. 481, 489 (1982); Comment, *Alternative Approaches to Municipal Antitrust Liability*, 11 Fordham Urb. L.J. 63 (1982) (Believing that "same treatment" is inappropriate, the student author advocates what he calls "qualified immunity" for local government. "At a minimum," he asserts, "anticompetitive municipal conduct involving 'integral operations in areas of traditional government functions should be exempt.' " *Id.* at 83 (quoting National League of Cities v. Usery, 426 U.S. 833, 852 (1976)).

29. 435 U.S. 389, 416 (1978).

30. 455 U.S. 40, 57 (1982).

31. 435 U.S. 679 (1978).

32. It seems especially unlikely that the Court meant to overrule, *sub silento*, *National Society of Professional Engineers v. United States* in *City of Boulder* because Justice Rehnquist discussed that possibility explicitly in his dissent. 455 U.S. 40, 65-68 (1982) (Rehnquist, J., dissenting).

33. *Cf.* Civiletti, *The Fallout from Community Communications Co. v. City of Boulder: Prospects for a Legislative Solution*, 32 Cath. U.L. Rev. 379, 387 (1983) (the former attorney general discusses the drawbacks of using the "reasonableness 'standard' "); Note, *Community Communications Co. v. City of Boulder: The Emasculation of Municipal Immunity from Sherman Act Liability*, 32 Cath. U.L. Rev. 433 (1983); Comment, *supra* note 28, at 81-82.

34. Lochner v. New York, 198 U.S. 45 (1905).

2

THE FALLOUT FROM THE "SAME TREATMENT" LESSON: THREAT AND REEXAMINATION

WHAT LOCAL GOVERNMENTS WILL DO IF THE ANTITRUST STATUTES ARE INTERPRETED AS THEY ARE NOW

As conscientious students of the Supreme Court's "same treatment" lesson, managers of local governments will find that many practices which they use routinely are subject to serious challenge and perhaps condemnation under the antitrust statutes as they are now interpreted. The most common ones are (1) agreeing with a supplier, or a purchaser, not to buy from, or sell to, one or more of his competitors;[1] (2) constraining the market behavior of a supplier;[2] (3) selling a good on the condition that buyers also purchase another one offered by the local government;[3] (4) selling services, and less frequently products, at prices that are "below costs";[4] and (5) treating an actual or potential supplier, or purchaser, less favorably than one or more of his competitors, or in ways proscribed by laws other than the antitrust statutes.[5] It is highly unlikely that any of these practices would diminish consumer welfare. Nevertheless, lawyers for those unhappy with the marketing or procurement decisions of local governments will have no trouble drafting complaints in which those practices are characterized as Sherman or Clayton Act offenses, like boycotting, resale price maintenance, tying, predatory pricing, or monopoly misuse.[6] Under the prevailing common law of antitrust, such complaints would most likely survive motions to dismiss and even motions for summary judgment based on limited discovery. Indeed, they might very well serve as the basis for a successful suit.

It would therefore become far more costly to use these practices. Managers of local governments who did so would personally bear substantial adverse risks. In the event of litigation they could have their time and energy diverted to unrewarding, and perhaps unpleasant, tasks like answering voluminous interrogatories or being deposed. In the event of an adverse judgment they could suffer considerable opprobrium and conceivably job loss. After all, an antitrust suit could financially cripple or even bankrupt most local governments.[7] Treasuries could be substantially depleted by the costs of defense and emptied by an award of treble damages, costs, and attorneys' fees (the probability of which the new legislation has reduced, but not to zero). Accordingly, well-adapted managers would tend to reduce their use of these practices.[8]

That reduction, however, would also be costly. Presumably, managers have used these practices primarily because they are the least costly means for achieving a variety of ends, ends which many seem to believe are desirable. Obviously, to pursue those ends without using these means would usually be more expensive—sometimes prohibitively so. Managers might substantially curtail, or even scrap, programs which they believed could not be implemented in a cost-effective manner without engaging in these practices. For example, agreeing, on behalf of all citizens, to purchase quick-response, advanced life support ambulance service (or any other collective good)[9] from one provider might be the only economical way to secure its availability.[10] If so agreeing would prompt a colorable antitrust claim from one or more of the provider's competitors, however, the managers of local governments might not attempt to secure the availability of such service. Or, for another example, granting territorially-limited franchises to cablecasters might be the key to ensuring, at reasonable cost, that they honor their commitments to provide state-of-the-art cable television service.[11] If granting such franchises would prompt those firms disappointed with their territories to file colorable antitrust claims, however, managers of local governments might permit relatively widespread welching. The same would be true for many services supplied by firms that would enjoy economies of scale and first-mover advantages.[12] Such programs are commonly considered desirable[13] and certainly inoffensive from an antitrust perspective. In any event, they are the stuff of local government. So, the Supreme Court's "same treatment" lesson might well change the very nature of local government if the antitrust statutes are interpreted as they are now.

WHAT JUDGES WILL DO IF LOCAL GOVERNMENT IS SO THREATENED

To sum up the preceding section, barring a major change in the common law of antitrust, managers of local government would tend to respond to the Supreme Court's "same treatment" lesson by reducing their use of several common practices that could be subject to serious, and perhaps successful, challenge as restraints of trade or monopolizing devices. It is unlikely, however, that they would forego those practices entirely. Managers might not themselves bear all of the costs of using them. Of the managers who do, some will be optimistic or ignorant and therefore underestimate those costs. Others will estimate the costs correctly but reckon that they will be exceeded by the benefits of using those practices to implement highly valued programs. Local governments, then, will continue to be named as defendants in antitrust suits.

Each trial judge presiding over such a suit will realize, or be made to realize, that permitting the suit to continue beyond quite preliminary stages may impair the financial health of the defendant local government and threaten the traditional functioning of all local governments. He will note, of course, that an adverse judgment would be more catastrophic still. These prospects will tend to make him uncomfortable. He will likely find it difficult to justify them in terms of his own values, the values subscribed to by the legal and lay communities in which he operates, or any purpose commonly attributed to the antitrust statutes. This discomfort is healthy. It is the kind that powers the evolution of the common law—adaptation by judges to changes in the economic, social, and intellectual environment.[14]

To avoid these uncomfortable consequences, some judges may

dispose of antitrust suits against local governments on intellectually suspect grounds unrelated to the merits of the plaintiff's complaint, although they may do so without any intention to deceive. They may do so in at least five ways. First, they may rule that the local government is immune on the basis of state legislation whose relationship to the challenged practice is primarily in the nature of word association. In these cases the local government will have used the practice in connection with the provisioning, purchasing, or regulating[15] of some service, and that service will have been the subject of state legislation. Although the legislation will not speak to the practice, explicitly or implicitly, the court will insist that the legislature "contemplated" its use.[16] Second, some judges may hold that they have no jurisdiction, blinding themselves to the obvious effect that the local government's conduct is likely to have on interstate commerce.[17] Third, they may refuse to see any combination between the local government and some other entity where there clearly is one.[18] Fourth, they may accord the local government defenses, like "good faith," not accorded private enterprises.[19] Fifth, they may rule that the challenged practice is "reasonable," purporting to weigh the anticompetitive effects of the challenged practice against the public interest being served by the local government.[20]

Some judges, however, will no doubt be more uncomfortable with such dispositions than with the consequences of permitting antitrust suits against local governments to proceed to full-fledged discovery, trial, and judgment. These judges may be prompted to reexamine the challenged practices in light of first principles. They will ask: What is the real objection to the challenged practice, even when it is engaged in by a private enterprise? Would sustaining the challenge on the basis of that objection be consistent with the purpose of the antitrust statutes?

NOTES

1. This practice is usually labelled a refusal to deal, a boycott (usually of the Klor's v. Broadway-Hale, 359 U.S. 207 (1959), variety), exclusive dealing, or, when used in connection with a highly specialized capital

asset (an "essential facility"), monopolization. It is discussed in Chapter 4.

2. This practice is usually labelled resale price maintenance, maximum price-fixing (of the Albrecht v. The Herald Co., 390 U.S. 145 (1968), variety), or a territorial or customer restriction on distribution. It is discussed in Chapter 5.

3. This practice is usually labelled tying. It is discussed in Chapter 6.

4. This practice is usually labelled predatory pricing. It is discussed in Chapter 7.

5. This practice is usually labelled a misuse (or abuse) of monopoly, a boycott, once again of the *Klor's* variety, or an unfair business practice. It is discussed in Chapter 8.

6. *See* Areeda, *Antitrust Immunity for "State Action" after Lafayette*, 95 Harv. L. Rev. 435, 439 (1981).

7. *Lafayette*, 435 U.S. at 440-441 (Stewart dissenting) (In that case Louisiana Power & Light sought $540 million ($180 million trebled) on only one of its claims against the defendant local governments. 435 U.S. at 440); *Federal Antitrust Laws and Local Government Activities: Hearings Before the Senate Comm. on the Judiciary*, 97th Cong., 2nd Sess. 2 (1982) (testimony of William F. Baxter, Assistant Attorney General, Antitrust Division); Washington Post, Mar. 19, 1982, at B3 (remarks of Sally Lackey of Maryland Municipal League); *id.*, Jan. 14, 1982, at A2; Comment, *Antitrust Treble Damages as Applied to Local Government Entities: Does the Punishment Fit the Defendant?* 1980 Ariz. St. L.J. 411.

8. *Boulder*, 455 U.S. at 60 (Rehnquist, J., dissenting); *Lafayette*, 435 U.S. at 439 (Stewart, J., dissenting); *Local Government Antitrust Liability—The Boulder Decision: Hearings Before the Senate Comm. on the Judiciary*, 97th Cong., 2nd Sess. (1982) (statements of Tracy Stallings, Mayor, City of Carrollton, Georgia, and Frank B. Gummey III, Florida Municipal Attorneys' Ass'n); Civiletti, *The Fallout from Community Communications Co. v. City of Boulder: Prospects for a Legislative Solution*, 32 Cath. U.L. Rev. 379, 386 (1983).

9. "*[C]ollective goods* are those for which consumption by one person in a given group of people does not diminish the amount of that good available for any other person in that group (once the goods are produced). For 'private' goods on the other hand, more for one person leaves less for someone else." A. Alchian & W. Allen, Exchange and Production: Competition, Coordination, and Control p. 122 (2d ed. 1977).

10. *See* Gold Cross Ambulance v. City of Kansas City, 538 F. Supp. 956 (W.D. Mo. 1982), *aff'd*, 705 F.2d 1005 (8th Cir. 1983), *petition for cert.*

filed ______U.S.L.W. ______(U.S. July 25, 1983) No. 83-138 (analyzed in Chapter 4).

11. *See* Community Communications Co. v. City of Boulder, Colo. (*Boulder II*), 660 F.2d 1370 (10th Cir. 1981) (analyzed in Chapter 5).

12. The phrase is Oliver Williamson's [O. Williamson, Markets and Hierarchies: Analysis and Antitrust Implications pp. 34-35 (1975); Williamson, *The Vertical Integration of Production: Market Failure Considerations*, 61 Am. Econ. Rev. 112, 116 (1971)], but I may have used it more broadly than he did. He used it to refer primarily to the information advantages, acquired in a learning-by-doing fashion, accruing to the initial contractor. I have used it to refer to other advantages as well. See the discussion in Chapter 5.

13. Civiletti, *The Fallout from Community Communications Co. v. City of Boulder: Prospects for a Legislative Solution*, 32 Cath. U.L. Rev. 387 (1983).

14. K. Llewellyn, The Common Law Tradition: Deciding Appeals (1960).

15. Regulating is often a form of purchasing. The local government, acting as an "agent" for the resident ultimate consumers, enters into what is in effect a long-term agreement with a provider which establishes the general framework pursuant to which a service will be bought and sold. Much of the implementation of that agreement is what we call "regulating." Goldberg, *Regulation and Administered Contracts*, 7 Bell J. Econ. 426 (1976).

16. *See, e.g.*, Gold Cross Ambulance v. City of Kansas City, 538 F. Supp. 956 (W.D. Mo. 1982), *aff'd*, 705 F.2d 1005 (8th Cir. 1983), *petition for cert. filed* ______U.S.L.W. ______(U.S. July 25, 1983) No. 83-138 discussed in Chapter 4.

17. *See, e.g.*, Heille v. City of St. Paul, Minn., 512 F. Supp. 810 (D. Minn. 1981), *aff'd*, 671 F.2d 1134 (8th Cir. 1982) (discussed in Chapter 7).

18. Venderstar, *Liability of Municipalities under the Antitrust Laws: Litigation Strategies*, 32 Cath. U.L. Rev. 395, 402-03 (1983). *See, e.g.*, Greyhound Rent-A-Car, Inc. v. City of Pensacola, 676 F.2d 1380 (11th Cir. 1982), *cert. denied*, 459 U.S. 1171 (1983) (discussed in Chapter 8). This approach has also been advocated by some commentators. *See, e.g.*, Slater, *Antitrust and Government Action: A Formula for Narrowing Parker v. Brown*, 69 Nw. U.L. Rev. 71, 77-78 (1974).

19. Rose, *Municipal Activities and the Antitrust Laws after City of Lafayette*, 57 Univ. Det. J. Urb. L. 483, 519 (1979); Posner, P., *The Proper Relationship Between State Regulations and the Federal Antitrust Laws*, 49 N.Y.U. L. Rev. 728–732 (1974). In effect, that may be what the court did in Mason City Center Associates v. City of Mason City, Iowa, 671 F.2d 1146, 1149 (8th Cir. 1982).

20. This substantive due process approach has been advocated, although not always by name, by some judges as well as commentators. *See, e.g.*, Cantor v. Detroit Edison Co., 428 U.S. 579, 610-13 (1976) (Blackmun, J., concurring); Klitzke, *Antitrust Liability of Municipal Corporations: The Per Se Rule vs. The Rule of Reason—A Reasonable Compromise*, 1980 Ariz. St. L.J. 253; Bangasser, *Exposure of Municipal Corporations to Liability for Violations of the Antitrust Laws: Antitrust Immunity after the City of Lafayette Decision*, 11 Urb. L. Rev. vii, xxxiii n.109 (1979); Posner, *supra* note 19, at 714; Slater, *supra* note 18, at 71, 102-09.

3

REEXAMINATION TO RETRENCHMENT: THE INTELLECTUAL PROCESS

To discover the true objection to a challenged practice, the judge will have to engage in a two-step intellectual process. Initially, he will have to ask: What functions are likely to be served by the practice? Once he ascertains them, he will then have to ask: According to what principles are those functions undesirable?

Neither question will be easy to answer, but the first will probably be more difficult than the second. To ascertain the functions likely to be served by the practice, the judge will have to grasp economic realities. That may prove an arduous task for which he may find himself inadequately trained. His principal mentors will have been law professors. In their work they tend to stress "macro-choices" to the exclusion of marginal ones, and, at least implicitly, to use models of human behavior that focus on static considerations instead of dynamic ones. These tendencies may be well suited to achieving certain pedagological goals. For example, using static models of behavior may yield considerable insight into doctrines that are based on them. But by so teaching, they reinforce habits of the mind that tend to obscure their students' vision of economic reality. This perceptual problem may be inadvertently compounded by those law professors who focus on what legislators and judges command people to do rather than on how people respond to those commands. This focus often leads students to confuse what economic actors ought to do and what they do do.

Even if the judge is up to the task of grasping economic realities, however, the allure of "literalistic jurisprudence" may lead him to stray from it entirely. By "literalistic jurisprudence" I mean resolving disputes largely on the basis of whether plaintiff's counsel "proves," by analogy necessarily, that some pejorative label "fits" a practice.[1] Such jurisprudence is a siren for the judge who is attempting to honestly navigate his way through the treacherous intellectual waters of an antitrust case. Antitrust labels, which skilled plaintiff's counsel can plausibly affix to almost any practice, tend to be appealing metaphors, like "boycott" or "predatory pricing." They usually invoke the image of the market as a jungle in which the large prey on the small.[2] The label used may be so appealing that the judge is tempted to accept it as the true objection to the challenged practice. If he gives in to that temptation, he will have been seduced by the siren's song.

If he resists it, however, then, in almost all cases in which a local government is a principal defendant, he will be able to make some general, but powerful, deductions about the functions that the challenged practice was likely supposed to serve. A description of how he would do that, however, must await an explanation of why he would focus on what the practice was supposed to do rather than what it did do. In brief the explanation is that that focus is consistent with, and probably dictated by, the consumer welfare goal of the antitrust laws. In most cases an inquiry into the actual impact of a particular practice would be extraordinarily time-consuming and, in the end, fruitless.[3] Even if that were not so, however, it would still be inefficient to make it. A practice would fail to serve its supposed function only if its users miscalculated or "misbehaved." If they miscalculated, then subjecting them to antitrust sanctions would be unnecessary since the market would punish them. Worse still, subjecting them to those sanctions would also deter some others from using the practice "correctly" because they would be unwilling to risk the possibility that they might also miscalculate or that a court might err in assessing the actual impact of the practice. If the users "misbehaved," took advantage of, or "sold out" their principals, then the antitrust laws would not even speak to their conduct. Those laws are simply not designed to limit opportunistic behavior on the part of agents.[4] They are certainly not designed to prevent local politicians and bureaucrats from taking advantage of or "selling out" their constituents. If they were so designed, then in applying them to local government defendants federal courts would have to operate as superlegislatures.

The judge's deductions about the function that the challenged practice was supposed to serve will rest on two foundations. One will be his observations about the economic context in which the practice was used. The other will be the assumption that local governments act to maximize the wealth of their residents, just as similarly situated private enterprise agents would do for their principals. That assumption may seem peculiar because, as a generally applicable statement of fact, it is hopelessly inaccurate. But it is mandated by *City of Lafayette* and *City of Boulder*. In those opinions the Court declared its intention to have them interpreted so that, except incidentally, they would not generally constrain the political process.[5] In particular, the Court made it clear that it did not want its decision on immunity to substantially limit local governments from taking actions that politicians believed promoted the interest of some or all of their constituents. The only effective way to honor both the Court's decision and its intention would be to evaluate the conduct of local governments on the assumption that it is designed to maximize the wealth of residents. If, on that assumption, the conduct amounts to an antitrust offense, then it is one; otherwise, it is not. The political context of the practice is irrelevant. Thus, although the mandated assumption is inaccurate, it is useful for the purpose of confining antitrust law to its proper sphere. Moreover, making it is consistent with the Court's reasoning that local governments should be subject to scrutiny under the antitrust laws precisely because of what they might do in pursuit of that wealth-maximization goal.[6] The Court's concerns were clearly prompted by predictions based on classical microeconomic theory, not public choice theory.

The remaining portion of this chapter describes and analyzes the general intellectual process by which a conscientious judge would use the mandated assumption, along with his observations about economic context, to deduce the likely functions of any practice.

Ordinarily, the practice will have been used as an integral part of a complex sales transaction in which the local government may have been the supplier, the purchaser, or, more likely, the agent for those occupying one of those positions.[7] In antitrust parlance, such practices are called vertical restraints.[8] On the basis of that observation alone, the judge will be able to deduce that the challenged practice was almost certainly supposed to serve some instrumental function in effectuating the transaction. Then, using the mandated assumption, he will realize that, generally speaking, that function must have been to secure the benefits which are the subject of the transaction or to reduce the costs of making it. Indeed, in a large number of cases it will be clear to the judge that without the practice the transaction would not have taken place because the benefits would have appeared ephemeral or the costs prohibitive. Of course, the judge will want to make more specific deductions about the function of the challenged practice on the basis of more intricate observations. With only his general deductions in hand, however, the judge will still be able to tackle the second inquiry: According to what principles is that function undesirable?

Whatever the principle may be, it must speak to the likely effects of the transaction, or of ones like it. Antitrust law is concerned with the effects of economic activity. Although some activity is condemned without an elaborate inquiry into its actual effects under the so-called "rule" of *per se* illegality, that is done only because those effects are so likely to be undesirable that making the inquiry would be wasteful.[9] Because of the instrumental relationship between the practice and the transaction, the only effects of interest here are those of the transaction. They will be of two kinds: those that relate to the creation of wealth, what antitrust scholars usually call consumer welfare, and those that relate to the distribution of wealth, who gains and who loses. It is commonly considered good to create more wealth. On that principle, however, the transaction, or ones like it, would almost certainly be deemed desirable. The parties to it will have perceived themselves as better off for having entered into the transaction unless one of them made a miscalculation.[10] Otherwise they would not have agreed to the exchange. The same observation may be made about the parties to any sales transaction. Thus, viewed statically, such transactions tend to create wealth.[11] Viewed dynamically, they certainly do. By entering into them, producers and consumers tend to shift resources to higher-value uses.

To say that sales transactions tend to be wealth-creating is not to say that everyone will be happy about them—quite the contrary. The parties themselves will be unhappy in the sense that they would have preferred to promise less than they did. In fact, if the penalty for acting opportunistically is small enough, some will renege on their promises while trying to hold others to theirs. Would-be parties will be unhappy in the sense that they would have preferred to participate in the transaction if they could have done so on their own terms. Such unhappiness reflects the fact that all of us wish that we could obtain what we want without giving up as much as we do. On each occasion that it is brought home to us that our wish is not going to be granted, we perceive ourselves as less well off than we would have been had it been fulfilled. That wishes are not fulfilled, however, does not mean that we have less wealth. To include wish fulfillment in the concept of wealth would rob the concept of any useful meaning. So to say that sales transactions tend to be wealth-creating is to say that after they are made the total personal value attached by the owners to the goods and services exchanged tends to be larger than it was before.[12]

Only two possible exceptions to the general rule that sales transactions create wealth merit discussion. First, certain sales transactions may be, in large part, transfer payments.[13] For example, a transportation enterprise owned by a local government might sell bus service to senior citizens at prices well below the marginal costs of providing it. In that event the local government might very well be making an in-kind transfer payment to those citizens. Transfer payments themselves have no impact on the creation of wealth (aside from endowment effects which are likely to be negligible), although the method by which they are financed, taxation in the case of governments, would almost certainly have one by reducing incentives to work or invest. Accordingly, on our principle, such transactions, while not necessarily desirable, are certainly unobjectionable.

The second exception consists of sales transactions that are strategic moves designed to secure market power which would then be used to restrict output. For example, in theory, the transportation enterprise described in the preceding paragraph could be selling its services to senior citizens at such low prices in order to drive competitors out of the market. Once it had succeeded it would attempt to raise its prices, concomitantly reducing the supply of bus service in response to the drop in the amount demanded, and obtain "monopoly profits." On our principle, those transactions would be highly objectionable.

It is rather unlikely, however, that judges hearing an antitrust suit against a local government would encounter such transactions. For reasons which have been thoroughly discussed elsewhere, most enterprises would not engage in such strategic moves because the expected losses from doing so would exceed the expected gains.[14] Even those scholars who seem to believe that such moves will be encountered often enough to raise serious antitrust concerns assume that only enterprises that are dominant or part of a collusive oligopoly are likely to engage in them.[15] It is particularly unlikely that local governments would engage in them. Their managers would have little incentive to even devise a strategy for obtaining market power because they would have considerable difficulty capturing the additional revenues which might be generated if such a strategy were successfully implemented. Moreover, it would be quite difficult to implement one since local governments tend to be plagued by greater turnover among top policy-makers and more cumbersome operating procedures than private enterprises of similar size.[16]

In almost every case, then, the effects of the transaction will be unobjectionable in terms of consumer welfare. They will be objectionable, if at all, only in terms of wealth distribution. That means that the judge will have to search for a controlling principle which provides that it is good to prefer one group to another. Both groups may be loosely defined and comprised of ever-changing populations as long as it may be plausibly argued that the plaintiff belongs to the favored group and the defendant to the disfavored. After all, the principle must require that the objecting party, the plaintiff, prevail if he proves his claim.

The judge will encounter three serious problems in conducting his search: a problem in logic, a problem with advocacy, and a problem of case analysis. The logic problem will be that no matter what principle of preference the judge considers, he will find that it does not require that the plaintiff prevail. The judge will have no difficulty designating any number of groups to which the parties belong. Let the plaintiff belong to group P and the defendant to group D. Presumably, P has many members in addition to the plaintiff and would-be parties who would accede to the particular transaction by virtue of a favorable disposition of the pending suit.[17] The judge will then consider the principle that it is good to prefer members of P to members of D. He must ask: Does that principle require that the plaintiff prevail if he proves his claim? The answer would be yes if penalizing the defendant for entering into the transaction would tend to make the members of P better off, and no if it would not. It would not. The reason inheres in the dynamics of markets.[18] First, consider the impact of penalizing the defendant from the P point of view. Members of that group who wished to bind themselves by making the promise which the plaintiff made would encounter a major obstacle. Everyone would realize that if he entered into a transaction in which a member of P made such a promise he would subject himself to the risks of paying substantial litigation costs and suffering an adverse antitrust judgment. That means that members of P would be unable to obtain the value of that promise; they would forfeit a "property right." Now consider the impact of penalizing the defendant from the D point of view. When contemplating transactions like the one involved in the suit, members of D would take into account the prospect that they might be penalized under the antitrust laws. They would expend resources to avoid that result. So the transactions would be more costly than they otherwise would have been. Therefore, members of D would tend to make fewer or less valuable offers to members of P. In short, penalizing the defendant for entering into the transaction would tend to make members of P, although not the plaintiff, worse off.[19]

The judge will find himself in the unenviable position of a scientist who conducts an experiment and then devises one hypothesis after another of a particular kind to explain the observed results, only to discover that none of them do so. The scientist would then reject that kind of hypothesis. The judge might not yet feel free to do so lest he be accused of casting aside precedent—the many antitrust cases which seem to have been resolved on the basis of some elusive principle of wealth distribution.[20] To continue his search for that principle, however, the judge will have to ignore the dynamics of markets. Such willed ignorance has been aptly called sentimentality.[21]

It will be critical to the plaintiff's case that the judge be sentimental. Yet even if he is, he will still probably obtain little meaningful assistance from plaintiff's counsel in conducting his search. Counsel will likely insist that what the case is all about is whether the challenged practice "denied plaintiff the opportunity to do business," "eliminated the plaintiff as a rival," "excluded the plaintiff from the market," "subjected the plaintiff to abuse," or "limited the freedom of the plaintiff to run his business independently." So characterizing the inquiry obscures rather than reveals the allegedly controlling wealth-distribution principle. That is the advocacy problem. Counsel will create it for two sound strategic reasons. One, he may then rely on that loosely Jeffersonian ideology which pervades so many antitrust opinions.[22] That ideology, which is so vague and yet so appealing, is likely to receive a more sympathetic reception than any particular wealth-distribution principle which it supposedly requires. Two, he may then invoke the authority of antitrust cases involving private enterprises engaged in arguably similar practices in which the inquiry was so characterized and the practice found suspect or condemned.

Unfortunately, the judge will almost have to turn to those cases for some help in conducting his search. He will probably find it difficult to distinguish the ideological rhetoric used in the opinions from the wealth-distribution principle which, market dynamics aside, dictated the results. That is the case analysis problem. Patient study will reveal, however, that that principle was that it is good to prefer private holdings of wealth, usually referred to as firms,[23] which are "smaller" or "less advantaged," to those which are "larger" or "more advantaged." That is the principle for which the judge will have been searching. It reflects a crude theory of public choice[24] and that collection of sentiments and beliefs known as populism.[25] The theory is that political behavior may be explained largely on the basis of the relative wealth of the private antagonists interested in influencing it; and populism holds that that behavior will be "better" the more widely dispersed and evenly wealth is distributed.[26]

Having finally completed his search, the judge will find, alas, that he undertook it in vain. Neither the principle discovered nor the public choice theory and ideology which it reflects will suggest that the judge rule against the defendant local government. The principle does not even speak to whether private holdings of wealth, of whatever size, should be preferred to public, or "collective," holdings, like those of local governments. The theory has little if anything to do with political behavior related to disputes between private enterprises and local government, and populism does not even hint that that behavior would be better if the former were made wealthier at the expense of the latter. Indeed, populism as it is commonly understood probably dictates that local government, and the taxpayers it purports to represent, be preferred to any firm. Local government is populist-preferred; in fact, there is probably no institution which occupies a higher place in the pantheon of populism. Thus, any objection to the wealth-distribution effects of the transaction would not be well taken.

There simply is no principle according to which the effects of the transaction might be considered undesirable, so the judge will be bound to reject the plaintiff's attack on the challenged practice since its principal function is to bring them about. Applying the Supreme Court's "same treatment" lesson, the same judge would also have to reject an attack on a substantially similar practice engaged in by a private enterprise.

A series of such holdings would mark a major retrenchment in the common law of antitrust. Thus, the implications of this reexamination process are rather startling. Part II of this book demonstrates how this process might work for the five practices engaged in by local governments that are most likely to be challenged as antitrust offenses.[27] Upon them, a host of nasty antitrust labels have been pinned. Indeed, the examples used for this demonstration are drawn from the reported cases. Yet, as will be shown, none of them should be considered illegal unless engaged in solely as part of a strategy for obtaining market power or as part of the operation of a classic cartel.

NOTES

1. For a more extended description and analysis of this type of judicial decision-making see my articles analyzing the opinions of the United States Court of Appeals for the Seventh Circuit: Lee, *Antitrust: Market Definition, The Section Two Offenses and Literalism*, 57 Chi.-Kent L. Rev. 25 (1981); Lee, *Economic Regulation of Business: The Seventh Circuit's Non-Economic Approach*, 56 Chi.-Kent L. Rev. 205 (1980); Lee, *Antitrust: A Collage of Vertical Territorial Restraints, Tying and Monopoly "Misuse," Arbitrability, and the General Dynamics Defense*, 55 Chi.-Kent L. Rev. 1 (1979).

2. R. Bork, The Antitrust Paradox: A Policy at War With Itself pp. 44-45 and generally at pp. 136-59 (1978).

3. *Id.* at 117, 123-29. *Cf.* United States v. Socony-Vacuum Oil Co., Inc., 310 U.S. 150 (1940).

4. *See* Chapter 8, pp. 157-59.

5. 435 U.S. 389, 405 n.31, 416-17 (1978), *quoted with approval* in 455 U.S. 40, 57-58 (1982).

6. 435 U.S. at 403-04, 412-13, *quoted with approval* in 455 U.S. at 51.

7. *Cf.* Omega Satellite Products Co. v. City of Indianapolis, 694 F.2d 119, 123 (7th Cir. 1982).

8. Because I am focusing on vertical restraints, I employ a transaction costs approach in this book. *See* Williamson, *Assessing Vertical Market Restrictions: Antitrust Ramifications of the Transaction Cost Approach*, 127 U. Pa. L. Rev. 975 (1979).

9. United States v. Container Corp. of America, 393 U.S. 333, 341 (1969) (Marshal, J., dissenting); Northern Pacific Railway Co. v. United States, 356 U.S. 1, 5 (1958).

10. Making miscalculations is likely to be a self-limiting activity and, therefore, an unimportant one in the aggregate. Because the market would punish miscalculations adequately and because using law to punish them would create risks likely to deter some efficient behavior, we ignore the possibility of such miscalculations when undertaking antitrust analysis.

11. A. Alchian & W. Allen, Exchange and Production: Competition, Coordination, and Control p. 28-31 (2d ed. 1977).

12. *See id.* at 30-31.

13. Some of these transactions may involve the sale of a durable good,

like a house, subject to resale limitations. *See* Strauss & Stegman, *Moderate-Cost Housing after Lafayette: A Proposal,* 11 Urb. Law. 209 (1979).

14. *See* Easterbrook, *Predatory Strategies and Counterstrategies,* 48 U. Chi. L. Rev. 263 (1981); R. Bork, *supra* note 2, at 144-60; R. Posner, Antitrust Law: An Economic Perspective pp. 184-96 (1976); Elzinga, *Predatory Pricing: The Case of the Gunpowder Trust,* 13 J. Law & Econ. 223 (1970); McGee, *Predatory Price Cutting: The Standard Oil (N.J.) Case,* 1 J. Law & Econ. 137 (1958).

15. *See, e.g.,* Williamson, *Predatory Pricing: A Strategic and Welfare Analysis,* 87 Yale L.J. 284 (1978); Williamson, *Predatory Pricing II,* 88 Yale L.J. 1183 (1979). (Williamson defines a dominant firm as one with 60 per cent of the relevant market and asserts that collusive oligopoly is likely to occur "mainly in mature, highly concentrated industries producing homogeneous products under uniform cost conditions and having significant barriers to entry." 87 Yale L.J. at 293. He suggests that highly concentrated industries are those in which four or fewer firms account for more than 70 per cent of output. 88 Yale L.J. at 1194.)

16. The approach described is, at least to this point, analogous to that advocated by Williamson. *See* Williamson, *supra* note 8, at 980.

17. Otherwise, the principle of wealth-distribution being tested would be anathema in our system of jurisprudence: the plaintiff should prevail in this dispute because he and those allied with him will be better off if he does. Moreover, it could not be tested since it is a mere tautology.

18. *See* A. Polinsky, An Introduction to Law and Economics pp. 107-10 (1983).

19. The illogic of applying a wealth distribution principle to resolve antitrust disputes makes for unpredictable outcomes. Unpredictable outcomes constitute evidence that the courts are making policy decisions that traditionally belong to legislatures. Thus, they raise the question of who governs. *See* R. Bork, *supra* note 2, at pp. 10, 418. That question is raised rather starkly in those cases in which a local government is the defendant.

20. For a recent example *see* Twin City Sportservice, Inc. v. Charles O. Finley & Co., 676 F.2d 1291 (9th Cir. 1982), *cert. denied,* 459 U.S. 1009 (1982).

21. *See* R. Bork, *supra* note 2, at pp. 54, 55; Will, *As I Was Saying,* Newsweek, Apr. 16, 1979, at 100.

22. C. Kaysen & D. Turner, Antitrust Policy: An Economic and Legal Analysis pp. 17-18 (1965); R. Bork, *supra* note 2, at pp. 54-56; 1 P. Areeda & D. Turner, Antitrust Law: An Analysis of Antitrust Principles and Their Application, pp. 22-23 and generally at pp. 7-31 (1978).

23. For the purposes of casual discussion, this reference is permis-

sible. It does not, however, reflect recent advances in the theory of the firm. *See, e.g.*, Alchian & Demsetz, *Production, Information Cost, and Economic Organization*, 62 Am. Econ. Rev. 777 (1972); Coase, *The Nature of the Firm*, 4 Economica 386 (1937). And, for the purposes of sophisticated analysis, the reference may be misleading, particularly when too much is made of the corporate legal form which many "firms" take.

24. For more sophisticated public choice theories *see, e.g.*, D. Mueller, Public Choice (1979); G. Tullock, The Logic of Law (1970); M. Olson, The Logic of Collective Action (1965); J. Buchanan & G. Tullock, The Calculus of Consent (1962).

25. Bork refers to them as "a jumble of half-digested notions and mythologies." R. Bork, *supra* note 2, at p. 54. They usually include a professed concern for the "free choice" of the "independent" businessman and his "opportunity to do business," what Bork calls the bondage theme, a stated preference for atomistic markets ("fragmentation for its own sake"), and a devotion to "fairness," which usually means equality of outcomes. *Id.* at 50-56.

26. *See* 1 P. Areeda & D. Turner, *supra* note 22, at pp. 7, 22-23; R. Bork, *supra* note 2, at pp. 54-55. Some of the leading antitrust opinions reflect both the theory and the ideology. *See, e.g.*, United States v. Von's Grocery Co., 384 U.S. 270 (1966); Brown Shoe Co. v. United States, 370 U.S. 294 (1962); and, especially, United States v. Aluminum Co. of America, 148 F.2d 416 (2d Cir. 1945).

27. Local governments do so much that their practices could be classified in any number of ways. Most commentators have classified them according to the type of enterprise in connection with which they were used. For example, the conduct of local governments related to the operation of airports is typically differentiated from that related to the operation of stadiums. *See, e.g.*, Rose, *Municipal Activities and the Antitrust Laws after City of Lafayette*, 57 Univ. Det. J. Urb. L. 483 (1979); Bangasser, *Exposure of Municipal Corporations to Liability for Violations of the Antitrust Laws: Antitrust Immunity after the City of Lafayette Decision*, 11 Urb. Law. vii (1979). That scheme has at least two important vices. One, it defines practices in ways that lack generality. Two, it suggests that it might be proper to treat economically-alike practices differently under the antitrust statutes. (Rose does acknowledge that some of the antitrust problems are "similar." Rose, *id.* at 495.) To cure those vices, I have classified the practices of local government according to the type of transaction in which they were involved. It is the transaction that is the fundamental unit of analysis when the explanation for alternative modes of organization is at issue, as it is here. Williamson, *Assessing Vertical Market Restrictions: Antitrust Ramifications of the Transaction Cost Approach*, 127 U. Pa. L. Rev. 953 (1979).

PART II

REEXAMINATION TO RETRENCHMENT: THE PROCESS ILLUSTRATED

4

"REFUSALS TO DEAL," "EXCLUSIVE DEALING," "MONOPOLIZING," AND "BOYCOTTS"

Every local government enters into agreements with suppliers, and some do so with purchasers, pursuant to which it declines to buy from, or sell to, some or all of their rivals. Of course, this practice displeases the rivals who all-too-frequently claim that it runs afoul of the Sherman Act. In fact, it has probably been the focus of more antitrust litigation against local governments than any other practice. The displeased rivals may pin one or more of several labels on it. "Refusal to deal" and "exclusive dealing" are favorites, as is the related catch-all, "boycott." Where the agreement is with a supplier, the rivals may also claim that the practice creates a monopoly in the "market" that consists of the local government's purchases.

The practice is used in countless contexts, but it serves a limited number of functions. Some of those functions are best illustrated by garden-variety uses and others by more striking ones.

FUNCTIONS RELATED TO THE USE OF AN EXISTING CAPITAL FACILITY

Consider first a garden-variety use, the one that was attacked in *Pinehurst Airlines, Inc. v. Resort Air Service, Inc.*[1] The Moore County (North Carolina) Board of Commissioners had apparently made arrangements with Resort Air Service for Resort to serve as a "fixed based operator" at the county's Southern Pines Airport. All fixed based operators sell aviation fuel and lubricants and aircraft maintenance and storage, and some of them sell and rent aircraft, charter flights, and offer flying lessons.[2] The Board apparently leased a portion of the airport to Resort, and Resort promised to sell a number of products and services to airport patrons. Having made those arrangements, the Board allegedly refused to make similar ones with Pinehurst Airlines, a would-be rival of Resort.[3] That refusal prevented Pinehurst from serving as a fixed based operator *de jure*. Pinehurst, however, was already a user of airport facilities and structures, so it could have easily sold airport patrons some of the products or services that Resort sold. To prevent Pinehurst from serving as a fixed based operator *de facto*, the Board allegedly took additional steps, like denying a request for maintenance space, that made it quite costly, perhaps prohibitively so, for Pinehurst to do so.[4]

Pinehurst claimed, *inter alia*, that the Board's course of conduct, a garden-variety use of the practice analyzed in this chapter, ran afoul of sections 1 and 2 of the Sherman Act. The Board, along with Resort, allegedly conspired to prevent Pinehurst from competing in the market for the services of fixed based operators at the Southern Pines Airport[5] and to monopolize that market.[6] Pinehurst might just as well have invoked other antitrust labels, like "monopolizing" or "attempting to monopolize" the market,[7] "boycotting,"[8] and "conspiring to exclude" Pinehurst from the market.[9] All describe the Board's course of conduct, albeit incompletely, and, because of the pejorative language, misleadingly; none reveal the true objection to it.

The court never ascertained the true objection. It need not have if it had properly analyzed the issues raised by the motions that were pending before it. None of those issues bore on the merits of Pinehurst's claim.[10] Unfortunately, the court analyzed one of them, the governmental exemption issue, as if it did.[11] The issue was whether the Board's alleged course of conduct could be scrutinized under the federal antitrust statutes.

Apparently,[12] the court reasoned that since the alleged course of conduct was "anticompetitive,"[13] it must not have been "authorized" or "directed" by North Carolina when the legislature empowered[14] counties to establish and operate airports and to lease portions of them in connection with those activities.[15]

Therefore, concluded the court, applying *City of Lafayette*, it was subject to scrutiny under the federal antitrust statutes.

That conclusion may have been correct, but the analysis was flawed. The court ignored the Supreme Court's cautionary language in *City of Lafayette* about inferring state authorization and direction. More importantly for present purposes, it confused legality with immunity.[16] Given that confusion, however, the court should have ascertained the true objection to the Board's course of conduct before pronouncing it anticompetitive.[17]

To do that, the court would have had to engage in the two-step inquiry described in the preceding chapter. First, it would ask: What function did the Board's course of conduct, the "practice," serve? To answer that question intelligently, the court would have had to carefully observe the economic context in which the practice was used. It would have seen that the practice was part of a transaction whereby the Board purchased a service from Resort. That may seem counter-intuitive since no transaction was entered into pursuant to which the Board transferred money to Resort, whereas under the lease, Resort did transfer money to the Board; so an explanation may be required.

The Board managed an airport on behalf of the taxpayers of Moore County, the "owners."[18] Presumably, the Board, like the management of any private enterprise, took actions calculated to maximize the value of the airport.[19] By "value of the airport," I mean the expected value, discounted to the present, of the stream of income which it could be used to generate. Apparently, the Board believed that the value of the airport would be increased if it made arrangements to have some of the facilities and personnel at the airport used to meet the demand of patrons for products and services which are typically sold at other airports by fixed based operators (fbo). Meeting that demand is itself a service which, for lack of a better name, I shall call fbo service.

The Board could have arranged for fbo service either hierarchically, by directing one or more of its employees to provide it, or across a market, by entering into a contract.[20] Regardless, the Board would have had to pay for that service. Had the arrangements been hierarchical, it would have been obvious that the Board was paying. Its employees would have been selling products and services to airport patrons, and they would have looked to the Board for their wages.[21] Under the more complex arrangements that the Board actually made, which were across a market, it was not so obvious. In fact, it might seem that the Board cleverly obtained fbo service for free. The Board probably did obtain that service for less than it would have paid had the arrangements been hierarchical. On the basis of our wealth-maximizing assumption we may presume that the Board arranged for the service across a market because it believed that it would be cheaper to do so.[22] But it did pay. When the Board entered into the contract with Resort, it gave up an opportunity, an opportunity to earn a stream of income from the sales which could have been made by its employees. Such opportunities are frequently called concessions or franchises. That concession was worth quite a bit of money, probably just a bit less than the present value of Resort's expected net revenues. The Board transferred it to Resort in return for fbo service.

The lease, pursuant to which Resort transferred money to the Board, can now been seen in proper perspective. It was really incidental to a more complex transaction, pursuant to which the Board transferred a concession to Resort. Thus, while it is true that Resort rented a portion of the airport controlled by the Board, it is equally true, and far more significant, in terms of value as well as antitrust law, that the Board "rented" some of the equipment and personnel controlled by Resort. When the Board engaged in the practice challenged by Pinehurst, it was purchasing fbo service from Resort. That was the economic reality which the court apparently failed to grasp.

Had it done so, it would have had grave doubts about the validity of Pinehurst's complaint since it would have been painfully obvious that the Board had no discernible interest in restricting the output of fbo service. It is rather unlikely that the Board entered into the transaction with Resort for the purpose of making a transfer payment. Fixed base operators are probably too successful to qualify for charity and too weak to command subsidies. It is even less likely that the Board entered into it for strategic purposes. The airport probably had no existing rivals to drive from the market nor any potential rivals to keep out. Even if it had, it is difficult to see how the Board's arrangements with Resort could have effectuated either goal. Given the relatively large number of would-be fixed base operators and the relatively small start-up costs of becoming one, those arrangements probably would have had no effect on the ability of an existing or potential rival airport to obtain fbo service.[23] As an ordinary purchaser, of course, the Board would have been interested in expanding output. The grave doubts engendered by these observations might have steeled the court against the allure of literalistic jurisprudence and prompted it to systematically study the functions that the challenged practice was likely supposed to serve.

The Board's refusal to make arrangements with Pinehurst for fbo service was almost certainly supposed to serve an instrumental function in the complex sales transaction between it and Resort. (Of course, in fact, the Board may have refused to make arrangements with Pinehurst because one of the members of the Board wanted to do a favor for his friend, a principal shareholder of Resort, but that is not what is important for the purposes of antitrust analysis.) Generally speaking, that function was to help secure the benefits which were the object of the transaction or otherwise reduce the costs associated with it. But specifically, how could that refusal do that?

It is child's play to develop an explanation for how the practice could do so *ex post* the transaction. By refusing to make arrangements with Pinehurst, the Board fulfilled a promise which it had made, explicitly or implicitly, to Resort. Had the Board reneged, Resort might have done likewise with respect to its promise to provide fbo service and sued for breach of contract. Thus, by using the challenged practice, the Board furthered two goals: securing the service which it believed would make the airport more valuable and avoiding a likely damage award.[24] Unfortunately, that explanation is unenlightening and useless for the purpose of antitrust analysis. It is unenlightening since a similar one could be offered for any conduct that was consistent with a promise which had been exchanged for another promise. Perhaps that is why similar explanations tend to be ignored by courts. It is useless for antitrust analysis because it tells us nothing about the likely consequences of the underlying agreement. That is a characteristic of all *ex post* explanations.[25] An *ex ante* explanation would be far better, but developing it requires a bit more sophistication.

Begin by focusing on the promise to make arrangements for fbo service with only one operator rather than the fulfillment of that promise. Then consider the ways in which the Board could have gained by so promising. There are two. First, it might have induced the most efficient provisioning of that service. Recall our presumption that the Board acts in a manner calculated to maximize the value of the airport. Necessarily, then, the Board would permit the use of airport-connected resources to provide fbo service only up to the point that they added more to the value of the airport than they would add if put to some other use. With those limited resources, it is plausible that that service could be most efficiently provided, *ceteris paribus*, by a single operator. That "natural monopoly" might reflect scale economies in "producing" the service. But it might also reflect economies either in coordinating the delivery of the service with other airport-related activities, like departures and arrivals, or in adapting that delivery to major changes in them which were prompted by significant maintenance projects or structural modifications.[26] The Board's promise would have assured the chosen operator of the opportunity to provide service efficiently throughout the entire term of the agreement. That assurance would have raised the expected value of the operator's net revenues and, thereby, the actual value of that portion of the airport which the operator was to lease. Thus the Board could have obtained more "rent." Of much greater significance, the Board could have also obtained more revenues from airport patrons since if the fbo service were efficiently provisioned, it would make its maximum possible contribution to the value of the airport. Thus, by making the promise, the Board may have helped secure its object in entering into the transaction.

Whether or not a single operator could have provided fbo service most efficiently, everything else being equal, the Board could still have gained by promising to make arrangements for it with only one. This second way of effectuating a gain is related not to efficiency in the provisioning of the service but in arranging for it. By making its promise, the Board could have avoided substantial transactions costs, which are among the things least likely to be equal. Most obviously, the Board bore fewer negotiating costs by entering into only one transaction rather than two or more.[27] Less obviously, but more importantly, the Board may have borne lower monitoring costs than it otherwise would have.[28] Monitoring, along with contract enforcement, is required in order to limit opportunism—"making false or empty, that is, self-disbelieved threats or promises,"[29] "cutting corners for undisclosed personal advantage, covering up tracks, and the like."[30] Limiting opportunism, the control of cheating, is the key to "the viability of a pattern of exchange."[31] That is not to say that all economic actors or even all fixed based operators would cheat. But some would, and it is expensive to sort out the cheaters and the non-cheaters.[32] Monitoring a fixed based operator by conventional methods, like inspection, may have appeared ineffectual or, if effectual, expensive. The Board may have believed that it would be more cost-effective to induce satisfactory performance by permitting the operator to earn returns to exclusivity which would be put at risk, like a hostage, if the operator acted opportunistically.[33]

The Board could have also used its promise to help it capture some of the quasi-rents generated by the investment in the airport. A "*quasi-rent* [is] [a]ny payment that does not affect the amount [of a good] *currently* available but will affect the *future* amount."[34] Specialized capital assets are prime generators of quasi-rents. By making its promise, the Board eliminated the possibility of any competition among fixed base operators at the Southern Pines Airport for the custom of airport patrons. By eliminating that possibility, the Board created an opportunity, albeit an evanescent one, for the chosen operator to appropriate some of those quasi-rents. Would-be operators could be expected to compete for that opportunity. They would do so by offering lump-sum or installment payments which might take the form of a franchise or license fee, or perhaps additional "rent."[35] It would be reasonable to expect that in the process of so competing, at least one of them would be driven to offer a payment almost as great in value as the quasi-rents which they hoped to appropriate.[36] The Board would accept such an offer and thereby capture those quasi-rents, or at least most of them, for itself and its constituent taxpayers. This may appear to be yet a third way for the Board to gain by making its promise, but this appearance is deceiving. The Board's gain would stem from the avoidance of substantial transactions costs. The Board could capture some of the quasi-rents as long as it contractually prevented unlimited competition between operators for the custom of airport patrons. A variety of stratagems would do that, but making the promise the Board allegedly made was likely the most cost-effective one.

To summarize the *ex ante* explanation, the challenged practice was most likely supposed to serve one or both of two basic instrumental functions. One, it might have helped secure efficiently provisioned fbo service. Two, it might have helped reduce the costs of (a) negotiating and, especially, monitoring and enforcing arrangements for that service,[37] and (b) capturing some of the quasi-rents generated by the taxpayers' investment in those portions of the airport used in providing that service.

A quite similar explanation could be developed easily in most instances in which a local government enters into an agreement with suppliers, or purchasers, pursuant to which it declines to buy from, or sell to, some or all of their rivals. That practice, of which the Board apparently made garden-variety use, is usually supposed to serve the same kind of functions as those which were likely supposed to be served by the Board's alleged promise.[38] Indeed, it is often supposed to serve those functions even when put to more striking use, as it apparently was when it was used by the cities of Dallas and Fort Worth in arranging for taxicab service at the D/FW Regional Airport, the focus of the controversy in *Woolen v. Surtran Taxicabs, Inc.*[39]

In the 1960's and early 1970's the cities of Dallas and Fort Worth had the Texas-sized, multiterminal D/FW Regional Airport (D/FW) built in the relatively undeveloped area betweeen them. They created an Airport Board to manage it. They also created the D/FW Surtran System (the System), a joint venture charged with the responsibility of seeing to it that an adequate ground transportation network served the airport. The network was to include an inter-terminal shuttle, one or more modes of mass transportation, and most important for present purposes, taxicab service.

The System discharged that responsibility, in part, by auctioning off the exclusive right to pick up passengers at the airport for carriage to all points in the ten surrounding counties. The right was made exclusive by virtue of an ordinance, enacted by Dallas, Fort Worth, and two smaller cities in which portions of the airport are located,[40] and a decision made by the Airport Board. The ordinance barred anyone who had not obtained a permit issued by the Airport Board from offering for-hire ground transportation from D/FW. The Board's decision was to issue a permit for taxicab service only to the winner of the System's auction. It is not clear from the court's opinion whether the ordinance was enacted and the decision made prior to the auction, but it cannot be seriously doubted that the participants in the auction were induced to prepare their bids on the basis that the winner would obtain an exclusive right.

The winner was Surtran Taxicabs, Inc. (Surtran), a joint venture of Yellow Cab of Dallas, Inc. and Fort Worth Cab & Baggage. Surtran offered to pay the System seventy-five cents per trip and 50 percent of all "profits" in excess of a 5 percent "operating profit."[41] It may have also offered to pay an additional lump-sum fee for the permit, but the court's opinion does not reveal whether it did or did not. Pursuant to the contract, which was signed following the auction, Surtran agreed, in essence, to supply, at set rates, something akin to the taxicab service requirements of arriving passengers at D/FW and to pay the System in accordance with the terms of its bid.

These arrangements were the source of considerable unhappiness among some of the taxicab operators licensed by the municipalities in the ten counties surrounding D/FW. Pursuant to them, Dallas and Fort Worth refused to let those operators pick up passengers at the airport. Several of those operators, including John Woolen, filed a class action suit challenging that refusal as violative of sections 1 and 2 of the Sherman Act.[42] The cities moved to dismiss the suit for failure to state a claim upon which relief could be granted.[43]

In support of their motion, the cities pressed two arguments which might have prompted the court to inquire into the function of the challenged practice. The first argument was that the practice was immune under *Parker v. Brown*. Unfortunately, the court responded with the same mistaken analysis employed by the *Pinehurst* court. Since the Texas legislature had not contemplated such an "anticompetitive" practice, reasoned the court, it was subject to scrutiny under the antitrust statutes.[44] Given that mistaken analysis, the court should have made the critical inquiry. It should have made it anyway since the cities' second argument, unlike their first one, went to the merits of the plaintiffs' claim. That argument, at least as the court apparently understood it, was that the practice was *per se* legal. The cities asserted that, as owners of D/FW, they could exclude any commercial enterprise from airport property without committing an antitrust offense. They observed that it had merely been alleged that the cities had so excluded the plaintiffs. Therefore, the plaintiffs were not entitled to any relief under the Sherman Act.

The court's response to this second argument was two-pronged. The first prong consisted of a line of analogical reasoning which, in the final analysis, was question-begging. It might be unlawful, began the court, for a monopolist, even one who had acquired his market power lawfully, to agree to sell his products exclusively to one distributor. For the purposes of the motion to dismiss, the court stated, the challenged practice was to be treated as analogous to such an agreement. The cities, taken together, were to be treated as a monopolist. After all, "ownership of land," stated the court, "may because of its unique location or other property attributes give to the landowner a specie of natural monopoly,"[45] meaning, presumably, the opportunity to obtain quasi-rents. Denying entry to such land to all but one vendor of a particular kind of service, continued the court, could have the same effect as a monopolist's exclusive distribution agreement. Therefore, the court concluded, the cities' refusal to let those taxicab operators unaffiliated with Surtran pick up passengers at D/FW might be unlawful.

The analogy is surprisingly apt.[46] The court did not explain, however, why a monopolist's exclusive distribution agreement should ever be considered unlawful. In fact, such an agreement would be objectionable on consumer welfare grounds only if the monopolist entered into it strategically for the purpose of disrupting the optimal distribution patterns of potential rivals.[47] Such behavior could not possibly be successful unless the dealers' activities required investments in rather specialized assets,[48] and so only under such circumstances, if at all, would it likely be observed.[49] Of course, the court may be forgiven for its omission since it may have reasonably believed that no explanation was necessary in the light of then existing authority.[50] Nevertheless, it is that omission which obscures the flaw in the court's line of reasoning. To provide the missing explanation, the court would have had to engage in a two-step inquiry: (1) what functions are likely served by a monopolist's exclusive distribution agreement? and (2) according to what principles might those functions be deemed objectionable? That is substantially the same inquiry as the one the court should have made in order to determine whether the cities' practice was *per se* legal. Thus, the first prong of the court's response was question-begging.

The second prong was no more than a *non sequitur*. The cities' property rights, stated the court, had to give way to the policy of the Sherman Act,[51] particularly when those rights had been "diluted" by the dedication of the airport to public purposes.[52] That statement is simply beside the point of the cities' argument, which was, in essence, that the way in which they exercised their property rights was necessarily consistent with that policy. Thus, the court, in effect, substituted two logical fallacies for an inquiry into the function of the challenged practice.

Had the court made the inquiry, it could have begun its analysis by observing that the practice was used by the cities in the context of purchasing a service. To them, the service was meeting the taxicab transportation requirements of arriving passengers at D/FW. The cities could have arranged for that service by using one of two basic methods. They could have purchased vehicles and hired drivers and then directed that the System provide the service hierarchically. Alternatively, they could have arranged for it across a market in a myriad of ways. For example, they could have permitted unrestricted use of airport roads and then relied on self-interested taxicab operators for the service. Or, the cities could have purchased the service pursuant to a more well defined contract.[53] Obviously, they chose to do the latter, presumably because it was more cost-effective. Thus, the cities did precisely what the Moore County Board did. They exchanged a concession for a service which would increase the value of the airport. An instrumental part of this sales transaction was the cities' promise to make arrangements for taxicab transportation from D/FW with only one company.

It might appear that making such a promise could not possibly have helped the cities secure efficiently provisioned taxicab transportation. After all, at most large airports, taxicab operators affiliated with several companies solicit business. Surely that would not be the case, one might reasonably assume, if taxicab transportation could be provided most efficiently by a single company. That assumption, however, could well be incorrect. A sole supplier of taxicab transportation at an airport might have an advantage over several companies because its response to congestion might be more nearly optimal than theirs. Suppose that congestion at an airport is such that, *ceteris paribus*, a reduction in the supply of taxicab transportation would be efficient. One would expect a sole supplier to make that reduction since he would reap most of the benefits of doing so, which, by supposition, exceed the costs, most of which he would bear. One would not necessarily expect several suppliers, acting independently, to do the same. Each one might hesitate to offer less taxicab transportation lest the others not follow his lead, or even offer more. Each one would fear the prospect of bearing many of the costs of making the reduction while reaping none, or a small fraction, of the benefits. Coordinated action might solve the problem, but the cost of arranging for it and then monitoring it might be prohibitive. If this advantage were quantitatively significant enough, a sole supplier might be able to provide taxicab transportation from an airport more efficiently than several suppliers. To exploit this advantage, however, a taxicab company would have to secure the exclusive right to pick up passengers at the airport, and the cost of securing that right might also be prohibitive. If the rights were purchased from other taxicab companies, enforcement costs might well be substantial. Moreover, such purchases would likely spur the strategic entry of other companies expecting to be bought out.[54] Thus, even though a single company might provide taxicab transportation more efficiently than several companies, one could still observe, as one would, that taxicab operators affiliated with several companies solicit business at most large airports. What that means, however, is that, by promising to make arrangements for taxicab transportation from D/FW with only one company, Dallas and Fort Worth may have helped themselves secure more efficiently provisioned service.

It is even more likely that by so promising, Dallas and Fort Worth helped reduce the costs of negotiating, and especially monitoring, their arrangements for the service. Had they made arrangements with several companies, they would have had to negotiate not only about more than one contract but also about the potentially delicate interrelationships between the operators affiliated with those companies.[55] Perhaps more importantly, to ensure satisfactory performance under the contracts, the cities might have had to engage in disproportionately more monitoring, like data gathering, supervision, and other relatively expensive activities, than they would have had they made arrangements with one provider and relied primarily on its fear of losing returns to exclusivity to induce satisfactory performance.

It is almost certainly true that by promising to make arrangements with only one company, the cities helped reduce the costs of capturing some of the quasi-rents generated by the taxpayer's investment in D/FW. By so promising, the cities practically assured themselves that the System's auction for the right to pick up passengers would elicit offers to make payments equal in value to those quasi-rents. Under the circumstances, one would be hard-pressed to conceive of a less expensive method of doing that.[56]

There is no evidence whatsoever that the cities' promise functioned to inefficiently restrict the output of taxicab transportation from D/FW. It would have been surprising had there been any. It is unlikely that the cities were making a transfer payment or a strategic move calculated to secure market power. It is unlikely for the same reasons that it is unlikely that the Moore County Board was doing so.[57] As the purchasers of a service in a complex sales transaction, the cities were interested in obtaining no less than an economically optimal output. That interest is no doubt what prompted the cities to insist that Surtran's rates be prescribed by contract.[58] Had the rates not been prescribed, Surtran would probably have found it profitable, as the sole supplier, (1) to charge higher rates, thereby causing a decline in the amount demanded, and (2) to restrict output inefficiently.[59] Under the terms of the contract, the less efficient the output, the less Surtran would pay the cities.[60] The cities would capture less quasi-rents and Surtran more.

That the cities' promise was supposed to serve the same kind of functions as the Moore County Board's promise suggests, without proving, that those kinds of functions are usually served when a local government enters into agreements with suppliers and purchasers pursuant to which it declines to buy from or sell to some or all of their rivals, regardless of whether that practice is put to a striking use or merely a garden-variety one. Of course, the cities' use of the practice seems striking only because we have come to expect taxicab operators affiliated with several companies to solicit our business at major airports. In contrast, most of us have no expectations about the number of fixed based operators we would likely find at any airport had we need for one. Those few of us who do have such expectations may well expect to find just one at smaller airports.

FUNCTIONS RELATED TO THE USE OF A CAPITAL FACILITY NOT YET BUILT

Occasionally, however, a local government's use of this practice seems striking not so much because the practice is used in an unconventional context, but because it really is supposed to serve some different, although not completely unrelated, functions. These functions are linked not to inducing efficient use of an existing capital facility but rather to inducing an additional investment in such a facility which itself would represent an efficient use of resources.

The prospect of obtaining quasi-rents induces investment. Thus, whether an investment is made will depend in large part on the amount of quasi-rents it is likely to generate and the proportion of those quasi-rents which the investors are likely to capture. Often, capture poses few, if any, problems. For example, Dallas and Fort Worth were assured of capturing some of the quasi-rents generated by the taxpayers' investment in D/FW by virtue of the rivalry between potential suppliers of taxicab transportation and the relatively low cost of replacing one supplier with another in the event the cities became dissatisfied with the service being rendered.[61] Without such assurance, the cities may have put less capital into the airport or none at all. Generally, in the absence of such rivalry and low transactions costs, investors might reasonably fear that any quasi-rents generated by their investment would be captured by others, or, to put it less technically, expropriated. They might then hesitate to make the investment, which they otherwise would have made, unless, before making it, they enter into an agreement which provides assurance that they will capture those quasi-rents.

A local government might wish to conclude such an agreement either because (1) one or more private enterprises wish to induce it to make an investment on behalf of its taxpayers that it is hesitant to make, or (2) it wishes to induce one or more private enterprises to make an investment that they are hesitant to make. In either case, an integral part of the agreement might very well be the common practice that was attacked in *Pinehurst* and in *Woolen*. That was certainly true of the agreements which were the focus of *Hecht v. Pro-Football, Inc.*,[62] and *Mason City Center Associates v. City of Mason City, Iowa.*[63]

In statutes enacted in 1957 and 1959, Congress authorized the District of Columbia Armory Board to build a stadium, subsequently named after Robert F. Kennedy, "in order to provide the people of the District . . . [with one] suitable for holding athletic events," including professional football games.[64] The Armory Board functioned as a city agency, and it was certainly treated like one by the courts.[65] The legislative history of the authorizing statutes shows, however, that Congress intended to have the Armory Board manage RFK Stadium as a private enterprise would.[66]

The Armory Board did not initiate construction immediately. Rather, in an effort to carry out Congress's intention, it initiated negotiations with the professional football and baseball teams which then played in the District of Columbia for a long-term lease of the proposed stadium. The football team was, and is, the Washington Redskins, whose corporate name is Pro-Football, Inc. Apparently, the Armory Board would not have built the stadium had the negotiations proved fruitless.[67]

But they were successful. The Armory Board entered into a

thirty-year lease with the Redskins, which commenced with the start of the 1961 professional football season, and then built the stadium under contract to the Department of the Interior, which leased the land to it. The lease contained a restrictive covenant that was the focus of the subsequent litigation. The covenant provided that the Armory Board would not lease RFK Stadium to any other professional football team.

In 1965 Norman Hecht and his associates applied to the American Football League (AFL) for an expansion franchise to be located in the District of Columbia. The AFL was then a rival of the National Football League (NFL) to which the Redskins belonged. To have his application seriously considered by the AFL team owners, Hecht had to make some arrangements for the use of a stadium at which his team could play its home games. Apparently, the only suitable one in the District of Columbia was the Armory Board's,[68] so Hecht offered to lease it for dates on which the Redskins were not scheduled to use it. The Armory Board expressed a strong interest in accepting Hecht's offer, as did its landlord, the Secretary of the Interior.[69] Reluctantly, however, the Board advised Hecht that it would reject his offer unless the Redskins waived their rights under the restrictive covenant. The Redskins refused to do so.

Hecht then sued the Armory Board and the Redskins, among others,[70] claiming that the restrictive covenant was a contract in restraint of trade and a device for monopolizing the professional football market in the District of Columbia. Initially, the District Court for the District of Columbia entered judgment for the defendants on the ground that, under *Parker v. Brown*, the restrictive covenant was not subject to scrutiny under the Sherman Act.[71] The Court of Appeals for the District of Columbia Circuit reversed and remanded for a trial on the merits.[72] To make those rulings, neither court had to address the merits of Hecht's complaint, and neither did. Therefore, prior to the remand neither court had to undertake an inquiry into the function of the restrictive covenant. Subsequent to the remand, however, both courts made rulings which should have been based on such an inquiry. Unfortunately, it does not appear, from the one opinion known to be issued, the court of appeals',[73] that either court undertook it.

The suit was tried to a jury, which reached a verdict for the defendants. The district court entered judgment accordingly, and Hecht appealed. Once again, the court of appeals reversed and remanded. During the trial Hecht had requested that the district court instruct the jury pursuant to the "essential facility doctrine." That doctrine is: "'where facilities cannot practicably be duplicated by would-be competitors, those in possession of them must allow them to be shared on fair terms' or stand condemned under the antitrust statutes."[74] Hecht asked that the jury be told that if it

> found (1) that use of RFK stadium was essential to the operation of a professional football team in Washington; (2) that such stadium facilities could not practicably be duplicated by potential competitors; (3) that another team could use RFK stadium in the Redskins' absence without interfering with the Redskins' use; and (4) that the restrictive covenant in the lease prevented equitable sharing of the stadium by potential competitors, then . . . [it] must find the restrictive covenant to constitute a contract in unreasonable restraint of trade, in violation of the Sherman Act.[75]

That instruction went to the merits of the complaint, so, before denying Hecht's request, the district court should have undertaken the critical inquiry.[76] For the same reason, the court of appeals should have undertaken it before reversing for failure to give the requested instruction.[77]

The inquiry would have revealed that the economic context in which the restrictive covenant was used was largely identical to that in which the cities of Dallas and Fort Worth made their controversial promise to Surtran. The similarity would have been somewhat easier to see had the Armory Board built RFK Stadium before trying to lease it. Suppose, for the purpose of analysis, that it had. It becomes clearer, then, that the Armory Board was trying to maximize the value of the stadium, a capital facility like an airport, by arranging to have professional football games exhibited there. The games added to the value of the stadium in the same way, although more dramatically than meeting the requirements of arriving passengers for taxicab transportation added to the value of the Dallas/Ft. Worth airport. To the Armory Board, the exhibition of those games was a "service" which it "purchased" from the Redskins in exchange for an opportunity to earn a stream of income. The Armory Board "hired" the Redskins just as much as the Redskins "hired" RFK Stadium. Suppose further that the Armory Board had "hired" the Redskins by auctioning off the exclusive right to exhibit professional football games at the stadium, and it becomes quite clear that the restrictive covenant was the same kind of practice as that challenged in *Woolen*. Under the supposed conditions, it would have likely served the same kind of functions as did the cities' promise to Surtran to make arrangements with no other supplier of taxicab transportation. In particular, it would have helped the Armory Board capture the quasi-rents generated by the investment in the stadium.

Under the actual conditions, it almost certainly did that, but it did much more. If the Armory Board had not been assured of capturing those quasi-rents, it would not have built the stadium. Thus, the restrictive covenant helped induce the Armory Board to make what we must presume was an efficient investment.[78]

Contrary to our supposition, of course, the Armory Board tried to lease the stadium before building it. It did so because rivalry on the supply side of the professional football market in the District of Columbia did not assure it of capturing those quasi-rents. Had the Armory Board built the stadium first, it would have found that the only folks interested in obtaining the short-term rights to use the stadium for professional football games were the Redskins. Long-term rights might have generated some interest among speculators hoping to resell them to teams that might be assembled in the future. Given the risk of non-resale, however, such speculators would probably not have offered to pay nearly as much for those rights as the Redskins were prepared to offer. An auction for the short term, or even the long term, rights would have been costly and fruitless. So, also contrary to supposition, the Armory Board tried to lease the stadium by negotiating directly with the Redskins.

Given the limited rivalry, if the Armory Board had built the stadium first, the Redskins would have likely offered to lease it for little more than the costs of operating it. That would be far less than the Redskins would have been willing to offer in order to make it worth the Armory Board's while to build it. The "low-ball" offer would have been accepted since the Armory Board would not have had a higher one to choose and since rejecting it would have made the Armory Board worse off. Thus, the Redskins would have captured most or all of the quasi-rents generated by the investment in the stadium.

Since rivalry in the professional football market would not assure the Armory Board of capturing those quasi-rents, it tried, before building the stadium, to make contractual arrangements which would. Those arrangements took the form of a lease.

To assure sufficient capture of those quasi-rents, the lease had to have two key features. First, it had to be long-term.[79] Presumably, the Redskins were willing to make yearly payments equal in value to only a fraction of the quasi-rents. If they had been willing to pay more, then they could have built the stadium themselves. The longer the term of the lease, then, the greater the capture.

A long-term lease also provided some assurance to the Redskins that they would capture the quasi-rents generated by their investment in goodwill. Those quasi-rents could be dissipated, in part, if the Redskins had to move their NFL franchise to another metropolitan area because they were unable to renew their short-term lease for the only stadium in Washington suitable for playing their home games.[80]

Of course, entering into a long-term lease was not costless to either the Armory Board or the Redskins. By doing so, each forewent future opportunities to earn more revenues by making alternative arrangements and each ran the risk of opportunistic behavior on the part of the other. But the Redskins would not have incurred such costs unless they expected the gains from entering into such a lease were greater. And, assuming that the Armory Board acted like a private enterprise, as we must, neither would it. Apparently, the sum of the expected gains exceeded the sum of the expected costs by the greatest margin for a lease term of thirty years. That the Armory Board obligated itself to repay the principal to its bondholders during the same period may reflect a similar trade-off. Presumably, the Armory Board expected that by doing so, it minimized its cost of capital.

The court of appeals implicitly recognized that the lease had to be long-term to assure sufficient capture of quasi-rents. It did so by acknowledging that the Armory Board would not have built the stadium unless it had entered into such a lease with the Redskins. The court did not similarly recognize, however, that the lease also had to be exclusive, the second key feature. It is easy to see why it had to be exclusive if one simply imagines what would have happened had it not been. The Redskins would have perceived a far greater chance that they would have to compete with another football team for ticket buyers sometime during the thirty-year term of the lease. They would then have been much less certain that they could charge those ticket-buyers enough to cover the quasi-rents generated by the investment in the stadium. Therefore, they would be unwilling to pay as much to the Armory Board. The Armory Board would capture substantially less of those quasi-rents, although, given the limited rivalry in the District of Columbia professional football market, it might have still captured some.

Moreover, exclusivity reduced the costs of entering into a long-term lease. Each side would be somewhat more reluctant to act opportunistically for fear of losing the returns to exclusivity. As in *Woolen*, those returns became "hostage."

So, the purpose of entering into a long-term lease—assuring sufficient capture of quasi-rents—would have been largely frustrated unless the lease had also been exclusive. Without such assurance, the Armory Board would not have built the stadium. Thus, the restrictive covenant functioned not only as did the cities' promise to Surtran but also to induce an investment which, presumably, represented an efficient use of resources.

In *Hecht* the practice helped induce the purchaser of a service to make an investment. In the appropriate situation, however, it could just as easily help induce the provider of a service to make one.[81] For example, consider again the situation in *Pinehurst*. When the Moore County Board was making its initial arrangements for fbo service at the Southern Pines Airport, it may have been searching for an operator who would expend resources either to develop goodwill or to acquire tangible, specialized capital assets, like a building or some durable equipment. It may even have been searching for one who would explicitly promise to make such investments. The Board may have reasonably believed, however, that its search would likely come to nought unless it allayed the fears of prospective operators that they would be unable to capture the quasi-rents that might be generated by such investments. Capture might be frustrated, on the one hand, by the post-investment franchising of one or more additional operators. They might take a "free ride" on any goodwill that had been developed or simply compete away the value of all the specialized capital assets that had been acquired. On the other hand, capture might be frustrated by opportunistic behavior on the part of the Board. By promising to make arrangements with only one operator, the Board may have hoped to allay such fears. Presumably, that promise would tend to foreclose the establishment of additional operators. Obviously that would dramatically reduce the threat posed by potential rivalry. Curiously, a dramatic reduction in that threat would tend to substantially reduce the other one. Opportunistic behavior on the part of the Board could very well provoke retaliation in kind by the operator. Such retaliation would be more costly in the absence of in-place alternative sources of fbo service. Thus, the Board would be less likely to risk it.

By providing some contractual assurance of quasi-rent capture, the Board's promise may have helped induce Resort to make an investment. One cannot be sure because it is not clear from the court's opinion whether any investment was sought. Typically, when the practice under discussion is put to garden-variety use, no significant investment is sought. So consider a more striking use of that practice, like the one challenged in *Mason City Center Associates v. The City of Mason City, Iowa*. In that case a sizeable investment was sought, the establishment of a downtown regional shopping center. The Mason City city council promised the developer of that center that it would use its powers to discourage the development of any other such centers within the city limits. That promise helped induce store owners to locate in the downtown center and thereby to make, collectively, the desired investment.

It seems that the citizens of Mason City, at least as a group, valued a downtown regional shopping center for itself, not just for the goods and services actually sold there. In 1943 their city council adopted a comprehensive land use plan which called for a compact central business district. When the plan was revised in 1965, it explicitly suggested that no regional shopping centers be developed on the edges of the city. In 1972 the city council began accumulating funds which it earmarked for the development of a downtown center. Five years later the council hired Holmen Development Corporation to undertake the development. In 1978 the council put to the citizens a bond issue to support the development, and 65 percent of those voting approved it. In light of the city council's actions, which we must assume were taken as the agent for its principals, the citizens,[82] and the vote on the bond issue, it appears that the citizens of Mason City, as a group, must have viewed the mere existence of a downtown center as a "service" from which they could derive substantial benefits. I shall refer to this service as central business district service.

It also appears, however, that those citizens perceived a shortage of that service.[83] Less of it was being supplied than they were willing to pay for. From their point of view, investment in a downtown regional shopping center was sub-optimal. That should seem puzzling. If the downtown center were so valued by the citizens of Mason City, then, as a rather specialized resource, it would tend to generate quasi-rents. *Ceteris paribus*, one would have expected investors to respond to the opportunity to earn them. An explanation is required.

It is true that if citizens valued central business district service, then presumably they would have been willing to pay for it provided that they could not have obtained it otherwise. But each citizen, as an individual, would have perceived that it would be equally available to him regardless of whether he paid. Downtown store owners could not have even begun to deny service to non-payers without negotiating an extraordinarily large number of contracts and then monitoring all of them. Prohibitively high transactions costs would have made it uneconomical for those owners to capture the quasi-rents which would be generated by their investments. Hence, they would have tended to make smaller ones than they would have made had transactions costs been negligible.

The citizens of Mason City could have obtained more investment by arranging for the store owners to capture those quasi-rents. The arrangements could have involved a promise to pay a separate fee, a promise to maintain patronage at the downtown stores even if their sales prices were raised to reflect those quasi-rents, or a combination of the two. As long as the cost of the arrangements was less than the value of the additional investment, the new level of investment would be more optimal than the old. Presumably, the citizens would have been interested in making such arrangements only if the cost had been that small. That reveals that by making such arrangements, the citizens would have been "purchasing" a service. It was in the context of such a purchase that the city council made its promise.

No arrangements would have been economical unless the citizens could have avoided some of the transactions costs which the owners would have had to incur in order to capture the quasi-rents. The citizens could have eliminated the costs of negotiating a very large number of contracts by acting through a previously designated agent with wide-ranging powers, the city council.[84] They would have had to do more, however, in order to reduce monitoring and enforcement costs because even arrangements made by the city council might have entailed substantial ones.

To illustrate, suppose that the council paid the owners a separate fee. If it promised to pay the entire fee before the investment was to be made, the risk of welching by the owners would rise. Indeed, the council might find itself without that for which it thought it was paying and no readily available means of securing compensation for its loss. The council might strongly prefer to pay periodically with most of the payments to be made following the investment. Unfortunately, it is more difficult for any government, including a local one, to bind itself than it is for a private enterprise to do so.[85] Those who deal with governments generally find it relatively expensive to make sure that promises are kept. Therefore, if the city council promised to pay periodically, it might have to pay the owners a premium for taking a risk. That premium might be significant in an age when a number of local governments teeter on the brink of insolvency. Moreover, by so promising, the city council would likely create incentives for store owners to inefficiently enter or refrain from exiting the downtown center.

Now suppose that the council promised, on behalf of all the citizens, that they would maintain their patronage of the downtown stores even if sales prices were raised to reflect quasi-rents. The costs of monitoring compliance with and enforcing such a promise boggle the mind. But those costs could be almost eliminated while achieving the same end if the council made a functionally equivalent promise. That promise would be to discourage the development of any other regional shopping centers where the residents might shop.

The making of that promise was the centerpiece of the arrangements which the city council actually made.[86] Presumably, making it made those arrangements cost-effective. Until the city council made that promise, its developer was notably unsuccessful in obtaining commitments from store owners to locate in the proposed downtown shopping center.[87] The promise helped induce an investment. That was the function it was supposed to serve.

Nevertheless, it was challenged as an antitrust offense by Mason City Center Associates (MCCA) and Beaver Farms, Inc. Unfortunately, that challenge never prompted any court to make the foregoing functional analysis. MCCA, a partnership formed in 1977, planned to develop a regional shopping center on the west edge of Mason City on land held by Beaver Farms. Almost two-thirds of that land, however, was zoned agricultural. Unless MCCA could get that land rezoned, it could not implement its plans. The Mason City Planning and Zoning Commission recommended that MCCA's rezoning request be denied. After a hearing and a debate, the city council voted to follow that recommendation. MCCA alleged that the city council's action was taken pursuant to the promise which it had made to the developers of the downtown center. It sued both the city and the developers.

Initially, the city moved to dismiss the suit on *Parker v. Brown* grounds. The district court denied the motion.[88] It assumed that the promise would have violated the antitrust laws if made by a private party. It was perfectly proper for the court to make that assumption for the purpose of highlighting the issue raised by the motion. That issue was immunity, not legality. The court, however, was not content to use the assumption for such a limited purpose. Instead, it bootstrapped the assumption into a resolution of that issue. The defendants were not protected by *Parker v. Brown,* ruled the court, in part because the Iowa legislature had not contemplated that "its municipalities would enter into anticompetitive agreements with private developers in connection with the exercise of their zoning powers."[89] Before so ruling, the court should have undertaken a functional analysis of the council's promise. Had it done so, it might have prompted the defendants to file a motion to dismiss on grounds related to the merits.

After the city's motion to dismiss was denied, it moved for summary judgment, which was also denied. The suit was tried to a jury. During the trial the plaintiffs moved for a directed verdict on the question of liability, which was denied. The jury found for the defendants, and the plaintiffs moved for judgment notwithstanding the verdict. The court denied that motion too and entered judgment for the defendants. The motion for a directed verdict obviously went to the merits, and the other motions probably did as well. Before denying any of them the district court should have undertaken that functional analysis. And since the propriety of each denial was questioned on appeal, the court of appeals should have undertaken it as well before affirming the judgment.

Functional analysis of the city council's promise could have yielded the same disposition as the one that was ultimately made. If undertaken by the district court early enough, however, the case could have been resolved much more quickly at far less expense to the parties and the judiciary. Moreover, if undertaken at all, the resolution of the case would have quite properly deterred the filing of similar claims and thereby reduced the chances that the horribles predicted by the dissenters in *City of Lafayette* and *City of Boulder* would come to pass.

FUNCTIONS SERVED WHEN A LOCAL GOVERNMENT "OWNS" OR WILL "OWN" THE CAPITAL FACILITY

In arranging for central business district service, the Mason City city council took steps to assure investors that they would capture the quasi-rents generated by any investment which they might make in downtown stores. Those steps reduced the costs that investors would otherwise have had to incur in order to effectuate that capture. Clearly, the council took those steps as the agent for the consumers of that service, the residents of the city. We must assume that a private enterprise agent in similar circumstances would have done the same. Presumably, it would have taken those steps only if by doing so it would have provided sufficient assurance at low enough cost so that those residents could obtain that service most cost-effectively by purchasing it from a privately owned provider, thereby paying the investors to bear the risk of non-capture, expropriation. We must therefore infer that what the council did provided that assurance.

Not all local governments attempting to arrange for that service would have been able to do likewise. For example, consider the city council of a city occupying far fewer square miles than did Mason City. On the one hand, had it taken the same steps as the Mason City city council, it might have provided negligible, if any, assurance. Moreover, it might not have had the power to take other ones that would have provided more. On the other hand, it might have been able to provide sufficient assurance but only by taking expensive steps, like making ancillary arrangements with the owners[90] of land lying beyond the city limits. Taking such steps might cost more than the additional central business district service was worth.

More generally, in arranging for any service requiring an investment, any local government might be unable to provide investors with sufficient assurance of quasi-rents capture[91] or unable to do so without incurring prohibitive costs. Prospective investors dealing with a local government that was so disabled would face a greater risk of expropriation. Presumably, they would not invest without being compensated for it, so they would demand a larger payment from the residents. That demand might make the "Mason City method" for obtaining service so much more expensive that an alternative method might be more cost-effective. That alternative would be purchasing the service from a collectively owned provider and bearing the risk of expropriation themselves.

Using that method, without more, might itself be so expensive, however, that residents would be better off simply doing without the service. Using it would entail more than "merely" arranging for the service to be provided. It would also entail (a) entering into a risk-bearing agreement, which might involve extraordinarily large negotiating costs, and (b) preventing each other from expropriating the quasi-rents,[92] which might involve even larger monitoring and enforcement costs. Presumably, residents would use this alternative only if they could adequately contain those costs.

The owners of a private enterprise could find themselves in a similar situation. They might wish to obtain a service, like wholesale distribution or retail marketing, that could only be provided if a substantial investment were made. Their management, however, might be disabled in the same way as our hypothetical local government was. They could then obtain the service most cost-effectively by creating their own service provider, which was subject to the commands of their management, and bearing the risk of expropriation themselves. Using that method to obtain the service, however, would still be expensive. Whether the owners used it or simply did without the service would depend upon how well they thought management could use hierarchical controls to contain those costs. Apparently, owners of private enterprises find themselves in such situations all the time and frequently believe that their managements can contain those costs. That is why we observe pervasive and persistent use of this method, which we call vertical integration.[93]

In such situations residents may be able to contain those costs best by acting through their local government. Indeed, in some instances that might be the only way in which they could avoid incurring prohibitive transactions costs. By having their local government bear the risk of expropriation, they could practically eliminate the costs of negotiating an agreement to do so. For that agreement, they could substitute, in effect, their governance arrangements by which the local government was constituted and empowered to act as the residents' "general agent."

Ironically, this action, which could practically eliminate negotiation costs, could raise monitoring and enforcement costs. By having the local government bear the risk, the residents would give themselves an incentive to take a free ride on the others and thereby expropriate the quasi-rents generated by their collective investment. A free-rider, as an individual consumer, would reap all of the gains from his behavior, while, as an "owner," he would suffer only a fraction of the losses which would be shared with all other residents. Monitoring residents who have such incentives and enforcing "anti-free-rider" ordinances against them would likely be prohibitively expensive, even if residents had their local government undertake those activities.

They might be able to effectuate the same end far more cheaply, however, by having their local government control the behavior, not of the potential free-riders, but of those with whom they would deal. That, of course, is precisely what the residents of Mason City had their city council do. As in that case, the local government will typically exert that control pursuant to an agreement with those responsible for actually performing the service or those who stand in their shoes financially. Under that agreement it will be obligated to refuse to make a similar one with some or all of their rivals. In short, it will use the same practice challenged in *Mason City* and *Hecht*. Its use will be distinctive in that it will be laced with coercion. Indeed, the practice may be complemented by an ordinance. It will, however, serve the same kind of functions as it served in those cases.

The fact that the local government "owns," or, more precisely for our purposes, acts for the "owners" of, the service provider, however, may obscure the practice itself and, especially, the functions it is supposed to serve. For example, suppose that the Mason City city council had "owned" the downtown stores. It might have then been difficult to even recognize that the council had entered into an agreement with the supplier of a service pursuant to which it had refused to deal with the supplier's rivals. It would certainly have been difficult to understand what functions were served by the council's promise to the developers and its related refusal to grant the plaintiff's request for rezoning. Since it would not have been at all clear that the council had acted on behalf of the consumers of central business district service, it might have appeared that the council's actions were designed to restrict output. Similar difficulties would have beset the analysis of *Hecht* had the District of Columbia Armory Board "owned" the Redskins.[94]

Where a local government does "own," or act for the "owners" of, the service provider, however, it is especially critical that the practice be recognized and that its functions be understood. It is so critical because such situations are particularly apt to arise in connection with services designed to promote the health and safety of residents. In arranging for them, a local government would find it most difficult to bind itself[95] and its residents[96] or to protect itself and them from being "held up" by a privately owned service provider.[97] Residents might, therefore, wish to obtain them from a collectively owned provider and bear the risk of expropriation themselves. But that might not be economical unless the practice were used to control the behavior of free-riders. Only local government can do that since only it can use the practice laced with coercion. Indeed, I would argue that it is a fundamental purpose of local government to so use the practice to make arrangements for just such services. In legal argot, such actions are called exercises of the police power. Thus, if the practice ran afoul of the antitrust statutes, local government as we know it would truly be transformed.

For this reason, it is worth illustrating the appropriate analysis of the practice when used by a local government which "owns," or acts for the "owners" of, the service provider. To that end, consider two instances of such use: one by Akron, Ohio, which was the subject of *Glenwillow Landfill v. City of Akron, Ohio,*[98] and the other by Kansas City, Missouri, which was the subject of *Gold Cross Ambulance v. City of Kansas City, Mo.*[99]

Glenwillow Landfill arose out of the efforts of Akron officials to develop a city-"owned" "recycle energy system" (RES). An RES is a solid waste disposal facility at which the materials deposited are incinerated in specially designed boilers to generate saleable energy in the form of steam or electricity. The officials decided to finance the RES through the sale of revenue bonds issued on behalf of the city by the Ohio Water Development Authority.

In connection with the sale of those bonds, Akron entered into an agreement with the Authority under which the city was obligated, until the bonds were redeemed, (1) to refrain from "establish[ing], construct[ing], operat[ing], or consent[ing] to the establishment, construction or operation of any facility" which would compete with the RES;[100] and (2) to require that collectors and haulers deposit all solid waste generated in the city at the RES[101] and pay the customary fees and charges for doing so.[102] In short, Akron promised that neither it nor its residents would make arrangements with anyone else for the disposal of solid wastes. That promise was made explicitly for the benefit of the bondholders who stood in the financial shoes of the service provider since their loans were secured solely by the revenues that the RES might generate. The city acted to fulfill its promise by adopting a complementary ordinance.[103] Thus, Akron used the practice analyzed in this chapter in the context under discussion.

The practice was challenged as an antitrust offense in a suit brought against the city and the Authority by sanitary landfill owners, a recycler, and solid waste collectors and haulers. After a bench trial the court entered judgment for the defendant governments because, in its view, their conduct was state action, "exempt from the operation of the Sherman Act" under *Parker v. Brown* and its progeny.[104] The court's view was based on two independent grounds. One was that when the Authority took action with respect to the issuance of revenue bonds for solid waste disposal facilities, it acted for the state as sovereign just like the Supreme Court of Arizona had done in regulating lawyer advertising, the conduct challenged in *Bates v. State Bar of Arizona*.[105] To the extent that the court's judgment was based on this ground, its soundness must be questioned. The Authority, unlike the Supreme Court of Arizona, derived all of its power from the Ohio legislature. And unlike the court's prohibition of lawyers' price advertising, the Authority's decision to issue bonds pursuant to an agreement with Akron which contained restrictive covenants did not reflect any discernible state policy. Moreover, even if the Authority's conduct were state action "exempt from the operation of the Sherman Act," it is not at all clear why that makes the city's conduct the same.[106] The second ground was that when Akron exercised its constitutional home rule powers, as it had done in financing the RES, it acted for the state as sovereign. To the extent that the court's judgment was based on that ground, however, it was simply wrong.[107] That judgment cannot be squared with *City of Boulder*. The Ohio cases invoked by the district court, which sustained the creation of municipal monopolies over solid waste disposal against a non-antitrust attack,[108] are inapposite. So, too, are the "Tenth Amendment values" invoked by the appellate court[109] when it affirmed the district court's judgment.

The Supreme Court did vacate that judgment and remand the matter for reconsideration in light of *City of Boulder*,[110] but the district court was barely moved.[111] It eschewed the home rule ground, but still reached the conclusion that Akron's conduct was exempt from antitrust scrutiny. One could not safely predict, however, that other courts would render like judgments on suits challenging like conduct. Thus, it is useful for purposes beyond illustration to evaluate Akron's practice on the antitrust merits.

Had it not been considered "exempt from the operation of the Sherman Act," Akron's practice might still have been deemed legal. That would have depended, or at least should have depended, on the functions which it was supposed to serve. Those functions can best be deduced by examining the economic context in which the practice was used and then applying the now-familiar mandated assumption that Akron officials acted to maximize the wealth of the city's residents.

Long before those officials even began to think about developing an RES, of course, Akron residents had been purchasing solid waste disposal service. By "solid waste disposal service" I mean all of those actions taken with respect to solid wastes after they are hauled away and deposited. They include not only burying the wastes in a sanitary landfill, the principal disposal method that had been used in Akron, but also controlling the harm that those wastes might do.

That service was costly. Valuable resources, including the burial site itself, were used in the operation of each landfill. Still more were used to monitor the landfills for compliance with regulations designed to protect the health and aesthetic sensibilities of Akron residents, and, when non-compliance was observed, to enforce those regulations. Even so, the health of some residents was no doubt impaired and the senses of some were no doubt offended by the solid wastes that had been deposited. Moreover, some of those wastes were themselves valuable resources which might have been recycled. Residents paid for this costly service monetarily and non-monetarily, both individually and collectively.[112]

Apparently, Akron officials came to believe that solid waste disposal service could be supplied more efficiently, and therefore more cheaply, if an RES were used. They did so despite the fact that a study which they had commissioned had reported that the unit cost of the actual processing of solid waste would likely be higher at an RES than at a sanitary landfill.[113] Nevertheless, their belief was not at all unreasonable. They might have expected, justifiably, that those additional processing costs would be more than offset by savings in land use, regulatory monitoring and enforcement, health and aesthetic sensibilities, and recycling. The RES which those officials were developing was going to be capable of handling virtually all solid waste generated in the city both when it was constructed and for a substantial period thereafter.[114] It would use the land on which it was situated far more intensively than would a sanitary landfill, thereby freeing other land for other uses. An RES might require considerably less regulatory monitoring and enforcement than would numerous sanitary landfills, especially since it could be centrally located rather than dispersed in outlying areas, and its highly automated operations might be less easily upset by difficult-to-detect shirking. Besides, incinerating solid waste in specially designed boilers might create fewer health hazards, eyesores, and noxious fumes than would burying it. Moreover, since the boilers would produce saleable energy, more solid wastes could be recycled and recyclables could be put to higher-value uses[115] at an RES than they could be at sanitary landfills or even at "transfer stations" where recycling is done.

If it were at all likely, however, that solid waste disposal service could be supplied more efficiently with an RES, then it is puzzling, at least superficially, that no entrepreneur had built one or, from all that appears in the relevant court opinions, even offered to do so. After all, a highly specialized facility like an RES would generate substantial quasi-rents if it were cost-effective to use, and quasi-rents are precisely what entrepreneurs seek. Of course, the solution to this puzzle might simply be that Akron officials had no good reason for believing that the RES would be as cost-effective as they apparently believed it would be,[116] but that seems unlikely. Even the *Glenwillow Landfill* plaintiffs made no such claim, and they would have had a powerful incentive to do so if any credible evidence could have been marshalled to support it. The more likely solution to this puzzle is that if an entrepreneur had built an RES, it would have been quite difficult for him to capture the quasi-rents that it generated. That which would have made it so difficult is a key part of the economic context in which the challenged practice was used, so we must understand it.

To that end, let us perform an intellectual simulation. Suppose that an entrepreneur had contemplated building an RES long before any government official had done so. The spot market for solid waste disposal service would have appeared a most unpromising source of quasi-rents. On the spot market for any good, selling yields all revenues, including any that are quasi-rents. Sales revenues are a function of the unit price and the quantity demanded, which in our case would be the tipping fee and the amount of solid waste deposited. The unit price and the quantity demanded are, in turn, functions of each other. These relationships imply that if sales revenues are to include any quasi-rents, the unit price must fall within certain limits. On the one hand, it must exceed some minimum lest each sale yield too little revenue. To use an extreme example, if the unit price were no greater than average operating cost, sales revenues could not possibly include any quasi-rents. On the other hand, the unit price must not exceed some maximum lest there be too few sales. Our entrepreneur would quickly conclude that on the spot market for solid waste disposal service, these limits would place him in a Catch-22 quandary. At any tipping fee high enough to permit him to capture some quasi-rents, so little solid waste would be deposited at the RES that he would, in fact, capture none of them.

His conclusion would rest on (a) an observation about the nature of the spot market, (b) a prediction about the behavior of solid waste haulers in that market, and (c) a comparison of his tipping fees with those of the owners of competing landfills. He would observe that on the spot market for solid waste disposal service, the amount deposited at the RES would depend upon the decisions of individual haulers about where to deposit the solid wates that they had collected. He would then predict that the individual hauler would make that decision almost entirely on the basis of where he would be charged the lowest tipping fee: the RES or a competing landfill.[117]

That prediction, while safe, is not so obvious as it may appear. It is not at all surprising, of course, that the size of the tipping fee would be important to a hauler in making his decision about where to deposit. That is because, everything else being equal, the lower the tipping fee, the greater would be his net revenues, and we would expect a hauler to try to maximize his net revenues. It is a bit surprising, however, that the size of the tipping fee would be determinative. After all, in many situations a buyer of a service can maximize his revenues by purchasing from a seller whose service is most valuable even if that seller charges a higher price for it than others do. In the situation we are simulating, however, haulers could not do that even though the service provided at an RES would be more valuable than that provided at a landfill. The reason is that, for the most part, the greater value of the RES service would have no effect on a hauler's bottom line. To illustrate, if solid waste were treated and incinerated at an RES rather than buried at a landfill, it is likely that less harm would be done to human health. That means that the service at the former would be more valuable than the service at the latter. To the individual hauler, however, it would appear that he could enjoy that additional value whether or not he chose to deposit any particular truck load of solid waste at the RES. Therefore, he would make his deposits wherever he would be charged the least for doing so.

So, our entrepreneur would compare tipping fees. In particular, he would compare the lowest RES tipping fee that might permit him to capture any quasi-rents, "his fee," with the tipping fees that he expected the landfill owners to charge once the RES was open for business, "their fees." He would find that his fee was significantly greater than theirs; in fact, he would probably find that his was greater than the tipping fees that they were charging while he was contemplating the building of the RES. Microeconomics and the available data tell us so.

Microeconomics reveals a floor below his fee and a ceiling

above theirs, and the available data show that that floor is higher than that ceiling. The floor for his fee would be "his marginal operating cost" when the RES was operating optimally from an engineering perspective (probably processing at least all of the solid waste produced in the Akron area at the time of the litigation). By "his marginal operating cost" I mean that portion of the marginal cost of operating the RES that he would have to bear.[118] In the absence of collusion, the ceiling for their fee would be the marginal landfill owner's marginal operating cost. We can safely ignore the possibility of collusion because even if the landfill owners had engaged in it (and nothing in the court opinions suggests that they had), the opening of the RES, a large rival with a considerably different cost structure,[119] would have upset their scheme.

The available data show that our entrepreneur's marginal operating cost would be greater than the marginal landfill owner's marginal operating cost. The court's description of RES and landfill operations suggests that many more resources were used to process solid waste at the former than at the latter. It also suggests, rather strongly, that a far greater proportion of the costs incurred as a result of processing would be borne by the owner of the RES than would be borne by the owners of the landfills. These suggestions are confirmed by the study commissioned by Akron officials which reported that the unit costs of processing solid waste would be higher at the RES than at the landfills. Unit processing costs are probably a good accounting proxy for that portion of marginal operating cost borne by the owner of a facility. The *Glenwillow Landfill* defendants had a powerful incentive to try to contradict the study. It would have then been easier for them to justify the challenged practice. Nevertheless, they did not even try to show that the reported cost relationship would be different when the RES operated optimally from the engineering perspective. It seems safe to assume that they did not try to do so because the evidence would not support such a showing.

We may thus conclude that the spot market would not have provided our entrepreneur with any assurance of capturing the quasi-rents that his RES would generate. So, he would not build it without first securing that assurance contractually. Unfortunately for him, securing that assurance contractually would have been prohibitively expensive.

Consider how costly it would have been for him to secure it from individual Akron residents. He would have had to negotiate tens of thousands of long-term service requirements contracts, each contingent on the signing of the others. These contracts might have been rather complex since he and the residents would probably have found it advantageous to leave many of the terms unspecified while agreeing to use some mechanism to specify them in the future.[120] Once these contracts were signed and the privately financed RES built, he would then have had to monitor residents or their agents for compliance. That would have been particularly problematic had residents, or at least some of them, been contractually free to purchase their own hauling from operators unaffiliated with the RES. Those operators would have had an incentive to haul their solid wastes to a landfill rather than to the RES if, *ceteris paribus*, a lower tipping fee were charged by one or more of the landfills or if the collection work itself, including pick-ups outside the city,[121] could have been performed more efficiently on routes ending at one or more of them. Of course, those operators might have been formally bound to ignore that incentive. A clause obligating them to ignore it could have been included in every agreement for the purchase of hauling. And such a clause probably would have been included, too, had the contracts between our entrepreneur and the residents so required. He could not have relied on the residents, however, to hold the operators to their formal obligations. It is unlikely that the individual purchaser of hauling would have bothered to track down the ultimate destination of his garbage. And an entrepreneur would have had to field a small police force to do so. In the absence of such monitoring costs, however, individual purchasing might otherwise have been most efficient. Finally, if non-compliance were observed, our entrepreneur would have had to take enforcement action. The costs of negotiating, monitoring, and enforcing such contracts might have exceeded the value of the quasi-rents whose capture by our entrepreneur they were designed to assure.[122]

Of course, Akron residents might have tried to induce private investment in an RES by taking steps, collectively, to reduce those transactions costs. Any such effort, however, might have been futile. It is true that they could have had the city, as their "agent," negotiate a single contract for waste disposal service, and that they might have been able to have the city use coercion to cost-effectively control those with whom free-riding residents would have dealt.[123] Taking such steps, however, would likely have been unintentionally counterproductive. Instead of providing assurance to our entrepreneur that they would capture the quasi-rents, such steps might instead have put them at greater risk. The reason is that once the RES was built, opportunistic behavior by city officials might dissipate those quasi-rents. For example, they might declare a medical emergency or simply abrogate the contract, or portions of it, or they might regulate RES rates. In light of the possible impact of waste disposal service on the health and welfare of Akron residents, a promise by the city that its officials would refrain from such conduct would almost certainly be unenforceable and would most likely be incredible. Thus, Akron residents might have been unable to induce private investment in an RES even by acting through their local government. It seems quite likely that in order to obtain the solid waste disposal service which could be more efficiently produced if an RES were used, they had to bear the risk of quasi-rent expropriation themselves.

They could do that through the Akron city government. If they did that, however, then they could expect to experience monitoring and enforcement problems analogous to those that would have helped deter our entrepreneur from building an RES. Once they had the government build it, each resident would likely have had an incentive to obtain solid waste disposal service from a provider who did not use the new facility. Those providers would have been the owners of sanitary landfills or transfer stations. For the reasons already discussed, they would probably have offered the service at a lower price than would the city of Akron. The resident who obtained service from such a provider could expect to gain as a consumer by pocketing the difference in price. He could also expect to lose as an owner-resident because his behavior would reduce RES revenues from tipping fees and the sale of recyclables and energy, and increase the risk of illness and aesthetic offense. Of course he would share those losses, with most, if not all, of the other residents of Akron so he could expect that his gain would exceed his loss. Only the costs of obtaining the service from an alternative provider would deter a resident from patronizing one.

Those costs might have been prohibitive for residents of one- and two-family dwellings who paid for pick-up and hauling collectively through their local taxes, but they would not have been for residents of multi-family dwellings acting through their landlords and, especially, owners of business establishments.[124] They were already making their own contractual arrangements for solid waste pick-up and hauling. It would have been a simple matter for them to make those arrangements with operators who planned to make their deposits at a site other than the RES. The fees paid to those operators would tend to reflect the lower monetary price of the alternative provider's service.

Presumably, the likelihood of such free-riding prompted the city's underwriters to advise it that lenders, who could look only to RES revenues for payment, would not make funds available unless the city entered into an agreement with the Authority that contained restrictive covenants having the effect of making it much more difficult to engage in such opportunistic behavior.

The restrictive covenants had that effect because they made it extraordinarily expensive for a rival provider of solid waste disposal service to operate in the city and for a hauler to carry solid waste to an operator located outside of the city. By making free-riding so much more difficult, the city assured investors that they would capture the quasi-rents generated by the RES. Thus, Akron's practice functioned to reduce the transactions costs of effectuating that capture, and that reduction was an integral, if not essential, part of purchasing efficiently produced waste disposal service. If serving that function were deemed undesirable according to the principles embodied in the antitrust statutes, then, and only then, should the practice be condemned as a violation of them.

Gold Cross Ambulance arose out of the efforts of Kansas City officials to create a publicly owned advanced-life-support/quick-response ambulance system. As part of those efforts, they entered into a contract with Ambulance Services, Inc. (ASI) for

Kansas City residents' requirements of ambulance service. ASI was obligated to use the city's emergency vehicles.[125] It was also obligated to provide service with specified medical-care and response-time characteristics. In fact, only if ASI's service had those characteristics, with the medical-care ones assessed by an advisory group of physicians, would ASI be paid. The city was obligated to actually make the payments that were due. ASI was thereby relieved of the task of collecting from resident users. The city also promised, explicitly or implicitly, that similar arrangements would not be made with any of ASI's rivals during the term of the contract. It fulfilled that promise by granting an operating license only to ASI and by adopting a complementary ordinance which provided that only those holding such licenses could pick up patients within the city limits. Thus, Kansas City used the same practice which Akron used in connection with the development of its RES.

That practice was challenged as an antitrust offense in a suit brought against the city and ASI by two privately owned ambulance companies, operating out of nearby Independence, which had been unable to compete for several large contracts to provide non-emergency ambulance service at institutions located in Kansas City. The city and its affiliates moved for summary judgment on the grounds, *inter alia*, that the practice was "permissible under the state action exemption to the antitrust laws."[126]

The court granted their motion, ruling that when the Missouri legislature enacted statutes which (1) permitted municipalities to own and operate ambulance systems[127] and (2) subjected private ambulance operators to licensure and related regulations,[128] the state had authorized, if it had not directed, Kansas City to use the challenged practice. On appeal, the Eighth Circuit affirmed.[129] Nevertheless, the ruling was erroneous since it does not appear that those statutes even speak to the practice much less reflect any discernible state policy favoring its use. Another local government that did what Kansas City did could not count on persuading another court that its conduct could not be scrutinized under the antitrust statutes. Thus, as with *Glenwillow Landfill*, it is useful for more than the purposes of illustration to consider the legality of Kansas City's practice.

Once again, legality turns, or ought to turn, on the function that the practice was likely supposed to serve. Analysis reveals that that function was the same as the one served by Akron's practice. We begin the analysis in the now-usual manner by carefully observing the economic context in which it was used.

Just as the residents of Akron had been purchasing solid waste disposal service long before the development of the RES, the residents of Kansas City had been purchasing ambulance service long before the creation of the advanced-life-support/quick-response system. In the years immediately preceding the system's creation they had been making their purchases from a number of providers on a spot market. Apparently, Kansas City officials came to believe that the service available on that market was substantially inferior, in terms of medical care and response time, to the service for which residents would have been willing to pay. That belief was reasonable since considerable transactions costs would have stood between the residents' willingness to pay and any provider's receipt of revenues. Those transactions costs would have been the costs of exclusion, search, and collection. Because of them, a provider of superior ambulance service would have had little, if any, chance of earning enough to cover his higher costs, much less enough to give him a return on his larger investment that was commensurate with his risk. Let's consider those costs *seriatum*.

The costs of exclusion would have prevented a provider of superior ambulance service from obtaining revenues from most of those who would have benefited by it. That may seem counterintuitive since those who are transported and cared for in ambulances are usually charged a fee. But those who are transported and cared for in ambulances would not have been the only ones who would have benefited by that service. Almost every resident of Kansas City would have benefited because in the course of producing it, a provider would have also produced another valuable good, the availability of that service. The provider would have found it rather expensive, however, to stop any resident from enjoying the benefits of that availability. In fact, the costs of exclusion would have probably been prohibitive—that availability would have been a "public good." As a result, no resident would have had any incentive to pay for it. A provider of superior service could have obtained revenues, then, only from those wishing to be transported and cared for in an ambulance.

And not all of them would have used the provider's service. The costs of search would have prevented the provider from obtaining the patronage of some who would have been willing to pay a premium for superior ambulance service. They would have been residents who were unaware[130] of the fact that they could secure such service from him. When summoning an ambulance, they might well have called a rival provider. Attempting to remedy such ignorance by supplying credible information about medical care and response time would have been quite expensive. Moreover, it might not have done much good since users rarely summon their own ambulances, and those who summon one for them might be ignorant, fail to appreciate the preferences of the user, or act opportunistically.[131]

Obtaining patronage, of course, does not itself fill the coffers of ambulance service providers. Collecting fees does. Their costs of collection, however, prevent them from obtaining revenues from all of their patrons. In large part, those costs are high because they usually seek payment after rather than before service is rendered. If a provider refused service, especially emergency service, until it had secured payment, or at least information suggesting that payment would be made in the near future,[132] residents would likely become aware of that practice[133] and, when summoning an ambulance for themselves or for others, tend to call a rival provider. Thus, there may be a substantial disparity between the revenues that an ambulance service provider earns and those that it receives. That disparity would have been especially painful to a provider of superior service because it would have been so costly to produce it.

These three transactions costs must have been large enough that they offset the economies of dispatching and positioning that a single provider would have enjoyed.[134] Otherwise, a single provider would have probably been able to drive all his rivals from the market. In any event, they were likely large enough so that the revenues obtainable on the spot market would have been insufficient to induce any provider to acquire the emergency vehicles, hire the trained personnel, and operate the sophisticated positioning and dispatching system necessary to supply advanced-life-support/quick-response ambulance service in an amount which would otherwise have been optimal.

Not surprisingly, then, Kansas City officials also came to believe that the amount of that service supplied would have been more nearly optimal if it were sold off the spot market. It does appear that by so selling a provider could have reduced the costs of exclusion, search, and collection. He could have reduced the costs of exclusion by selling his service pursuant to a requirements contract, and he could have reduced the costs of search and collection by including provisions in that contract that (a) specified the characteristics that his service would have to have and (b) placed the risk of non-payment on the buyers. But, then, why didn't any provider do just that? The explanation is that the costs of negotiating, monitoring, and enforcing such a contract were prohibitive.

The provider would have had to negotiate contracts with perhaps hundreds of thousands of residents in order to make the non-payment provisions palatable. Each contract would have had to contain complex performance standards. Each would have had to have been long-term and contingent upon the signing of all of the others. Once the contracts were signed, the provider would have had to identify non-signers and prevent them from using the service. That would have been difficult since many users would have been unable to identify themselves, even by their location since they might have been away from their homes, and denial of service would have had catastrophic consequences. If the demand charge, or option fee, were low enough, the provider would also have had to prevent signers from using rival providers. Otherwise, he would fail to cover those capacity costs reflected in his schedule of user fees, the charges for transportation and care. Moreover, the provider would have to assure residents that they would receive the service for which they had contracted. That would not have been easy since residents would have been hard-pressed to assess the provider's performance and even harder pressed to take action against the provider if the service were found wanting since a recalcitrant provider might respond to enforcement with a curtailment.

Kansas City residents could have reduced these costs had they taken collective action through the city. The city could have struck the necessary agreements on their behalf and thereby dramatically reduced negotiating costs. The city could have also used coercion to prevent would-be rivals, who had not entered into an agreement, from selling ambulance service to them. That would have substantially reduced the costs of monitoring the behavior of residents and enforcing anti-free-rider provisions against them. Finally, the city could have hired personnel to assess the service that was provided and, if its quality did not meet contractual standards, to withhold payment or otherwise secure better service. That might have reduced monitoring and enforcement costs somewhat since the city would have likely enjoyed some scale economies in carrying out those tasks. Monitoring and enforcement costs would still have probably been prohibitive, however, unless the city had made arrangements with only one provider. If the city had made arrangements with more than one, each provider would have had an incentive to act opportunistically to try to avoid runs on which it would have been more difficult to meet performance standards.

Although taking such collective action would have reduced the costs of negotiating, monitoring, and enforcing requirements contracts for ambulance service, it would probably not have provided sufficient assurance to investors of quasi-rent capture to induce the investment necessary to create an advanced-life-support/quick-response system. In fact, it is likely that those actions would have inadvertently put the prospective owners of the system at greater risk for the same reason that analogous actions taken by the residents of Akron would have put the prospective private owners of an RES at greater risk. The probability of opportunistic behavior on the part of the city would have been substantial, and the costs of enforcing its promise to refrain from such behavior would have been prohibitive. The premium that the owners would have demanded for bearing this moral hazard risk probably would have amounted to a substantial fraction of the value of the service. The residents would have likely been reluctant to pay it. They would have been particularly reluctant since they would have had to bear the parallel moral hazard risk that the provider would hold them up—reduce the level of service provided or threaten to do so in order to obtain more revenues. That risk would have been particularly acute if, to economize on monitoring and enforcement costs, the city had entered into a service agreement with only one provider, because the effect of doing so would have been to make it much more difficult to quickly replace the provider.

Thus, it was quite reasonable for Kansas City officials to believe that no privately owned provider would supply the kind of service that could be produced with an advanced-life-support/quick-response system. The costs of capturing the quasi-rents generated by such a system would have been prohibitive. So, if the residents were to obtain that service, for which they would be willing to pay, they would have to obtain it from a publicly owned provider. They could do so, without negotiating a risk-bearing agreement, by having the city acquire the necessary emergency vehicles and contract with a privately owned firm to use those vehicles to actually make the runs. That would mean, however, that they would bear the risk of quasi-rent expropriation themselves. The quasi-rents generated by the system could have been expropriated by residents who welched on the implicit agreement to purchase their requirements of ambulance transportation and care from the city-owned provider.

Many residents would have had an incentive to do just that. By purchasing service from a non-city-owned provider, a resident could have pocketed any difference in rates. There would have likely been a difference because the city-owned provider's rates would probably have reflected more capacity costs than the other provider's would. The city could have eliminated any potential gain by setting its provider's rates so that they did not reflect any capacity costs. If it had done so, however, residents might very well have had to bear even more costs than they would have borne as a result of welching. They would have had to bear additional taxes to cover those capacity costs, and they would have had to bear the expense of inefficient behavior prompted by that taxation. Generally, residents would have been tempted to try to reap the gain from rate differences whenever they preferred the price/performance of the non-city-owned provider to that of the city-owned one. They would have been especially likely to have had that preference when they believed that they did not need emergency service. And obtaining non-emergency service from a non-city-owned provider would have been easy. The costs of making the purchase would have been almost zero. The chances of being caught would have been small, and it seems likely that if one were caught, the penalty would have been less than harsh. Of course, whenever a resident purchased ambulance service from a non-city-owned provider, he would have also suffered a loss. The city-owned provider would have realized fewer revenues, and so the value of his interest in it would have been diminished. Since he would have shared that revenue shortfall with so many others, however, his gain would have almost certainly exceeded his loss. Thus, the incentive to welch, at least when obtaining non-emergency service, would have been strong. Unless the response to this incentive were checked, it is quite likely that collective risk-bearing, even through the city, would have been prohibitively expensive.

By making it much more costly for non-city-owned providers to operate in Kansas City, the agreement between Kansas City and ASI and the complementary ordinance did check that response. Thus, the challenged practice served an instrumental function in securing more nearly optimal ambulance service for the residents of Kansas City.[135] If that function were deemed undesirable according to the principles embodied in the antitrust statutes, then, and only then, should it have been condemned as an offense.

ALL FUNCTIONS ARE UNOBJECTIONABLE

In *Pinehurst, Woolen, Hecht, Mason City, Glenwillow Landfill,* and *Gold Cross Ambulance,* the legal problems of the defendant local government grew out of its efforts to purchase a "service," broadly conceived, at the lowest possible price. Each tried to make the purchase by entering into a complex sales transaction, an integral part of which was it promise not to buy from any of the supplier's rivals. That practice, which is used by virtually every local government, is almost invariably supposed to serve one or more of the four functions it served when used by the defendants in the illustrative cases. Most of those functions are related to the avoidance of transactions costs, and that is no accident. Individuals and groups generally enter into complex sales transactions instead of making their purchases on a spot market for that very purpose.[136] The four functions are: (1) to help secure efficiently provisioned service by permitting the supplier to enjoy either production or transactions economies; (2) to help reduce the transactions costs, particularly monitoring and enforcement costs, of arranging for the service; (3) to help reduce the transactions costs of capturing quasi-rents; and (4) by reducing them, to help induce investment when providing the service requires that an additional one be made.

Serving those functions is consistent with the principle that it is good to maximize consumer welfare. That should not be surprising since the practice is invariably used as part of a sales transaction, and sales transactions generally tend to increase consumer welfare. In fact, as already noted,[137] the only ones that do not are those which are largely transfer payments and those which are strategic moves designed for the acquisition of market power. Only transactions that are strategic moves tend to reduce consumer welfare, and they are likely uncommon—especially among local governments. There is certainly no evidence that the defendant local governments in the illustrative cases engaged in them.

When this most common practice is supposed to serve functions 1 and 2, it obviously tends to maximize consumer welfare. It tends to reduce the total costs incurred in making available a given output of a particular service. That cannot be said about the practice when it is supposed to serve only function 3. Viewed statically, the practice tends to maximize consumer welfare only in the sense that it may be the most cost-effective means by which investors can capture the quasi-rents generated by a service-related investment, an activity in which they are likely to engage in any event. Total costs will not vary with the identity of the individuals who can economically effectuate that capture. Viewed dynamically, however, total costs will so vary. Unless potential investors can economically effectuate capture, they may not make the service-related investment, and without it, the total costs incurred in making available a given output of the service may be much greater than they would otherwise be. Indeed, they may be infinite. Thus, when the practice is supposed to induce investment, function 4, it tends to promote efficiency. To put the point a bit more technically, whichever function the practice is supposed to serve, it tends to lower the supply curve. In a sense, it thereby "liberates" resources for other uses, which may include the production of more of that particular service or of something else entirely. That means that as a result of its use, the total personal value of all goods and services produced will tend to be higher than it would otherwise be. Thus, the practice is unobjectionable on grounds related to wealth creation.

It could be objectionable, if at all, only on grounds related to wealth distribution. In any particular instance of its use, one could certainly identify those who seem to be worse off as a result of the transaction of which it was a part. They are the rivals of the chosen supplier who would have liked to do business with the local government, or, in the case of "Johnny-come-latelies," who would like the local government to welch on its promise. Presumably, they are the ones who should benefit by the application of any wealth-distribution principle, according to which the functions served by the practice are undesirable. It is easy enough, then, to describe the general characteristics of such a principle. There are two. The principle must be based on an intellectually acceptable distinction between a group that includes those who seem to be worse off and some other group that includes the chosen supplier and the local government, even if the latter is included only as a confederate. It must also provide that it is good to prefer the first group to the second one. Finding a principle with these characteristics that will help resolve a specific dispute, however, is difficult at best.

For example, consider the problems one would have in finding such a principle for the *Pinehurst* dispute. One could identify those who seem to be worse off as a result of the arrangements between the Moore County Board and Resort. They are fixed based operators, not including Resort, who, upon reasonable notice, could begin providing fbo service at Southern Pines Airport, and others, like Pinehurst, who could have done so without incurring heavy start-up costs even though they were not already established as fixed based operators. It is no simple task to distinguish in an intellectually acceptable way between that group and another one which includes Resort. Even if we suppose that that could be done, however, one would still be confronted with an intractable problem in logic. The principle that it is good to prefer the first group to the second one will not help resolve the dispute since penalizing the Board for engaging in the practice would not make the preferred group any better off. Penalizing the Board would deter fixed based operators from agreeing to provide fbo service in reliance on the kind of promise which the Board made to Resort. In the absence of such an agreement, fbo service would seem more costly to the Board and other airport-owning local governments. They could be expected, therefore, to purchase less of it, or to offer less in exchange for it, than they otherwise would. In either event the preferred group would not be better off, but worse off. The dynamics of markets will cause the search for a wealth-distribution principle to yield about as much as a snipe hunt.

One could willfully ignore those dynamics and search for the principle on the basis of analogy. The cases are legion in which similar challenges to the practice were entertained, or even sustained, when engaged in by private enterprises.[138] Unfortunately, they are almost as unhelpful as they are bountiful. Most of the opinions do little more than affix one or more antitrust labels to the practice. The labels do colorfully describe the obvious: the plaintiffs were made worse off as a result of a contract which, literally, restrained their trade. They do not expressly disclose the wealth-distribution principle upon which the cases were decided.

But that principle must have been that it is good to prefer private holdings of wealth which are "smaller" or "less advantaged" to those which are "larger" or "more advantaged." As suggested previously, that principle seems to be rooted in a two-part rationale. Recall that one part is the public choice theory that political behavior may be explained largely on the basis of the relative wealth of the private antagonists interested in influencing it, and the other part is populist ideology, which holds that that behavior will be "better" the more widely dispersed and evenly wealth is distributed.

Searching on the basis of analogy will yield a wealth-distribution principle, but that principle is inapplicable to disputes between plaintiff private enterprises and defendant local governments. Even if we ignore the dynamics of markets, it is inapplicable on its own terms. It simply does not tell us that it is good to prefer some private holdings of wealth to any public holdings. One could try to expand the principle so that "larger" or "more advantaged" public holdings of wealth would be included in the non-preferred group. Local governments using the practice could then be included in that group if they arranged with a supplier for a "large" quantity of service or if parties to the arrangements were *ipso facto* deemed "more advantaged" than non-parties. Even if the principle were so extended, and one would almost have to compromise one's intellectual honesty to do so, it would still be inapplicable in light of the rationale on which it is based. The crude public choice theory does not even purport to tell us what effect the distribution of wealth between private enterprises and local governments will have on political behavior. Certainly, populism does not even hint that that behavior will be better if wealth is redistributed from local governments, and the taxpayers they represent, to private enterprises. Indeed, local government is a populist-preferred institution.

There simply is no principle, of wealth distribution or wealth creation, according to which the functions served by this practice are undesirable. The practice is, in and of itself,[139] lawful when engaged in by local governments. And under the principle of same treatment, established by the Supreme Court in *City of Lafayette* and *City of Boulder*, the practice must also be lawful, in and of itself, when engaged in by private enterprises. A holding to that effect, which would be contrary to the holdings in so many cases, would itself mark a major retrenchment in antitrust law.

NOTES

1. 476 F. Supp. 543 (M.D.N.C. 1979).
2. *Id.* at 548.
3. The opinion does not reveal whether Pinehurst alleged that the Board refused to make such arrangements pursuant to an explicit agreement. *See* 476 F. Supp. at 549 n.4. Pinehurst may have merely alleged that the Board acted upon an implicit understanding. It is plausible that the Board and Resort may have perceived that the Southern Pines Airport had limited facilities suitable for a fixed based operator and that the construction of new ones would be rather expensive. Believing that

the other party shared those perceptions, they may have understood that the Board would refuse to make arrangements for fbo service with any enterprise other than Resort. Legally, little, if anything, turned on which allegation Pinehurst had made, and functionally, nothing turned on it.

4. 476 F. Supp. 543, 555 nn.19-20 (M.D.N.C., 1979). Pinehurst also alleged that the Board had denied it a fuel facility to serve aircraft other than Pinehurst's and had treated it quite differently than Resort in regard to improvements generally. Moreover, Pinehurst claimed that the Board had made deceptive and false representations about it to the F.A.A., levied "inflated" electricity charges against it, required it to file financial statements and generally helped Resort harass it. Finally, Pinehurst asserted that the Board had insisted that it deal with the airport through Resort, presumably adding insult to injury. *Id.* at 555 nn.19-20.

5. *Id.* at 554.

6. Resort's motion to dismiss for failure to state a claim upon which relief could be based was grounded, in part, on what it argued was Pinehurst's failure to allege the relevant geographic and product markets. 476 F. Supp. at 551. The court rejected that argument, observing that Pinehurst did allege that (1) "[t]he Airport is the only one in Moore County that is federally funded and equipped to service passenger air service for the Southern Pines resort community," and (2) "Resort enjoys the position as the sole FBO at the airport." *Id.* Apparently, the first observation suggested to the court that the airport was the geographic market; and the second one suggested to the court that the alleged product market was the one for all goods "required and used by customers of the airport FBO." On that "analysis," almost every exclusive franchise at a major public facility would constitute a monopoly.

7. The same practice was so labelled in Pueblo Aircraft Service, Inc. v. City of Pueblo, Colo., 498 F. Supp. 1205 (D. Colo. 1980), *aff'd*, 679 F.2d 805 (10th Cir. 1982), *cert. denied*, 103 S. Ct. 762 (1983); Alphin v. Henson, 392 F. Supp. 813 (D. Md. 1975), *aff'd*, 538 F.2d 85 (4th Cir. 1976), *cert. denied*, 429 U.S. 960 (1976), *amended*, 552 F.2d 1003 (4th Cir. 1976), *cert. denied*, 434 U.S. 823 (1977); Metro Cable Co. v. CATV of Rockford, Inc., 375 F. Supp. 350 (W.D. Ill. 1974), *aff'd*, 516 F.2d 220 (7th Cir. 1975); Murdock v. City of Jacksonville, Fla., 361 F. Supp. 1083 (M.D. Fla. 1973); and E. W. Wiggins Airways, Inc. v. Massachusetts Port Authority, 362 F.2d 52 (1st Cir. 1966), *cert. denied*, 385 U.S. 947 (1966).

8. The same practice was so labelled in Corey v. Look, 641 F.2d 32 (1st Cir. 1981); and Metro Cable Co. v. CATV of Rockford, Inc., 375 F. Supp. 350 (W.D. Ill. 1974), *aff'd*, 516 F.2d 220 (7th Cir. 1975).

9. The same practice was so labelled in Pueblo Aircraft Service, Inc. v. City of Pueblo, Colo., 498 F. Supp. 1205 (D. Colo. 1980) *aff'd*, 679 F.2d 805 (10th Cir. 1982), *cert. denied*, 459 U.S. 1126 (1983); Guthrie v. Genessee County, N.Y., 494 F. Supp. 950 (W.D. N.Y. 1980); and Huron Valley Hospital, Inc. v. City of Pontiac, 466 F. Supp. 1301 (E.D. Mich. 1979), *vacated and remanded*, 666 F.2d 1029 (6th Cir. 1981).

10. Both the private and governmental defendants moved for dismissal pursuant to Federal Rules of Civil Procedure 12(b)(1) & (6). The motions raised issues related to standing, exhaustion of remedies, primary jurisdiction, subject matter jurisdiction (nexus to interstate commerce), statute of limitations, and market definition, as well as state action "immunity."

11. 476 F. Supp. 543, 551-56 (M.D.N.C. 1979).

12. The court's unfocused discussion of the "governmental exemption" issue permits only a qualified statement of the court's reasoning. Moreover, the court's much ado about the North Carolina statute empowering local governments "to determine . . . the terms and conditions under which . . . properties [which they control] may be used, provided that in all cases the public is not deprived of its rightful, equal, and uniform use of such property," N.C. Gen. Stat. § 63-53(5) (1975), is particularly confusing. The court said that this statute showed that the North Carolina Legislature had not contemplated the challenged practice since that practice prevented equal and uniform use by the public. 476 F. Supp. at 554-55. But the court must not have meant what it said, for the practice only limited the equal and uniform use by would-be airport concessionaires.

13. 476 F. Supp. at 551 & 553. What the court meant by "anticompetitive" is not clear. "Competition may be read as [1] the process of rivalry; . . . [2] the absence of restraint over one person's or firm's economic activities by any other person or firm; . . . [3] that state of the market in which the individual buyer or seller does not influence the price by his purchases or sales; . . . [4] the existence of 'fragmented industries and markets' preserved 'through the protection of viable, small, locally owned businesses'; or . . . [5] a term of art designating any state of affairs in which consumer welfare cannot be increased by moving to an alternative state of affairs through judicial decrees." R. Bork, The Antitrust Paradox: A Policy at War with Itself pp. 56-61 (1978). For the reasons suggested by Bork, only the latter is suitable for the purposes of antitrust law. If, however, the court meant that the transaction between the Board and Resort decreased consumer welfare, then it was mistaken.

14. N.C. Gen. Stat. § 63-53(3) (1981) empowers a local government

"[t]o determine the charge or rental for the use of any properties under its control . . . and the terms and conditions under which such properties may be used. . . ." Those "[c]harges," the statute provides, "shall be . . . established with due regard to the property and improvements used and the expense of operation to the municipality." It could be argued, persuasively I think, that § 63-53(5) directs local governments to try to capture the quasi-rents generated by the properties they control as cost-effectively as possible, which is what the Moore County Board was apparently doing.

15. Compare Guthrie v. Genessee County, N.Y., 494 F. Supp. 950 (W.D.N.Y. 1980). Guthrie complained, *inter alia*, that the County had violated the antitrust laws by (1) making arrangements with Prior Aviation Service to replace Guthrie's Batavia Aviation as the fixed base operator at the County's airport and then refusing to make similar arrangements with him, and (2) taking additional steps in concert with Prior, who also served as the airport manager, to make sure that Batavia could not continue to use the airport to sell any products or services to airport patrons commonly sold by fixed base operators. The county moved to dismiss the complaint for failure to state a claim upon which relief could be based. One of the grounds for its motion was "that the Sherman Act does not apply to conduct undertaken by a local government . . . pursuant to state legislation which authorizes a restriction of competition." *Id.* at 953. In fact, N.Y. Gen. Mun. Law § 352(5) (Consol. 1982) expressly provides for the exclusive lease of portions of airports so that various services could be provided there. Nevertheless, the court denied the motion on the same analysis employed by the *Pinehurst* court.

16. *See* Areeda, *Antitrust Immunity For "State Action" after Lafayette*, 95 Harv. L. Rev. 435 (1981).

17. The opinion contains the assertion that "[t]he [c]ourt expresses no opinion as to whether any antitrust violation has occurred, . . ." 476 F. Supp. at 555, but that assertion is belied by the key role played by the "anticompetitive" label in the court's reasoning as well as the tenor of the opinion.

18. Identifying the taxpayers as the owners and the local government as their agent is consistent with the mandated assumption that local governments act to maximize the wealth of those whom they represent. Of course, as individuals, the taxpayers held rather limited rights in the airport, to say the least. For example, if a taxpayer wished to divest himself of his "interest" in the airport, he would have had to leave Moore County. Nevertheless, as a group, the taxpayers possessed the usual incidents of ownership. They even have the collective right to

any residual income generated by the operation of the airport whose value they could capture via a reduced tax assessment.

19. Recall the mandated assumption that local governments act to maximize the wealth of their residents.

20. The distinction between the two is not nearly so stark as the text may imply. In fact, they merely identify two ends of a continuum. *See* O. Williamson, Markets and Hierarchies: Analysis and Antitrust Implications (1975); Klein, Crawford & Alchian, *Vertical Integration, Appropriable Rents, and the Competitive Contracting Process*, 21 J. Law & Econ. 297 (1978); Coase, *The Nature of the Firm*, 4 Economica 386 (1937).

21. Wages reflect only the most obvious costs, those for labor, for which the Board would have had to pay.

22. That belief may have been based on the fact that pursuant to the contract Resort would have the same incentives to provide fbo service that the Board had, thus obviating the need for expensive monitoring. *See* Alchian & Demsetz, *Production, Information Costs, and Economic Organization*, 62 Am. Econ. Rev. 777 (1972).

23. It is also rather unlikely that Resort was engaged in a strategic move not only because of the reasons stated in the text but also because the Board would have likely captured all of the expected monopoly revenues in the form of "rent."

24. Moreover, it maintained or increased the value of its promises generally, thus enabling it to obtain as much or more for them in subsequent transactions. Given the difficulty which governments have in binding themselves, that is no mean feat. *See* K. Dam, Oil Resources: Who Gets What How (1976), especially pp. 173-179. *See generally* T. Schelling, The Strategy of Conflict pp. 21-52 and especially pp. 22-28 (1960).

25. Unfortunately, these problems have not deterred some courts from coming to judgment in reliance upon such *ex post* explanations. *See, e.g.*, Hecht v. Pro-Football, Inc., 570 F.2d 982 (D.C. Cir. 1977), *cert. denied*, 436 U.S. 956 (1978) (analyzed in the section "Functions Related to the Use of a Capital Facility Not Yet Built").

26. These planning economies provide one of the principal inducements for entering into requirements contracts, of which the arrangement between the Board and Resort is one example. *See generally* Standard Oil Co. of California (Standard Stations) v. United States, 337 U.S. 293 (1949).

27. Of course, the Board might have found itself bearing additional negotiating costs in the future if it decided to replace the single provider. There is no reason to believe, however, that the Board would make the decision to replace any more often if it had a single provider than if it had several providers.

28. "'Monitoring' connotes several activities in addition to its disciplinary connotation. It connotes measuring output performance, apportioning awards, observing the output behavior of inputs as means of detecting or estimating their marginal productivity and giving assignments or instructions in what to do and how to do it. (It also includes . . . authority to terminate or revise contracts.)" Alchian & Demsetz, *supra* note 22, at 777, 783 (monitoring and the importance of monitoring costs in determining economic organization is the central focus of this article).

29. E. Goffman, Strategic Interaction p. 105 (1969).

30. Williamson, *Assessing Vertical Market Restrictions: Antitrust Ramifications of the Transaction Cost Approach*, 127 U. Pa. L Rev. 953, 957 (1979).

31. Hirshleifer, *Economics from a Biological Standpoint*, 20 J. Law & Econ. 1, 27 (1977).

32. Williamson, *supra* note 30.

33. *See* Klein, Crawford & Alchian, *supra* note 20, at 297, 303-07.

34. A. Alchian & W. Allen, Exchange and Production: Competition, Coordination, and Control p. 99 (2d ed. 1977). Quasi-rents are closely related to economic rents which are "market receipts that affect neither the present nor the future amount of that good." *Id.* For an excellent analysis of quasi-rents as a determinant of economic organization *see* Klein, Crawford & Alchian, *supra* note 20.

35. Here I use the word in its lay rather than in its technical sense. Sometimes, but not always, "rent" payments reflect quasi-rents.

36. *See generally* Demsetz, *Why Regulate Utilities?* 11 J. Law & Econ. 55 (1968).

37. A. Alchian & W. Allen, *supra* note 34, at p. 110.

38. It probably did so when used by the local government defendants in Corey v. Look, 641 F.2d 32 (1st Cir. 1981); Pueblo Aircraft Service, Inc. v. City of Pueblo, Colo., 498 F. Supp. 1205 (D. Colo. 1980), *aff'd*, 679 F.2d 805 (10th Cir. 1982), *cert. denied*, 459 U.S. 1126 (1983); Guthrie v. Genessee County, N.Y., 494 F. Supp. 950 (W.D. N.Y. 1980); Alphin v. Henson, 392 F. Supp. 813 (D. Md. 1975), *aff'd*, 538 F.2d 85 (4th Cir. 1976), *cert. denied*, 429 U.S. 960 (1976), *amended*, 552 F.2d 1003 (4th Cir. 1976), *cert. denied*, 434 U.S. 823 (1977); Murdock v. City of Jacksonville, Fla., 361 F. Supp. 1083 (M.D. Fla. 1973); and E. W. Wiggins Airways, Inc. v. Massachusetts Port Authority, 362 F.2d 52 (1st Cir. 1966), *cert. denied*, 385 U.S. 947 (1966); and the local government involved in Metro Cable Co. v. CATV of Rockford, Inc., 375 F. Supp. 350 (W.D. Ill. 1974), *aff'd*, 516 F.2d 220 (7th Cir. 1975). See Appendix.

39. 461 F. Supp. 1025 (N.D. Tex. 1978).

40. The cities are Irving and Grapevine, Texas.

41. 461 F. Supp. 1025, 1027 (N.D. Tex. 1978). "Profit" has so many meanings that it is not clear from the court's opinion precisely how the word was used in the agreement between the System and Surtran. "Operating profit" is, if anything, more nebulous.

42. The opinion does not reveal what labels, if any, plaintiff's counsel tried to affix to the practice. Perhaps that is because, mercifully, the court did not completely succumb to the allure of literalistic jurisprudence, although it did make some related errors. See text immediately following.

43. Surtran also moved to dismiss on related grounds.

44. 461 F. Supp. 1025, 1028-33 (N.D. Tex. 1978).

45. *Id.* at 1037.

46. Pursuant to an exclusive distribution agreement, a monopolist would deny the use of his product to all but one vendor of wholesaling or retailing service.

47. Williamson, *supra* note 30, at 952, 960-66. For an excellent economic analysis of exclusive dealing generally, see Marvel, *Exclusive Dealing*, 25 J. Law & Econ. 1 (1982).

48. Williamson, *supra* note 30, at 964.

49. Bork argues that it is so unlikely that exclusive dealing would be used strategically and so likely that it would be used to economize on transactions costs that it should be deemed unqualifiedly legal under the antitrust laws. R. Bork, *supra* note 13, at pp. 156-57.

50. *See, e.g.*, L. Sullivan, Handbook of the Law of Antitrust pp. 429-31 (1977) and cases cited therein.

51. It is not at all clear why property rights would ever have to give way to the policy of the Sherman Act unless that policy were one calling for wealth redistribution. *See generally* Coase, *The Problem of Social Cost*, 3 J. Law & Econ. 1 (1960).

52. 461 F. Supp. 1025, 1038 (N.D. Tex. 1978). Even assuming that it is clear how property rights and the policy of the Sherman Act are to be balanced, the relevance of dedication to public purposes is not. The airport solicitation cases discussed by the court are inapposite.

53. Permitting unrestricted use of airport roads and then relying on self-interested taxicab operators for the desired service may be usefully characterized as a less well defined contract pursuant to which the unrestricted use is exchanged for the service.

54. If the rights were purchased from an airport board which had in the past permitted unrestricted use, realignment costs might have been quite large. *See* Demsetz, *Some Aspects of Property Rights*, 9 J. Law & Econ. 61, 65-67 (1966).

55. Disputes related to those delicate interrelationships may them-

selves give rise to antitrust litigation which might ensnare local governments. *See, e.g.*, All American Cab Co. v. Metropolitan Knoxville Airport, 1982-1983 Trade Cases ¶ 65,163 (E.D. Tenn. 1982).

56. *Cf.* K. Dam, Oil Resources: Who Gets What How? (1976).

57. *See* pp. 50-51.

58. The rates were probably part of the bid specifications. *See* Chapter 5.

59. *Id.* This would be an instance of the general phenomenon of "subgoal pursuit." *See* Williamson, *supra* note 30, at 955.

60. *See* Chapter 5.

61. In the absence of collusion, the System could expect the potential suppliers to compete for the exclusive right to pick up passengers at the airport by offering to purchase that right for a payment almost equal in value to the quasi-rents which they hoped to capture. Given the number of those potential suppliers, collusion was unlikely. The System could also expect the chosen supplier not only to offer the desired service but also to actually provide it, because the supplier would know that, if it welched, there were others who would be only too happy to replace it and could do so quickly.

62. 570 F.2d 982 (D.C. Cir. 1977), *cert. denied*, 436 U.S. 956 (1978).

63. 468 F. Supp. 737 (N.D. Iowa 1979), *aff'd in part, rev'd in part*, 671 F.2d 1146 (8th Cir. 1982).

64. D.C. Code Ann. §§ 2-1720,-1721 (1967).

65. 444 F.2d at 939.

66. *Id.* at 946.

67. *Id.*

68. It is not clear from the opinions what happened to Griffith's Park, the stadium where the Redskins, as well as the Washington Senators baseball team, had been playing their home games.

69. Note the all-too-ready willingness to welch, to act opportunistically, on the part of this office-holder. That reduced the value of the promises made on behalf of the government he served. The implications of this phenomenon are discussed in Chapter 4 in connection with Mason City Center Associates v. The City of Mason City, Iowa, 468 F. Supp. 737 (N.D. Iowa 1979), *aff'd in part, rev'd in part*, 671 F.2d 1146 (8th Cir. 1982), and in the next section in connection with Glenwillow Landfill v. City of Akron, Ohio, 486 F. Supp. 671 (N.D. Ohio), *aff'd*, Hybud Equipment Corp. v. City of Akron, Ohio, 654 F.2d 187 (6th Cir. 1981), *vacated and remanded*, 455 U.S. 931 (1982) (for reconsideration in light of *City of Boulder*), *remanded mem.*, 701 F.2d 178 (6th Cir. 1983), and Gold Cross Ambulance v. City of Kansas City, Mo., 538 F. Supp. 956 (W.D. Mo. 1982), *aff'd*, 705 F.2d 1005 (8th Cir. 1983), *petition for cert. filed*, No. 83-138 (U.S.L.W. July 15, 1983).

70. Hecht also sued the individual members of the Armory Board and the National Football League.

71. 312 F. Supp. 472 (D.C. 1970).

72. 444 F.2d 931 (D.C. Cir. 1971).

73. 570 F.2d 982 (D.C. Cir. 1977), *cert. denied*, 436 U.S. 956 (1978).

74. *Id.* at 992 (quoting A. Neale, The Antitrust Laws of the United States p. 67 [2d ed. 1970]). This peculiar notion, that the antitrust laws require those with market power to share it with at least some of their would-be rivals, is also known as the bottleneck doctrine. Apparently, the disposition of a number of reported cases has turned on this notion. *See, e.g.*, United States v. Terminal Railroad Ass'n of St. Louis, 224 U.S. 383 (1912); Associated Press v. United States, 326 U.S. 1 (1945); International Boxing Club of New York v. United States, 358 U.S. 242 (1959); Gamco v. Providence Fruit & Produce Bldg., 194 F.2d 484 (1st Cir. 1952), *cert. denied*, 344 U.S. 817 (1952); Rogers v. Douglas Tobacco Board of Trade, 266 F.2d 636 (5th Cir. 1959), *cert. denied*, 361 U.S. 833 (1959); United States v. Standard Oil Co., 362 F. Supp. 1331 (N.D. Cal. 1972), *aff'd on appeal*, 412 U.S. 924 (1973).

75. 570 F. 2d at 993.

76. Unless the defendants proceeded in a manner almost unique in the annals of antitrust litigation, they probably moved for a dismissal, a summary judgment, or a directed verdict on grounds related to the merits of Hecht's complaint. On the basis of the court of appeals' opinion, however, one cannot be sure that such motions were made: The opinion does not mention any of them, which is not surprising since Hecht, not the defendants, took the appeal. If they were made, the district court should have undertaken the critical inquiry before ruling on them as well.

77. The court predicated its reversal on other grounds as well: (1) the failure of the trial judge to instruct the jury that the relevant geographic market was metropolitan Washington, D.C., rather than the United States, 570 F.2d at 933-89, and (2) the failure of the trial judge to instruct the jury that the defendants, rather than Hecht, bore the burden of persuading the jury that professional football was a "natural monopoly" in that market, 570 F.2d at 990-92.

78. Since we must assume that the Armory Board acted to maximize the wealth of those whom it represented, the mere fact that it was willing to pay for the stadium shows that the value of the stadium in use exceeded the price.

79. *See* Williamson, *The Vertical Integration of Production: Market Failure Considerations*, 61 Am. Econ. Rev. 112, 116-17 (1971).

80. The costs of making the move itself might be substantial, and the

costs of building the loyalty of fans in the new locale might be even greater.

81. It is rather unlikely that the practice helped induce the Redskins to make any investment.

82. Once again I invoke the mandated assumption. Although in some instances this assumption seems to clash with reality, here it seems to complement it.

83. Masonites probably perceived the shortage more in terms of the quality than the quantity of central business district service.

84. Of course, the agent might not serve the interests of the principals as well as they might like, but that is a problem endemic to the agency relationship. Williamson, *The Modern Corporation: Origins, Evolution, Attributes*, 29 J. Econ. Lit. 1537 (1981); Fama, *Agency Problems and the Theory of the Firm*, 88 J. Pol. Econ. 288 (1980); Jenson & Meckling, *Theory of the Firm: Managerial Behavior, Agency Costs and Ownership Structure*, 3 J. Fin. Econ. 35 (1976).

85. *See supra* note 69 and accompanying text; T. Schelling, *supra* note 24. The members of the council might have also found it substantially more expensive politically to pay the owners than to prevent the development of competing regional shopping centers.

86. The city council also made some payments. It hired the developer and funded, with bonds, some of the development.

87. 671 F.2d at 1148.

88. 468 F. Supp. 737 (N.D. Iowa 1979), *aff'd in part, rev'd in part*, 671 F.2d 1146 (8th Cir. 1982).

89. 468 F. Supp. at 743.

90. Among those owners would likely have been the residents of other cities who exercised their rights, including the power to zone, collectively, through their local governments. Making arrangements with such owners would have been especially expensive because enforcement costs might be infinite.

91. More precisely, the cost of providing it would have been infinite.

92. If the residents did not collectively prevent each other from individually expropriating the quasi-rents, then, in the end, the majority of the citizens would probably pay substantially more for the service than it was worth to them. That would be obvious where the local government had borrowed the funds to make the investment from bondholders. See the analysis of *Glenwillow Landfill* which follows.

93. Klein, Crawford & Alchian, *supra* note 20, at 297.

94. That is not as far-fetched as it might seem, as the resident "owners" of the Green Bay Packers football team can attest.

95. For example, a promise not to regulate the providers of such

services would probably be unenforceable and would certainly be incredible. *See generally* T. Schelling, *supra* note 24, at pp. 43-46.

96. Politicians and bureaucrats who attempted to directly control the choices of residents with respect to such services would probably succeed only in getting themselves voted out of office or fired.

97. A local government that was "held up" would find itself in a "hostage" situation, with those demanding the service serving as the hostages. It is rather difficult to respond to that situation with a "we-will-not-negotiate" posture, which is one reason why we find governments that do so consistently, like the Israeli national government, noteworthy.

98. 485 F. Supp. 671 (N.D. Ohio 1979), *aff'd sub nom.* Hybud Equip. Corp. v. City of Akron, Ohio, 654 F.2d 1187 (6th Cir. 1981), *vacated and remanded,* 455 U.S. 931 (1982) (for consideration in light of *Boulder*), *remanded mem.*, 701 F.2d 178 (6th Cir. 1983), *on remand,* 1983-1 Trade Cases ¶ 65,356 (N.D. Ohio 1983), *aff'd,* 742 F.2d 949 (6th Cir. 1984).

99. 538 F. Supp. 956 (W.D. Mo. 1982), *aff'd,* 705 F.2d 1005 (8th Cir. 1983), *petition for cert. filed,* No. 83-138 (U.S.L.W. July 25, 1983).

100. 485 F. Supp. at 689-90. In fact, the city was obligated to do what it could to prevent the establishment, construction, and operation of a competing facility. 485 F. Supp. at 690.

101. The RES was not equipped to handle some kinds of unusual waste, and, under the agreement, the city could permit collectors and haulers to deposit those kinds elsewhere.

102. Akron promised to "use its best efforts to establish rates and charges for the disposal of [s]olid [w]aste through the [RES] at a level which assures an adequate supply of [s]olid [w]aste for the purpose of the [RES] and, subject to the foregoing, shall be comparable with competitive charges for such services." 485 F. Supp. at 690.

103. Akron, Ohio, Ordinance 841-76 (Oct. 4, 1976).

104. 485 F. Supp. 671, 675-78 (N.D. Ohio 1979).

105. 433 U.S. 350 (1977).

106. Unless it was "innocent by association."

107. State *ex rel.* Moock v. Cincinnati, 120 Ohio St. 500, 166 N.E. 583 (1929), *cert. denied,* 280 U.S. 578 (1929); City of Canton v. Van Voochis, 61 Ohio App. 419, 22 N.E.2d 651 (1939), *cited at* 485 F. Supp. 671, 677 (N.D. Ohio 1979).

108. Springs Ambulance Service, Inc. v. City of Rancho Mirage, Cal., 1983-2 Trade Cases ¶ 65,646 pp. 69,285-69,287 (C.D. Cal. 1983), *rev'd in part and remanded in part,* 1984-2 Trade Cases ¶ 66,261 (9th Cir. 1984); Omni Outdoor Advertising, Inc. v. Columbia Outdoor Advertising, Inc., 566 F. Supp. 1444, 1446-47 (D.S.C. 1983). *But see* Pueblo Aircraft

Service, Inc. v. City of Pueblo, Colo. 679 F.2d 805 (10th Cir. 1982), *cert. denied,* 103 S. Ct. 762 (1983).

109. 455 U.S. 951 (1982), *remanded mem.*, 701 F.2d 178 (6th Cir. 1983).

110. Hybud Equipment Corp. v. City of Akron, 1983-1 Trade Cases ¶ 65,356 (N.D. Ohio 1983).

111. 654 F.2d 1187, 1196 (6th Cir. 1981).

112. Those who lived in multi-family dwellings and those who owned business establishments indirectly paid for the service, in part, by paying haulers to pick up their solid wastes. The haulers paid the landfill owners a "tipping fee" for the privilege of depositing the solid wastes which they had picked up. Those who lived in one- and two-family dwellings made similar payments, but they did so collectively rather than individually. They paid taxes to Akron which used some of those funds to pay haulers. In fact, all residents paid for the service collectively, in part, since the city used tax funds to operate its own landfill and to issue licenses to, make inspections of, and challenge regulatory infractions allegedly committed by, the operators of other landfills. These monetary payments may have paled by comparison with nonmonetary ones. Some residents may have suffered illness, offense, or the threat of one or both, as a result of the disposal of solid wastes.

113. 485 F. Supp. 671, 694 (N.D. Ohio 1979).

114. According to the district court, 1,300 tons of solid waste per day were being brought to the city's Hardy Road Landfill. 485 F. Supp. at 671. Since 1975 that landfill had been the only public disposal facility operating in the Akron area capable of disposing of solid waste, and private haulers of solid waste generated in that area were disposing of most of what they collected there. 485 F. Supp. at 695. Teledyne, the contract operator of the RES, planned to process 1,400 tons per day, but the facility was designed to process 2,240 tons per day.

115. In fact, they may not have even believed that the RES would be particularly cost-effective. I ignore this cynical solution to the puzzle, however, in part because I find it rather unconvincing. It is not supported by the data reported in the relevant opinions. Indeed, it seems inconsistent with the refusal of Akron officials to embark on the RES project in the 1960's for reasons related to cost-effectiveness (a study which those officials commissioned predicted too little demand for the energy that would be generated at the proposed facility). 485 F. Supp. at 694. I ignore this cynical solution also because my purpose is to demonstrate the proper analysis of a practice that might very well be used in good faith by some local government officials in a similar context.

116. If they could not be put to higher-value uses, they would be bid away by other users of recyclables, assuming (a) that Akron was acting

to maximize the wealth of its residents, as we must, and (b) that the costs of transacting sales in recyclables were small, as seems likely.

117. He would expect that the individual hauler would take into account any savings in collection that might be generated by operating on a route ending at one disposal site rather than another. He would also expect, however, that a difference in tipping fees would dwarf any such savings.

118. Some of the marginal operating costs would take the form of foregone payments from those adversely affected by his activities, but he would not bear as many of those as he would have in a world of zero transactions costs. Thus, to speak of "his marginal operating costs" is not to make the Pigouvian error of ignoring foregone opportunities as costs.

119. "Among the problems of fixing a mutually satisfactory price are the conflicting interests of sellers having different costs—the optimum cartel price will be lower for a seller with lower costs." R. Posner, Antitrust Law: An Economic Perspective p. 51 (1976). On the economics of price-fixing generally *see id.* at 47-77; G. Stigler, *A Theory of Oligopoly,* in The Organization of Industry 39 (1968); *cf.* Kuhlman, *Nature and Significance of Price Fixing Rings,* 2 Antitrust L. & Econ. Rev. 69 (1969).

120. *See* Goldberg, *Regulation and Administered Contracts,* 7 Bell J. Econ. 426 (1976).

121. 485 F. Supp. at 685 (Finding of Fact ¶ 6).

122. The costs need only be high relative to the value of those quasi-rents to make the RES an unattractive investment.

123. Given the nature of the service, however, a promise by the city to do so would probably not have been as credible as the analogous promise made by the Mason City city council.

124. *See supra* note 112.

125. Initially, the city leased the vehicles from ASI and then subleased them back. By the time of the second contracting, the city had purchased them outright. Gold Cross Ambulance v. City of Kansas City, 705 F.2d 1005, 1009 (8th Cir. 1983), *petition for cert. filed,* No. 83-138 (U.S.L.W. July 25, 1983).

126. The city also moved for summary judgment on the ground that its regulations were insulated from the antitrust laws by the Tenth Amendment to the Constitution. (The ambulance owners moved for summary judgment on the grounds that their activities were in the nature of lobbying insulated from the antitrust by the First Amendment.) With respect to the plaintiffs' Fourteenth Amendment claims, the city asserted that the uncontroverted facts showed that (1) it had properly exercised its police powers in regulating ambulance compa-

nies, and (2) the plaintiffs did not have a property right in a license to operate an ambulance company. Finally, regarding the plaintiffs' equal protection claim, the city claimed that the plaintiffs were not in fact similarly situated as other ambulance companies since plaintiffs did not have a license to operate. 538 F.2d 956, 967, 969-73 (W.D. Mo. 1982).

127. Mo. Rev. Stat. § 67.300 (Vernon 1983).

128. *Id.*, §§ 190.105, .115, .120, .125, .145, .175.

129. 705 F.2d 1005 (8th Cir. 1983), *petition for cert. filed*, No. 83-138 (U.S.L.W. July 25, 1983).

130. Ignorance or disbelief could render a resident unaware of the superiority of a particular provider's ambulance service.

131. For example, the dispatcher at a nursing home might summon an ambulance from a particular provider because he was paid by it to do so. Jack Stout, one of the defendants in *Gold Cross* and a consultant to cities on ambulance service, told me that he was aware of ambulance companies who strongly encouraged their female personnel to date male dispatchers for that purpose.

132. The provider might insist, for example, that the would-be user prove that he owned (1) an effective insurance policy which covered ambulance service or, in the alternative, (2) durable assets not exempt from execution, of sufficient value to exceed the costs of the service and collection.

133. It may seem inconsistent to assert that, on the one hand, many residents would have become aware of a provider's refusal to render ambulance service prior to receiving payment while, on the other, those same residents would have remained unaware of the superiority of that service. But it is not. The difference between the two assertions simply reflects the different costs of acquiring and verifying different information. To acquire and verify information about the quality of ambulance service (response times and medical care), residents would have had to undertake an arduous study. To acquire and verify information about a pay-before-you-go-to-the-hospital practice, however, they would have had only to open a local newspaper or tune to a local broadcasting station for a report on the resulting deaths.

134. If transactions costs were negligible, one firm could provide dispatching and positioning service and other firms could make the ambulance runs. The transactions costs, however, would be considerable, in large part because the firms providing the runs would tend to resist directions from the dispatcher that would likely result in their making the most costly ones. Center for Economic and Management Research, University of Oklahoma, "A Process for Setting Community and State Policies Regarding EMS System Performance Capabilities" (unpublished paper, 1974).

135. It enabled Kansas City to solve a problem of organizational design that confronts every firm: "the need to organize transactions in such a way as to economize on bounded rationality while simultaneously safeguarding the transactions in question against opportunism." Williamson, *supra* note 30, at 958.

136. "The basic presumption of the transaction cost approach"—which is the approach taken here—"is that successive interfaces are organized in a manner that economizes on transactions costs." Williamson, *supra* note 30, at 958.

137. *See* Chapter 3.

138. For recent examples *see* Twin City Sportservice, Inc. v. Charles O. Finley & Co., 676 F.2d 1291 (9th Cir. 1982), *cert. denied*, 459 U.S. 1009 (1982); and Fishman v. Estate of Wirtz, 47 Antitrust & Trade Reg. Rep. 57 (N.D. Ill. 1984).

139. Of course, if non-immune local governments somehow found a way to use it solely as a part of a strategic move to become a monopolist or as part of the operations of a classic cartel, they would run afoul of the antitrust statutes.

5

VERTICAL "PRICE-FIXING" AND TERRITORIAL RESTRAINTS

In making arrangements on behalf of the residents of a community for the purchase of a service, local governments often take actions which place a ceiling over the provider's maximum price or a floor below his minimum one, or which limit his sales territory, the class of customers to whom he may sell, or the like. Such actions are all species of the second practice which we shall consider: constraining the marketing behavior of the provider. That practice may be challenged, usually by the provider himself, as an antitrust offense. In light of the Supreme Court's "same treatment" lesson, however, such challenges could well prompt a reexamination of the legality of the practice which will focus on the functions that it is supposed to serve. In turn, that reexamination might result in another major retrenchment in antitrust law.

Analysis will show that for the most part the principal functions served by this second practice are the same as those served by the first one we considered.[1] In fact, local governments often use the two jointly. In arranging for some services, the costs of monitoring and enforcing the service agreement or of capturing quasi-rents would not decline significantly and might even rise if the first practice were used alone. Monitoring might be hindered by the difficulty of comparing the exclusive provider's performance with anyone else's; enforcement might be thwarted by his threat to curtail service; and the capture of quasi-rents might be frustrated by the provider who would have not only the incentive to try to capture them for himself, but also, by virtue of exclusivity, the opportunity to do so. A local government could ameliorate all of these problems by employing the second practice. Since it serves the same principal functions as the first practice, both have, or should be deemed to have, the same antitrust merit.

This chapter demonstrates the process of reexamination to retrenchment for this second practice using four examples, each of which is drawn from a decided case. The first two examples are drawn from cases that have already been described: *Woolen v. Surtran Taxicabs, Inc.*,[2] which was analyzed in connection with the first practice, and *Community Communications Co. v. City of Boulder* (*Boulder I*),[3] which was one of the Supreme Court's seminal decisions regarding the antitrust "immunity" of local governments. The last two examples are drawn from cases new to the reader of this book. One of those cases is the sequel to *Boulder I*, *Community Communications Co. v. City of Boulder* (*Boulder II*).[4] It focused on additional restrictions placed on the offering of cable television service by the Boulder municipal government which were complementary to those involved in *Boulder I* and adopted subsequent to them. The other case is *Kurek v. Pleasure Driveway and Park District*,[5] apparently the first antitrust suit against a local government to go to trial on the merits following the Supreme Court's decision in *City of Lafayette*.

MAXIMUM "PRICE-FIXING": *WOOLEN V. SURTRAN TAXICABS, INC.*

Recall that in arranging for taxicab transportation from D/FW Regional Airport, the cities of Dallas and Fort Worth, through their joint venture, the Surtran System, solicited bids for the opportunity to provide patrons with their requirements of that service. It is likely that the System selected the winning bid on the basis of how much the firm making it promised to pay rather than how much it promised to charge. If so, then to ensure that the bids received could be compared easily, it is also likely that under the terms of the solicitation, the System prescribed the rates that the winning bidder would be permitted to charge its patrons. In any event, the contract between the System and Surtran Taxicabs, Inc., prescribed them.

Rate prescription was not the gravamen of the complaint filed by Woolen and his fellow hacks. Indeed, it probably could not have been. Woolen and his fellow hacks would have probably lacked standing to file such a complaint since they would have been outside the "target area" of the rate prescription "offense." Even if they had had standing, such a complaint would have likely been dismissed for failure to allege any "antitrust injury."[6] Surtran or a government agency, however, might have challenged rate prescription as *Albrecht*[7]–style maximum "price-fixing."[8]

In theory, the prescription of rates placed a floor below Surtran's minimum selling price as well as a ceiling above its maximum one, but only the ceiling had any practical economic significance. If Surtran had wished to charge rates lower than those prescribed, the System would have no doubt acquiesced. After all, Surtran had promised to pay the System 50 percent of those "profits" exceeding a 5 percent "operating profit" plus seventy-five cents per trip.[9] Presumably, Surtran would have wished to charge lower rates only if it expected to earn additional revenues by so doing. Since those additional revenues would have been reflected in additional "profits," the System would have gained because it was entitled to 50 percent of them. It would have also gained by virtue of the fact that at lower rates, more trips would be demanded by airport patrons. For each additional trip, the System would have received another seventy-five cents. Thus, the System would have acquiesced to Surtran's wish to charge lower rates because if Surtran could expect to earn additional revenues by charging them, then so too could the System.

That symmetry would not have held, however, if Surtran had wished to charge higher rates. In that event they might well have had different expectations because of their different perceptions of the marginal revenue curve for taxicab service from D/FW. To Surtran, the curve would have appeared below and to the left of where it would have appeared to the System (see Figure 1). Therefore, Surtran might have wished to charge higher rates, because it expected to earn more as a result, while the System might have objected to them because, if it acquiesced, it would have earned less. The System might have earned less

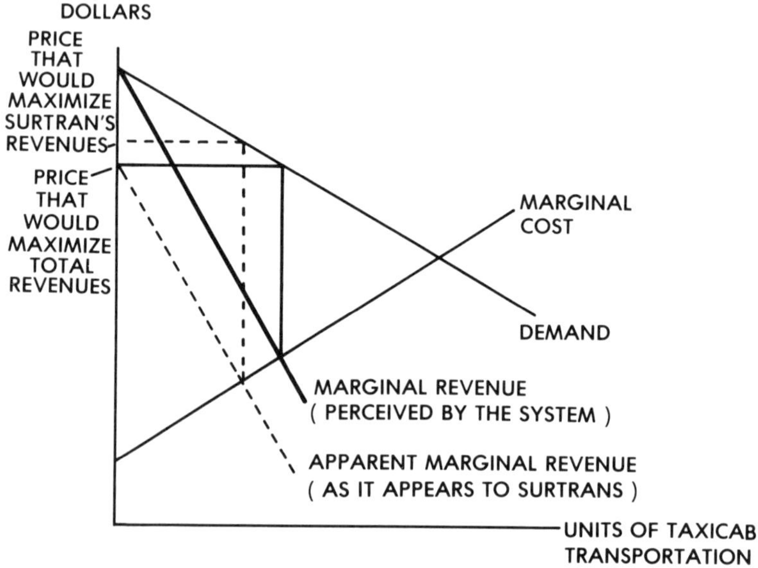

Figure 1. Conflicting Perceptions of Marginal Revenue and Price Preferences.

by virtue of the fact that whatever it gained from 50 percent of the additional "profits" would have been offset by that which it lost from foregoing seventy-five cents per trip for all of those trips not taken because of the the higher rates. Rate prescription ensured that the System's objections to higher rates would prevail over Surtran's wish to charge them.

If the rate prescription had been challenged in an antitrust suit as a ceiling on Surtran's maximum selling price, a conscientious judge would have ascertained the function that that practice was supposed to serve before ruling on its legality. He could have done so most easily by first predicting what Surtran's behavior would likely have been had its rates not been prescribed. A crystal ball would not have been needed; simple microeconomic analysis would have done. Once Surtran had been contractually designated as the exclusive provider of taxicab transportation from D/FW, its perception of its own marginal

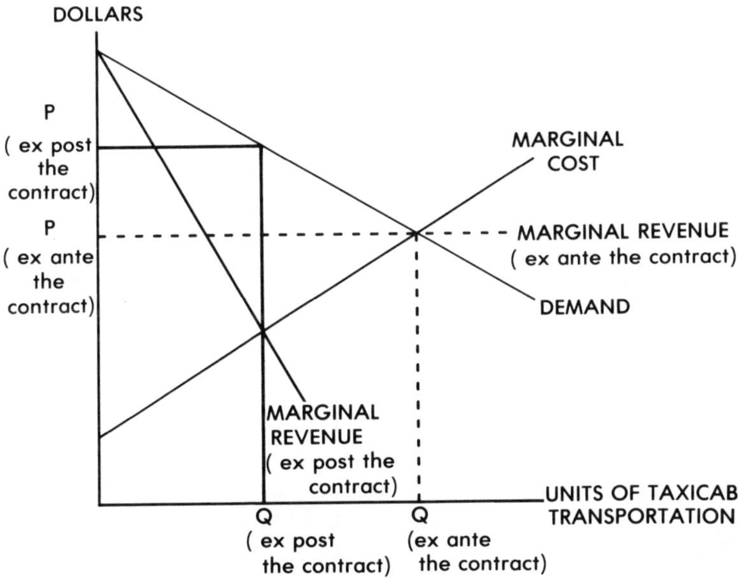

Figure 2. Supplier's Price Preferences Before and After Contracting for Exclusivity.

revenue curve would have changed. Before, in the face of competition for the market, the curve would have appeared horizontal, but afterwards it would appear downward-sloping. This change would have prompted another one. Surtran would have perceived that its revenue-maximizing price had risen (see Figure 2). Of course, at higher rates, airport patrons would have demanded fewer trips, and Surtran would have responded accordingly by curtailing the supply.

This behavior would have had two important results. One, the amount of taxicab transportation from D/FW would have been sub-optimal and therefore economically inefficient, and so it would have added less than it otherwise would have added to the value of the airport. Two, Surtran, rather than the cities and their residents, would have captured more of the quasi-rents generated by virtue of the investment which they had made in the airport. If the amount of quasi-rents that Surtran stood to capture had been large enough, the cities might not have built D/FW, an otherwise efficient investment. The amount was probably not that large in this case, but it might be in others. If a local government expected that a service provider would act as Surtran might have acted, it might refrain from making certain investments unless it could protect itself.

The System could have avoided these two results in any one of a number of ways,[10] but surely the most cost-effective one was simply to place a ceiling on Surtran's maximum selling price—to prescribe rates. Thus, that practice served the same functions as the practice which was the subject of the actual case, agreeing to arrange for taxicab transportation from D/FW with Surtran but not with any of Surtran's rivals. Those functions were securing efficiently "produced" service and reducing the costs to investors of capturing the quasi-rents generated by their investment. If those functions are undesirable according to the principles embodied in the antitrust statutes, then, and only then, should the practice be deemed an offense.

RESTRICTING SALES TERRITORIES: *BOULDER I* AND *BOULDER II*

In arranging for cable television service on behalf of Boulder's residents, the Boulder city council wished to solicit bids for the opportunity to provide it, just as the cities of Dallas and Fort Worth had done in arranging for taxicab transportation from D/FW. The solicitation, and its contractual aftermath, however, did not themselves prompt litigation, as they had in Texas. Rather, two closely related, but preliminary actions taken by the council did so.

When Community Communications Company (CCC), the only cablecaster who was then doing business or even had a permit to do business in Boulder, announced that it planned to wire unserved areas in the city, the council was not prepared to make arrangements with it or any other cablecaster. While the council debated about the appropriate arrangements in general and the terms of the solicitation in particular, it placed a temporary moratorium on the implementation of CCC's plan. The moratorium expired twice while the debate continued, and the council renewed it twice. Finally, the council reached a decision. For present purposes, the pertinent term of the solicitation was that the firms making the winning bids would each be awarded an "exclusive franchise" for a portion of the city, like Surtran's at D/FW. One such portion, comprising approximately one-third of Boulder, was the area that CCC had already wired. As part of this "districting" scheme, the council permanently prohibited CCC from wiring any additional areas without its express permission to do so. As the reader already knows, CCC claimed that the moratorium was an antitrust offense, and, as the reader has no doubt surmised, it made the same claim, albeit in a separate suit, about districting and the related permanent prohibition. The moratorium was the focus of *Boulder I*, and the districting/permanent prohibition was the focus of *Boulder II*. Both actions were challenged as limitations on CCC's sales territories.

The function each was supposed to serve may be ascertained by employing the same intellectual apparatus brought to bear on rate prescription in *Woolen*. First, on the basis of microeconomic theory, predict what CCC's likely behavior would have been had the Boulder city council refrained from taking the challenged actions. Second, deduce the consequences of such behavior for the residents of Boulder who subscribed to cable television. Third and finally, observe the link between those actions and the avoidance of those consequences.

As technological developments shifted the marginal cost curve of producing cable television service downward and to the right (see Figure 3), CCC apparently perceived that it would maximize its revenues by selling its service to more Boulderites than simply those who resided in the University Hills community, where poor over-the-air reception made cable television especially valuable. It therefore announced its plans to wire additional areas, and it surely would have implemented them had the city council not done what it did. In fact, CCC did wire substantial additional areas despite the moratorium and districting/permanent prohibition.[11]

Consider now what CCC's pricing output decisions likely would have been had it implemented its plans. CCC would have perceived its marginal revenue curve as sloping downward rather

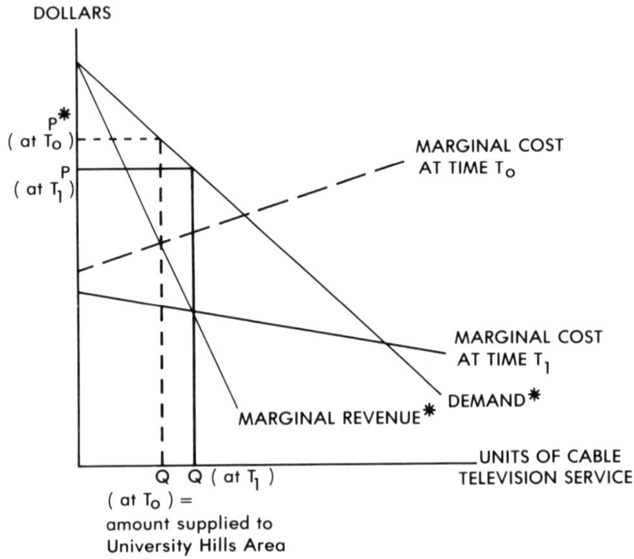

* The Demand and Marginal Revenue curves are drawn as if they were constant over time. If, instead, they had shifted upward and to the right, as they likely did, then the effect on the quantity supplied (and the price) illustrated here would be even greater.

Figure 3. Supplier's Response to Technology-Based Reductions in Marginal Cost.

significantly, in the long run as well as the short run. That perception would have been based on two quite reasonable expectations. First, CCC would have expected to encounter no ongoing rivalry from other cablecasters in those areas it served since it would have enjoyed substantial scale economies of "production." Second, CCC would have expected little threat of displacement since it would have enjoyed a substantial "first-mover advantage."[12] As a practical matter, a rival cablecaster could have displaced CCC only by luring away a large number of subscribers with promises of a superior "product," lower prices, or both. He would have found that quite difficult to do. Subscribers would have discounted the promises of a superior "product" due to lack of verifiable information and the problems of ensuring that the promises were kept. If the rival had been providing service in some other city, he might have been able to supply subscribers with some verifiable information, but it would have still been expensive to do so. Besides, even if he had incurred that expense, his promise would still have been discounted because of the monitoring and enforcement problems. A promise of a lower price would not have been discounted quite as much,[13] but even if it were taken at face value, it might not prompt many subscribers to switch. The price of cable television service is typically two-part. The first is a one-time charge and the second is a periodic one. Unless the rival's promised total price was lower than CCC's periodic charge, subscribers would not perceive it as lower. The first-mover advantage was apparently great enough that CCC was willing to run the risks associated with flouting municipal ordinances in order to have it.

Given its perception of its marginal revenue curve, CCC would have likely established a price for its cable television service substantially in excess of the marginal cost of producing it. Boulder residents who subscribed to it would have suffered the obvious consequences: production of the service in an economically inefficient manner.

Had those residents privately negotiated an agreement with CCC or, for that matter, with some other cablecaster, pursuant to which it would have provided cable television service at a price nearly equal to marginal cost, they could have avoided those consequences. That they did not may be explained by the fact that the benefits to be derived from such an agreement would almost surely have been dwarfed by the costs of (1) undertaking joint negotiations, (2) obtaining a suitable offer, and (3) monitoring compliance with, and enforcing the terms of, any agreement.

Undertaking joint negotiations would have been expensive for two reasons. A very large number of residents with different tastes would have had to act together, and they would have had to address themselves to rather complex terms, like those providing for price renegotiation during what surely would have been the long term of the contract.[14] Of course, residents could have avoided bearing most of the costs of undertaking joint negotiations simply by acting collectively through the Boulder city council, which is what they did. To avoid some of the other costs, however, they would have had to have the city council take additional steps, which they also did.

Obtaining a suitable offer would have been fairly easy as long as there were competition for the market. Because of first-mover advantages, however, the city council could expect such competition only for unwired portions of Boulder, and then only if those portions comprised a large enough and densely populated enough area that a cablecaster operating only in them could have enjoyed the scale economies available to a cablecaster operating in adjacent areas as well. CCC's expansion plans threatened to eliminate such competition and thereby make obtaining a suitable offer quite problematic.[15]

To overcome those problems, the city council could have attempted to solicit offers and negotiate agreements in the days immediately following CCC's announcement of its plans. Acting with such haste, however, the city council would have been more likely to err. For example, it might have made a mistaken assessment of the demand schedule of Boulder residents for cable television service. Even if the city council avoided any major error, its haste would likely have been self-defeating. It would have had almost no chance of identifying a large number of reliable potential cablecasters, soliciting them, and providing them with the information that they required, but unless it did so, the probability of obtaining a suitable offer would have been small indeed.

The alternative to hasty action was delay in the implementation of CCC's plans, which, of course, is what the city council achieved through the moratorium. The moratorium preserved a market for which rival would-be cablecasters would compete, and thereby made it likely that the city council could cost-effectively obtain an offer for efficiently provisioned cable television service. The primary function that the moratorium was supposed to serve was to secure just such service.[16]

The moratorium was supposed to serve a secondary function as well. That function was the same as the one served by districting, which, along with the related permanent prohibition, could not have been implemented without the moratorium. It was to reduce the costs of monitoring compliance with, and enforcing the terms of, agreements to provide cable television service.

Without such monitoring and enforcement, Boulder residents could not have secured efficiently produced service even if their city council had obtained an offer for it and negotiated an agreement with the cablecaster who made the offer.[17] The cablecaster would have had both the incentive and the opportunity to promise the technological moon but deliver only video green cheese. By so welching, he could have frustrated the residents' efforts to obtain efficiently provisioned cable television service. Monitoring and enforcement, however, would have been costly. Indeed, since production economies of scale and, especially, the first-mover advantage would have probably eliminated any significant rivalry in the market, they probably would have been prohibitively expensive. Monitoring would have been costly because of the problems of assessing the quality of such complex service without the benefit of easily made comparisons at (a) any particular time and, especially, (b) over substantial periods during which residents would almost surely expect the cablecaster to modify the service by incorporating advances. Enforcement would have been costly because of two problems. First, it would be difficult to prevent the cablecaster from raising rates opportunistically. The agreement would likely provide for increases in rates to reflect increases in the cablecaster's costs.[18] Without having the benefit of easily made comparisons, agents for the residents would be hard-pressed to know when to challenge the operator's costs as overstated or imprudently incurred.[19] Second, without the benefit of on-going rivalry, it would be difficult to quickly replace an unsatisfactory cablecaster and, hence, to credibly threaten to do so.[20] If a decision to replace were made, it would be difficult to evaluate the assets of the existing cablecaster and arrange for their transfer to the new one.[21] Moreover, politicians and bureaucrats might be locked in to their choice of cablecaster and therefore unwilling to take enforcement action. These tendencies might be less pronounced if the politicians and bureaucrats could replace an unsatisfactory cablecaster with another whom they had also chosen.

The benefits of easily made comparisons and on-going rivalry could be had, and thus these myriad problems ameliorated cost-effectively, by negotiating service agreements with several cablecasters while limiting the sales territory of each. Of course, that is precisely what the city council attempted to do by taking the action that was challenged in *Boulder II*. The function that districting and the related permanent prohibition was likely supposed to serve was to reduce the costs of monitoring and enforcing the service agreements. By taking that action, the council might have effectuated a savings that exceeded any foregone production economies of scale.

MINIMUM "PRICE-FIXING": *KUREK V. PLEASURE DRIVEWAY & PARK DISTRICT*

Taking action to make monitoring and enforcement easier, as the Boulder city council did in arranging for cable television service, is only one of several methods for reducing the costs of those tasks. Another one is engaging in them less often while ensuring that the market gives suppliers sufficient incentive to perform satisfactorily. That might be more cost-effective in arranging for some services, particularly those provided by suppliers who would face considerable rivalry in the market and could be replaced at low cost. The Peoria Park District Board might well have found it so when the Board arranged for concessionaire service at the five public golf courses which it owned.[22] Out of those arrangements arose *Kurek v. Pleasure Driveway and Park District*.[23]

Presumably, the Board arranged for concessionaire service in order to maximize the value of the golf courses.[24] The arrangements were of the kind all too familiar to the reader of this book. The Board purchased the service by conveying to the concessionaires the opportunity to earn a stream of income from sales that they made to their patrons and extracting from them a payment, or the promise of one.

For many years the Board had asked for a lump-sum payment. For example, in 1972 each concessionaire paid the Board six hundred dollars, except the one responsible for the nine-hole course, who paid only three hundred dollars. The Board became dissatisfied with the revenues it derived from these payments.

Rather than ask for a larger lump sum, however, it demanded, in 1973, a percentage of each concessionaire's gross sales receipts.

Changing the method of payment, not just the amount of it, must have held the promise of greater revenues. The additional revenues could have been generated as a result of three changes that would have been wrought when the Board began taking a percentage of the gross sales receipts.[25] First, the Board would have eliminated the costs that would-be concessionaires would have incurred in order to secure a larger lump sum. The Board could have expected to reap the benefit of that saving because would-be concessionaires would have tended to respond to it by bidding more for the concessions. If the bids were higher in an amount that exceeded the loss incurred by foregoing the return on the lump sum, the Board would have earned more revenues. Second, the Board would have given would-be concessionaires more assurance that critical services, like timely golf course maintenance, would be provided. Such services tend to increase gross receipts, so would-be concessionnaires would recognize that the Board could gain by providing them. The additional assurance would have made the concessions more valuable, and so the Board could have expected to obtain larger total payments from concessionaires, and therefore more revenues. Third and finally, the Board would have assumed a portion of the risk associated with operating the concessions. If it could have borne that portion of the risk more efficiently than could have the would-be concessionaires, it could have expected compensation for doing so in an amount exceeding its cost, and, thereby, earned more revenues.

The promise of greater revenues would not have been realized, however, had the concessionaires shirked their duties, and that is precisely what the new method of payment gave them an incentive to do. The new method of payment would have changed the concessionaires' perception of the marginal revenue that they would expect to earn on each additional sale (see Figure 4). Suppose, as seems likely, that they were price-takers.[26] Had they not had the obligation to pay the Board a percentage of their gross sales receipts, they would have perceived their marginal revenue as equal to the price of each item sold. Since they had it, however, they would have perceived their marginal rev-

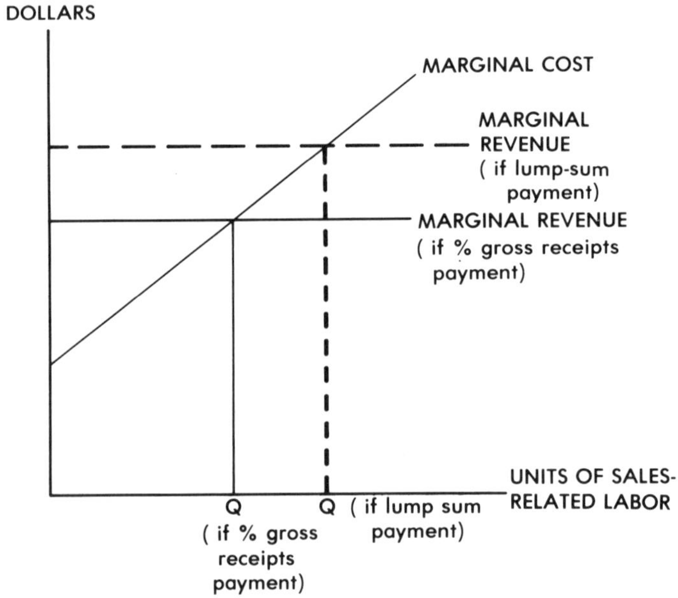

Figure 4. Percentage of Gross Receipts Leasing and Conflicting Perceptions of Optimal Supply.

enue as less than that. That perception, in the absence of other constraints, would have dictated the amount of sales-related labor that they would provide. They would have provided only that amount for which the marginal cost of providing the last unit was no greater than the marginal revenue that they could expect to earn by doing so. Because of the concessionaire's perception of marginal revenue, the amount of sales-related labor provided would have been less than that for which the Board would have thought it was paying when it conveyed the concession. From the Board's point of view, the difference would have reflected shirking.

Such shirking would have reduced the value of the product/service mix available to patrons, so concessionaires' prices would likely have been lower than they otherwise would have been. The Board, of course, would not have earned the revenues promised by the new method of payment. Moreover, since the reduced-output/lower-price combination would be sub-optimal from the point of view of the patrons, it would not have maximized the value of the golf courses. Thus, the Board's purpose in making the arrangements would have been frustrated.

The Board could have reduced the concessionaire's shirking by specifying performance standards in the concession agreement, monitoring compliance with them, and when appropriate, enforcing them. Doing so, however, would have been costly, perhaps costly enough to dwarf the benefits of engaging in such activities. In any event, it surely would have been more cost-effective to engage in far less monitoring and enforcement while ensuring that the market gave the concessionaires sufficient incentive to perform satisfactorily. The Board could have ensured that the market did just that by simply placing a floor beneath the concessionaires' sales prices. With such a floor in place, concessionaires would have to provide more sales-related labor in order to make the sales that would maximize their revenues.

The five professional golfers who had held the concessions in 1972 alleged that the Board attempted to place just such a floor beneath their sales prices. After some unharmonious negotiations, they had agreed to pay the Board 1.5 percent of their gross sales receipts in 1973. In 1974, the Board decided to auction off the opportunity to provide concessionaire service. It received only one bid and that was from Golf Service Management (GSM). GSM offered to pay the Board 5 percent of its gross sales receipts. The Board did not immediately accept that offer. Instead, it negotiated with the five golf professionals for a matching one. They argued that they could not afford to make it. When the Board's negotiators countered by suggesting that they could if they raised their sales prices, they dismissed that suggestion as unrealistic. The negotiations proved fruitless so the Board accepted GSM's offer. According to the golf professionals, the suggestion made by the Board's negotiators along with the threat of accepting GSM's offer, which they claimed was solicited only for strategic purposes,[27] constituted the attempt to place a floor beneath their sales prices. Since the placing of such a floor is functionally equivalent to, and formally analogous to, resale price maintenance, they claimed that the Board had committed a *per se* antitrust offense.

After a trial on the merits, the district court held that the five professional golfers had failed to prove their allegation. Had they proved it, however, the court should not have held that the placing of such a price floor was an antitrust offense, much less a *per se* one, unless it believed that the function that that practice was supposed to serve, reducing the costs of monitoring and enforcing a sales agreement, was undesirable according to the principles embodied in the antitrust statutes.

As the analysis of these cases suggests, the second practice, constraining the market behavior of a supplier, is rather likely supposed to serve some of the same efficiency-enhancing functions as the first one, agreeing with a supplier (or a purchaser) not to buy (or sell, in the case of a purchaser) from one or more of his competitors. When it is supposed to serve one of those functions, it is, of course, no more objectionable on any antitrust principle than is the first. As a practical matter, the only other function that the second practice might serve would be to facilitate a wealth transfer, and then only if it took the form of a ceiling on resale prices. To illustrate, consider the sale of a house by a local housing authority at a below-market-clearing price to a low-income resident on the condition that the resident refrain from reselling the house except to another similarly situated resident and at a similarly low price. In that case the ceiling on the resale price of the house would help the managers of the authority redistribute the wealth of their constituent taxpayers among the objects of their charity. That function is unobjectionable on consumer welfare grounds, and it would be unobjectionable on populist grounds, if they were applicable. Of course, only a strategic function would be objectionable, and the second practice is even less likely to serve one than the first practice because its use could not possibly help a local government obtain market power. Thus, it should be deemed *per se* legal.[28]

NOTES

1. Those functions are: (1) to help secure efficiently provisioned service by permitting the supplier to enjoy either production or transactions economies; (2) to help reduce the transactions costs, particularly monitoring and enforcement costs, of arranging for the service; (3) to help

reduce the transactions costs of capturing quasi-rents; and (4) by reducing them, to help induce investment when providing the service requires that an additional one be made. (It is less likely that this second practice would serve the investment-inducing function than it is that the first practice would do so.) The second practice may also serve an additional function.

2. 461 F. Supp. 1025 (N.D. Tex. 1978).

3. 455 U.S. 40 (1982).

4. 660 F.2d 1370 (10th Cir. 1981), *cert. dismissed*, 456 U.S. 1001 (1982).

5. 583 F.2d 378 (7th Cir. 1978), *cert. denied*, 439 U.S. 1090 (1979). I served as the antitrust consultant to the prevailing party in *Kurek*, the Peoria Park District.

6. *See* Brunswick Corp. v. Pueblo Bowl-O-Mat, Inc., 429 U.S. 477 (1977).

7. Albrecht v. Herald Co., 390 U.S. 145 (1968).

8. No such challenge has yet been the subject of any reported case.

9. 461 F. Supp. 1025, 1027 (N.D. Tex. 1978).

10. For example, the service agreement could have specified the quantity and quality of service to be provided, and the System could have monitored Surtran's behavior to ensure compliance with those specifications.

11. 630 F.2d 704, 710 (10th Cir. 1980); 660 F.2d 1370, 1373 (10th Cir. 1981).

12. Omega Satellite Products Co. v. City of Indianapolis, 694 F.2d 119, 125 (7th Cir. 1982).

13. The longer the term of the service agreement, the more the promise of a lower price would have been discounted.

14. *See* Williamson, *Franchise Bidding for Natural Monopolies—In General and with Respect to CATV*, 7 Bell J. Econ. 73 (1976).

15. Acting individually, residents would have had little, if any, incentive to hold out in the hope of obtaining an offer of service from a competitor of CCC.

16. The moratorium may have also helped Boulder residents capture some of the quasi-rents that had been or would be created by two investments: (1) the collective investment in the city itself, particularly its thoroughfares, and (2) the private investment of the cablecasters in their receiving stations and wiring. The moratorium could have served that function by preserving Boulder's opportunity to conduct an auction for operating rights during which it could expect non-colluding bidders to offer payments or services whose value represented some of those quasi-rents (presumably, the moratorium would not have helped the residents capture so much of the quasi-rents generated by the private investment that no operator would have made it).

17. The residents of Dallas and Fort Worth, in contrast, did not face that problem in securing efficiently produced taxicab transportation from D/FW. *See* Chapter 4, n.61.

18. *Ceteris paribus*, that would be efficient. Williamson, *supra* note 14, at 82. *See generally* Goldberg, *Regulation and Administered Contracts*, 7 Bell J. Econ. 426 (1976).

19. *See* Goldberg, *supra* note 18, at 426, 444-46; *see generally* Averch & Johnson, *Behavior of the Firm under Regulatory Constraint*, 52 Am. Econ. Rev. 1052 (1962).

20. *See* Williamson, *supra* note 14, at 81-82.

21. *Id.* at 84-90.

22. By "concessionaire service" I mean standing ready to sell golf-related products along with complementary information to patrons of the course and other members of the playing public.

23. The litigation began in 1974 in the Illinois state courts. The Park District sued the five golf pros for possession of the concession shops that they managed. The golf pros secured a jury verdict and judgment in their favor. 27 Ill. App. 3d 60, 61, 325 N.E.2d 650, 652 (1975). The Park District, however, successfully appealed and obtained an order for possession. *Id.* at 69, 325 N.E.2d at 657. The Illinois Supreme Court denied the golf pros' leave to appeal. 51 Ill. App. 3d 182, 185, 367 N.E.2d 111, 114 (1977). The Park District then brought an action against the golf pros for damages resulting from the wrongful holdover of the concession shops. The golf pros counterclaimed for the allegedly wrongful termination of their employment. After a bench trial, the Park District was awarded $127,605 in damages, and it prevailed on the counterclaim. *Id.* at 184, 367 N.E.2d at 113. The judgment was affirmed on appeal. *Id.* at 191, 367 N.E.2d at 118. Once again, the Illinois Supreme Court denied leave to appeal. 574 F.2d 892, 893 (7th Cir. 1978). After the Park District attempted to collect the damage award, the golf pros brought suit for malicious prosecution and abuse of process. The trial court dismissed the claim and the appellate court affirmed. 50 Ill. App. 3d 1033, 1036, 1042, 365 N.E.2d 1191, 1193, 1198 (1977).

While the parties were litigating in the state courts, the golf pros brought suit in federal court. The golf pros claimed that the Park District had violated not only the federal antitrust laws but also the federal civil rights laws. Both claims were dismissed by the district court, but the Seventh Circuit reversed and remanded. 557 F.2d 580, 595 (7th Cir. 1977). On writ of certiorari, the Supreme Court vacated the appellate court's decision and remanded the case for reconsideration in light of City of Lafayette v. Louisiana Power & Light Co., 435 U.S. 389 (1978). 435 U.S. 992 (1978). Once again, the Seventh Circuit reversed and remanded. 583 F.2d 378, 380 (7th Cir. 1978), *cert. denied,* 439 U.S. 1090 (1979). After a trial on the merits, judgment was entered for the Park District, and, on appeal, that judgment was affirmed. Neither the opinion of the district court for the central district of Illinois nor that of the Seventh Circuit was published.

24. Once again, I invoke the mandated presumption that local governments act to maximize the wealth of their residents.

25. Rubin, *Theory of the Firm and the Structure of the Franchise Contract* 21 J. Law & Econ. 223 (1978).

26. Making the unrealistic assumption that they were price-searchers would complicate the analysis without altering the conclusion.

27. Even after GSM took over their concessions, the golf professionals still contended that the Board had solicited GSM's offer solely for the purpose of improving its negotiating position. On the basis of this contention, their lawyer labelled the offer a sham. He no doubt anticipated that GSM would move to dismiss their complaint on the basis of the *Noerr-Pennington* doctrine, which insulates from antitrust scrutiny conduct designed to induce government action. *See* Eastern Railroad Presidents Conference v. Noerr Motor Freight, Inc., 365 U.S. 127 (1961); United Mine Workers v. Pennington, 381 U.S. 657 (1965). Labelling GSM's offer as he did, he could invoke the "sham" exception to that doctrine to defeat such a motion. *See* California Motor Transport Co. v. Trucking Unlimited, 404 U.S. 508 (1972).

28. Richard Posner has already argued that restrictions on competition among distributors of a good should be *per se* legal. Posner, *The Next Step in the Antitrust Treatment of Restricted Distribution: Per Se Legality,* 48 U. Chi. L. Rev. 6 (1981).

6

"TYING"

When a local government restricts the marketing behavior of a supplier, it almost invariably does so pursuant to a purchase agreement in which the supplier obligates himself to refrain from specified conduct. The practice to be analyzed next, selling a good on the condition that the purchaser buy another one, may occasionally take the same form. It did so, for example, when used by the city of Pueblo, Colorado.[1] Pueblo arranged for fixed base operator (fbo) service at its airport by entering into purchase agreements with several operators. The terms of the agreements were, for the most part, fairly standard. Pueblo promised to convey an fbo franchise, and in return the operators promised to pay the city a sum of money and to provide certain products and services to airport patrons. Some of the terms, however, were a bit more unusual. They provided that Pueblo would maintain and operate a fuel storage facility at the airport from which it would supply each operator, and that operators would purchase their fuel requirements from the city. Thus, in these purchase agreements the suppliers, the operators, obligated themselves to refrain from purchasing fuel from anyone else. The form of these agreements was the same as the form of those that were attacked, or might have been attacked, in *Woolen, Boulder I* and *II*, and *Kurek*, but what Pueblo did pursuant to them was arguably different. It sold fbo franchises on the condition that the purchasers, the operators, buy their fuel from the city.

Typically, such conditional selling, labelled tying by those hostile to it, takes a less complex form. For example, according to the allegations that provided the factual predicate for the Supreme Court's seminal decision in *City of Lafayette*, the City of Plaquemine, Louisiana, simply refused to provide water or gas connections to would-be customers unless they purchased their requirements of electric power from its municipal distribution company. Whatever the form of the practice, however, its legality under the antitrust statutes should turn on the functions which it is supposed to serve. We can deduce those functions by employing the now-familiar intellectual apparatus employed in making parallel deductions in the preceding chapters. Pueblo's and Plaquemine's tying provide convenient illustrations.

Turning first to Pueblo's, consider what the fixed base operators would have likely done had Pueblo not sold them their fbo franchises on the condition that they purchase their fuel requirements from it. Presumably, they would have done that which the practice bound them not to do, purchase fuel from other suppliers or, at least, credibly threaten to do so. Observe that they would not have even considered doing the former, and they could not have done the latter, unless the price charged by Pueblo were higher than the price charged by one or more of those other suppliers (assuming that the quality of the fuels was nearly identical and that the probability of delivery was about the same). If we can ascertain why Pueblo's fuel price might have been so high, then we will be able to see why the city wanted to bind the fixed base operators as it did, and thus understand the function its tying was supposed to serve.

It may appear that Pueblo might have set its fuel price high for any one of three reasons: (1) to cover higher marginal costs, (2) to obtain monopoly rents generated by the airport, or (3) to capture quasi-rents generated by the fuel storage facility. That appearance, however, is deceiving. It is deceiving because it fails to reflect the fact that a fixed base operator interested in servicing the Pueblo airport would have anticipated Pueblo's higher price and reduced his bid for a franchise accordingly. So, setting a higher fuel price would not have permitted Pueblo to cover higher marginal costs in any economically meaningful sense. If its marginal costs had indeed been higher, it would have maximized revenues by simply exiting from the fuel-selling business, a business in which other suppliers enjoyed a comparative advantage. Setting a higher fuel price would have permitted Pueblo to secure more rents than it could have secured through the franchise bidding process only if securing them through fuel sales would have economized on transactions costs.

Securing monopoly rents through fuel sales would probably not have economized on transactions costs. In fact, it might well have done just the reverse. After all, it would have meant relying on the quantity of fuel purchases as a measure of the value attached by each fixed base operator to his franchise,[2] and considering all of the services provided by an operator, that measure would have likely been rather crude. Thus, fuel sales could have easily yielded less for Pueblo than the franchise bidding process would have yielded.

With respect to quasi-rents, however, Pueblo might very well have found itself in a different position. By securing them through fuel sales, the city would have given itself an incentive that it would not have otherwise had to refrain from behaving opportunistically in connection with the storage facility—opportunistic behavior might have resulted only in reduced sales. Potential fixed base operators would have perceived the resulting reduction in the risk of such behavior as a reduction in monitoring and enforcement costs. Since that reduction would have been of considerable value, Pueblo could have expected them to pay for it.

In reality, then, Pueblo would have probably set its fuel price higher than that of other suppliers for only one reason: to capture some of the quasi-rents generated by the investment in the fuel storage facility,[3] a highly specialized capital asset.

It therefore had to bind the fixed base operators to purchase their fuel requirements from it. If they had been contractually free to make purchases from other suppliers or to credibly threaten to do so, Pueblo would have been confronted with the choice of reducing its price or foregoing sales. To maximize its revenues, it would have reduced its price so long as that price exceeded the short-run marginal costs of providing the fuel. This turn of events would have greatly reduced the expected return on investment in the facility. Pueblo would have therefore likely had an incentive to disinvest, probably by curtailing maintenance and repair work. In the short-run, a decision to curtail such work would have had little effect. In the long-run, however, it would have led to the facility being unavailable for use.

The city could have avoided that presumably inefficient result, at little cost, by entering into long-term requirements contracts with the operators at the same moment that it sold them their franchises. Of course, that is precisely what Pueblo did by virtue of tying. Thus, the practice was evidently supposed to serve two familiar functions. It permitted Pueblo taxpayers, through their city government, to cost-effectively capture the quasi-rents generated by their investment in the storage facility, and by permitting that capture, the practice induced them to continue to invest in it.

Pueblo Aircraft Corp., which had been one of three fixed base operators at the city's airport, challenged the practice as an antitrust offense. When Pueblo Aircraft's franchise expired, the city put it up for auction, and one of the other two operators acquired it. Unhappy with this outcome, Pueblo Aircraft brought an antitrust suit against the city in which it claimed, *inter alia*, that the provision in their agreement obligating it to purchase all of its fuel from the city ran afoul of not only section 1 of the Sherman Act, but also section 3 of the Clayton Act which prohibits the "lease or . . . sale of goods . . . on the condition . . . that the lessee or purchaser thereof shall not use or deal in the goods . . . of a competitor or competitors of the lessor or seller, where the effect of such lease [or] sale . . . may be to substantially lessen competition or tend to create a monopoly."[4]

The city moved for summary judgment on that claim. Although the court granted the motion on grounds related to the merits, it failed to consider the functions that the practice was supposed to serve. Indulging in a transparent *non-sequitur*, the court ruled that since Pueblo had acquired the fuel storage facility as part of the legitimate purchase of the airport property from the federal government, since that facility was the only one of its kind at the airport, and since no fixed base operator had ever offered to build and maintain a substitute facility, Pueblo's practice did not constitute an antitrust violation.

Had the court focused on the functions that the practice was supposed to serve, it could have reached the same result, but it would have done so on the basis of sound reasoning. It would have begun by observing that the principles embodied in the antitrust statutes speak to consumer welfare, not to the distribution of wealth between entities of different "sizes." On those principles, Pueblo's tying was unobjectionable since it tended to promote, or at least not impair, consumer welfare. Besides, no populist notion about the appropriate distribution of wealth requires that fixed base operators serving a city airport at any particular time be enriched at the expense of that city and its taxpayers.

On the same reasoning, Plaquemine's tying, the sale of water and gas service to customers residing outside the city limits on the condition that they purchase their requirements of electric power service from the municipal distribution company, did not constitute an antitrust offense. It was probably supposed to serve the same kind of functions served by the analogous conduct in which the City of Pueblo engaged.

Suppose that Plaquemine's managers had contemplated selling electric power service separately. Presumably, they would have offered it to customers residing outside the city limits only at a price high enough to permit the capture of quasi-rents generated by the investment in the facilities needed to provide it. The managers would have realized, however, that even if those customers accepted Plaquemine's offer, they might prove fickle once the investment was made. That would certainly be true if another enterprise was in a position to become an alternative supplier of that service, and if we credit the allegations in Louisiana Power & Light's counterclaim, then it must have been in just that position. Then Plaquemine's non-resident customers could have purchased, or credibly threatened to purchase, electric power service from LP&L. If they had done so, Plaquemine would have found that its financial self-interest dictated a price reduction and, as in Pueblo's case, that price reduction would have probably dictated disinvestment. If, in anticipation of this turn of events, Plaquemine's managers had offered the service at a price high enough to compensate the city for bearing the risk of customer fickleness, there might have been so few takers that little or no investment would have been made in the first place.

In the absence of significant transactions costs, Plaquemine's managers could have avoided these inefficient results by doing what Pueblo did with its fixed base operators, enter into long-term requirements contracts with non-resident customers. The costs of enforcing such contracts, however, might have been prohibitive. It seems unlikely that any court would be willing to order a welching customer to continue to make purchases from the city or to pay the city lump-sum damages equal to the present value of the quasi-rents foregone. Indeed some courts might refuse to enforce the contracts at all, perhaps finding them "unconscionable" or inconsistent with the perceived policy of the relevant regulatory statutes. In any event, the costs of making sure that customers purchased electric service from no other enterprise would have far exceeded the costs of simply confronting them with the credible threat that their supply of water or gas service would be cut off if they did. From all that appears in the relevant court opinions, other enterprises were not in a position to offer such services. Therefore, by confronting their electric power customers with that credible threat, the city managers could count on them to remain faithful even after the investment in the facilities needed to serve them had been made. By engaging in the challenged practice, then, Plaquemine could enjoy the principal benefits of long-term requirements contracts without incurring the costs of enforcing them. Thus, the practice likely permitted Plaquemine's taxpayers to cost-effectively capture the quasi-rents generated by their investment in addition to their electric power distribution network, and by so doing, induced them to make it.[5]

It is also possible, although far less likely, that Plaquemine's tying was supposed to serve one of two other functions that were not served by Pueblo's. These may be most easily deduced by inquiring how else it is that the city could have possibly gained by doing what it did. In theory, it could have done so by using the tie to subtly discriminate between groups who valued the tied services differently. For example, suppose that Plaquemine's managers correctly believed that among potential non-resident customers desiring gas as well as electric service there were two groups of equal size who valued the services quite differently.[6] One group, ABC, would be willing to pay only $40.00 for a connection to the electric power distribution network, but as much as $80.00 for a connection to the gas distribution network. The other group, XYZ, would be willing to pay $50.00 for an electric power connection but only $60.00 for a gas connection. Now suppose further that, although the managers were sure that the two groups existed, they could not ascertain who belonged to ABC and who belonged to XYZ. If they sold the services separately, they would maximize revenues by charging customers $40.00 for a gas connection and $60.00 for an electric power one. Customers with both connections would pay $100.00 each. If they sold the services as a unit, however, they could charge those customers $110.00 without losing any business.[7] This subtle discrimination would yield more revenues and those additional revenues might constitute monopoly rents. Conceivably, Plaquemine's practice permitted the city's taxpayers to capture them. This function bears some resemblance to that of permitting capture of quasi-rents. In theory, the two are quite different because the prospect of capturing quasi-rents is the *sine qua non* of investment, while the prospect of capturing monopoly rents is not. In practice, however, it may be rather difficult to distinguish between monopoly rents and quasi-rents.

The city could have also gained by tying the sale of one service to the sale of another, *at the prices it was charging*, if it could provide them together at a lower cost than it could provide them separately. Lower costs might reflect savings in simultaneous installation of the distribution networks or in joint meter reading. Thus, the practice may have simply prevented non-resident customers from obtaining either service at a price below the marginal cost of providing it. This function is analogous to that of securing efficiently provisioned service by permitting the supplier to enjoy either production or transactions economies.

If the practice was supposed to serve either one of these functions, it could not have been condemned outright on grounds related to consumer welfare. That is obviously true if it served the second one, but it is also true if it served the first. Although discriminatory pricing may permit the capture of monopoly rents, it may also yield a larger output at an average price no higher than that which would otherwise prevail.[8] Besides, forbidding the capture of monopoly rents would create powerful disincentives to efficient investment. Tying and related practices like requirements and output contracts and reciprocal dealing should almost invariably be deemed legal under the antitrust statutes.

NOTES

1. Pueblo Aircraft Service, Inc. v. City of Pueblo, Colo., 679 F.2d 805 (10th Cir. 1982), *cert. denied*, 459 U.S. 1126 (1983).

2. It would have then been using the tie to subtly discriminate between operators. For an analysis of this use of tying, see the discussion of *City of Lafayette* which follows.

3. If (a) the costs to the operators of obtaining a lump sum from the money market to pay Pueblo had been peculiarly high, and (b) the city were forbidden from loaning it to them directly, then the city might have had another incentive to tie the sale of fbo franchises to the sale of fuel and to charge more for the fuel than other suppliers would have charged. There is no reason to believe, however, that either condition prevailed.

4. Clayton Act § 3, 15 U.S.C. § 14 (1976).

5. It is possible, although certainly less likely, that tying also permitted Plaquemine's taxpayers to cost-effectively capture some of the quasi-rents generated by their investment in extensions of the water and gas distribution networks. It might have served that function if capture had been effectuated through the rates for electric power service rather than those for water and gas service. That rate structure might have prevailed within the city limits because Plaquemine's managers believed that it tended to distribute wealth in ways of which they approved, and they might have decided to extend it beyond the city limits, along with the distribution networks, in order to comply with anti-price-discrimination laws or to economize on billing costs. If the demand for electric power service had been sufficiently inelastic, this seemingly round-about method of capturing quasi-rents would have worked as long as the city's water and gas customers could not practically turn to a rival provider for electric power. The city's managers could have easily used coercion to prevent customers residing within Plaquemine from doing so. They could have simply refused to grant any such entity permission to lay wires across public thoroughfares. Coercion would have been unavailing, however, with respect to customers residing outside of Plaquemine. To capture those quasi-rents from them, the city's managers would have had to do more. They could have charged higher rates for water and gas service, but presumably that would have meant

raising those rates for customers residing within the city. Sudden changes in rates can be quite costly, and inefficiently so. 1 A. Kahn, The Economics of Regulation: Principles and Institutions p. 84 (1970). (Moreover, elected officials and bureaucrats might find it politically expensive to suddenly change the rates for a municipally supplied service even if it were not otherwise costly to do so.) It might have been more cost-effective in the short run to simply make sure that customers residing outside of Plaquemine purchased their electric power requirements from the city, and that is precisely what Plaquemine's tying did.

6. *See* Stigler, *A Note on Block Booking*, in The Organization of Industry (1968).

7. Plaquemine could have done the same sort of thing with per-unit prices for gas and electricity by virtue of the fact that the two products are substitutes for one another, albeit imperfect ones.

8. R. Posner, Antitrust Law: An Economic Perspective p. 64 (1976); W. Bowman, Patents and Antitrust Law: A Legal and Economic Appraisal pp. 111-13 (1973). Discriminatory pricing that yielded a larger output at an average price lower than that which would otherwise prevail could still be economically inefficient if it substantially changed the competitive relationship between users of the discriminatorily priced good. Such second order effects would have likely been negligible, however, in the case of Plaquemine's alleged tying.

7

"PREDATORY" PRICING

When local governments sell goods, they may, and probably often do, set prices that are "below costs" —below average total costs[1]—or perhaps even below marginal production costs, or rather some accounting surrogate for them.[2] Such pricing, usually labelled predatory by those attacking it, is the fourth practice to be considered. It has been challenged as an antitrust offense by private suppliers of the services that have been so priced. For example, when Bi-State Development Agency, a unit of local government in the metropolitan St. Louis area, allegedly sold bus transportation to students at "below-cost" prices, a private school bus operator, Ladue Local Lines, Inc., claimed that Bi-State had monopolized or attempted to monopolize its market.[3] And when the City of St. Paul, Minnesota, allegedly sold trash collection on similar terms to senior citizens, widows, and low-income families, a private trash collector, Heille, claimed that the city had engaged in predatory pricing, which had the effect of excluding it from the market.[4]

This practice can be wealth-maximizing in the short run. Prices that are below average total costs might simply be all that the market will bear. And because of the potentially wide disparity between marginal production costs and accounting surrogates for them, the same observation may be made about prices that are below those accounting surrogates. Of course, such prices are unobjectionable on any commonly accepted antitrust principle.

Where "below-cost" pricing is not wealth-maximizing in the

short run, it may, in theory, serve any one of three functions. First, as a transfer payment device, it could simply enable the local government to redistribute wealth from taxpayers to the recipients of the low-priced service. Second, as a promotional device, it could induce purchasing and thereby help the local government provide potential customers with information about the good—obviously, the kind of information that could be obtained by using the good. Third, as a strategic device, it could help drive competing private suppliers out of business, or deter them from engaging in rivalrous behavior, and thereby permit the local government to raise its price and capture monopoly rents.

In practice, however, a local government's "below-cost" pricing is almost bound to serve the transfer payment function. Consider two pieces of supporting circumstantial evidence. One is that law-makers in the post-Depression era have acted as if transferring wealth is one of the principal tasks of government. The recipients of low-priced services tend to be either those with political clout or the natural objects of their bureaucratic bounty, like parents with school-age children in the St. Louis metropolitan area or senior citizens, widows, and those with low incomes in St. Paul. The second and more important piece of evidence is that law-makers need not take any additional action if "below-cost" pricing is to serve the transfer payment function. In contrast, if the practice is to serve either the promotional or strategic functions, law-makers must do more than set prices. At the very least, they must subsequently raise them at an opportune time. Taking such action would likely prove difficult since the law-makers would have to overcome bureaucratic inertia and the efforts of the favored groups to retain their benefits, and do so with a speed and a constancy of purpose that is rare in government.

The transfer payment function is unobjectionable on the principle that, as between private holdings of wealth, "smaller" or "less advantaged" ones should be preferred to "larger" or "more advantaged" ones. As previously explained, that populist principle is inapplicable when the challenged practice is used by a local government, particularly if the ideological underpinnings of that principle are considered. (Even if the local government were treated as if it were a private holder of wealth, the transfer payment function would still not be objectionable on that principle.) That means, or course, that the other two functions that "below-cost" pricing might serve are similarly unobjectionable.

The transfer payment and promotional functions are also unobjectionable on consumer welfare grounds. Transfer payments themselves have no effect on consumer welfare and presumably wealth-maximizing promotion tends to increase it. Only the strategic function is objectionable on those grounds, and it is especially unlikely that a local government's "below-cost" pricing would serve that function.

Law-makers would have little reason to resort to such problematic tactics just to drive private suppliers out of business or to discipline them when they could probably achieve the same end more easily by using their coercive powers. For example, they might find plausible-sounding reasons for failing to renew the necessary operating permits and for denying them to would-be new entrants. It is not surprising, then, that neither Ladue Local Lines, Inc., nor Heille alleged that their local government competitors used "below-cost" pricing strategically. Both private plaintiffs merely complained that prices were too low and therefore injurious to them. Thus, neither complaint stated a claim upon which antitrust relief could be based.

Generally, a local government may set prices "below cost" without committing an antitrust offense unless the practice is designed to serve a strategic function. Under the Supreme Court's "same treatment" lesson, a private enterprise should be permitted to do likewise.[5]

NOTES

1. It is not my intention here to enter into the debate over the appropriate cost standard, if any (*see* Williamson, *Predatory Pricing: A Strategic and Welfare Analysis*, 87 Yale L.J. 284 [1978]) for determining whether prices are "predatory." The latest round of the debate began with Areeda & Turner, *Predatory Pricing and Related Practices under Section 2 of the Sherman Act*, 88 Harv. L. Rev. 697 (1975), and it continues unabated. *See, e.g.*, R. Posner, Antitrust Law: An Economic Perspective pp. 184-96 (1976); Scherer, *Predatory Pricing and the Sherman Act: A Comment*, 89 Harv. L. Rev. 869 (1976); Scherer, *Some Last Words on Predatory*

Pricing, 89 Harv. L. Rev. 901 (1976); Williamson, at 284; R. Bork, The Antitrust Paradox pp. 144-60 (1978); Williamson, *Predatory Pricing II*, 88 Yale L.J. 1183 (1979); National Commission for the Review of Antitrust Laws and Procedures, Report to the President and the Attorney General pp. 149-51 (1979); Posner, *The Chicago School of Antitrust Analysis*, 127 U. Pa. L. Rev. 925, 939-44 (1979); Joskow & Klevorick, *A Framework for Analyzing Predatory Pricing Policy*, 89 Yale L.J. 213 (1979); Baumol, *Quasi-Permanence of Price Reductions: A Policy for Prevention of Predatory Pricing*, 29 Yale L.J. 1 (1979); McGee, *Predatory Pricing Revisited*, 23 J. Law & Econ. 289 (1980); Hay, *A Confused Lawyer's Guide to the Predatory Pricing Literature*, in Strategic Predation and Antitrust Analysis (S. Salop, ed., 1981).

2. Average variable costs are the most commonly used surrogate.

3. Ladue Local Lines, Inc. v. Bi-State Development Agency of the Missouri-Illinois Metropolitan District, 433 F.2d 131 (8th Cir. 1970). The district court dismissed Ladue's suit and, on appeal, the Eighth Circuit affirmed, holding that Bi-State was "exempt" from the antitrust laws because of its status as a unit of local government.

4. Heille v. City of St. Paul, Minn., 512 F. Supp. 810 (D. Minn. 1981), *aff'd*, 671 F.2d 1134 (8th Cir. 1982). Holding that Heille's antitrust claim lacked the nexus with interstate commerce required for subject matter jurisdiction, the district court dismissed it.

5. *See* R. Posner, *supra* note 1.

8

"MONOPOLY MISUSE" AND KLOR'S-TYPE "BOYCOTTS"

The fifth and final practice to be considered is the selling or buying of goods on such terms and under such conditions that (a) some *potential* competitors, purchasers, or suppliers find that they are unable to economically enter their respective markets, or (b) some *existing* ones are more successful than others. This definition may strike the reader as rather inclusive. Indeed, understood literally, it includes conduct that could be classified as one of the other four practices. I intend, however, that it be understood in context so that it includes only that selling or buying that could not neatly be so classified.

Even when so understood, this definition may also strike the reader as rather amorphous. It is. What makes the definition amorphous is that it speaks in terms of effects rather than just conduct, and, arguably, these particular effects are caused by every sale or purchase. While this is a vice for the purposes of semantics, it is a virtue for the purposes of understanding the impact that municipal liability and the Court's "same treatment" lesson could have on the common law of antitrust. Only such an amorphous definition could encompass all of the conduct upon which courts have frequently pinned the same pejorative labels and then, following in the long antitrust tradition of literalistic jurisprudence, treated alike. Those all-important labels are "monopoly misuse" or "abuse,"[1] and, especially in the absence of any allegation or proof of market power, "boycott,"[2] which is sometimes referred to by the less colorful, but synonymous, "conspiracy to exclude."[3]

When a local government uses the fifth practice, there will usually be little, if any, doubt about the functions that it is likely supposed to serve. In typical cases, the bulk of which involve the local government as purchaser, even a casual observer would readily see that the practice should help secure the desired good at the lowest obtainable price.[4] In that sense *Greyhound Rent-A-Car v. City of Pensacola, Fla.*[5] was a typical case.[6] The city, which held title to the Pensacola Regional Airport, was in the market for at-the-terminal car renting service. It planned to purchase the service, as it had in the past, by conveying four franchises, in return for a cash payment, to firms that would actually rent the cars. To that end, it solicited bids for these franchises from firms that (a) would accept payment from patrons through nationally recognized credit cards; (b) had a national reservation system; (c) would rent cars with the understanding that patrons could return them in other cities; (d) would provide primary liability insurance for bodily injury and property damage, insurance that covered the principal loss, not merely that portion of the loss that exceeded the limits of the patron's personal liability insurance; and (e) had engaged in the car rental business on a national scale for the immediately preceding five years. Five firms responded to the solicitation. Greyhound Rent-A-Car, Inc., submitted the third-highest bid, but the city did not award it a franchise. Instead, the city awarded a franchise to the lowest bidder, Dollar Rent-A-Car Systems, Inc. Dollar had questioned Greyhound's compliance with the credit card, reservation, and insurance specifications of the city's solicitation and, in particular, had objected that Greyhound had not operated its car rental business on a national scale for the immediately preceding five years. Greyhound had been renting cars for some time in only Florida, Georgia, Louisiana, and Arizona, and had recently begun to do so in Nevada, California, and Colorado. The city manager apparently believed that Dollar's objection was well taken, for on the basis of it, he recommended that the city award a franchise to Dollar rather than Greyhound, and his recommendation was accepted by the city council.

That the franchise was awarded to Dollar rather than Greyhound shows that Pensacola used the fifth practice. It purchased at-the-terminal car rental service on such terms that suppliers who qualified for a franchise were more successful than those who did not. By using that practice, Pensacola helped secure the kind of service deemed desirable by its managers at the lowest obtainable price. The specifications of its solicitation evidenced that function. Specifications (a), (b), (c), and (d) obviously did so. Each one described a characteristic of the desired service, like its availability for purchase through major credit cards. Presumably, Pensacola's managers believed that at-the-terminal car renting service with those characteristics would tend to maximize the value of the airport. Specification (e), the principal one upon which Greyhound's bid foundered, described a characteristic of the supplying firm rather than of the desired service. Nevertheless, it still evidenced the same function as the other specifications.

A car rental firm operating on a national scale would have had a difficult time surviving for five years, as required by specification (e), unless it had habitually satisfied the travelling public. Pensacola's managers could have reasonably believed that firms that had so performed in the past were *ceteris paribus* more likely to do so in the future than were firms that had not. Of course, there can be little doubt that some of the firms disqualified by specification (e) had also habitually satisfied the travelling public; and that some of those who had not, perhaps because they were new entrants, would have done so in Pensacola had they been awarded a franchise. The costs of identifying the firms in the first group, however, probably would have exceeded the benefits of making them eligible to bid. The costs of identifying the firms in the second group would have been even greater. Pensacola could have specified performance standards for the desired service, accepted bids from anyone wishing to make one, and then monitored the winning bidders for compliance with those standards, and, in the event of non-compliance, taken effective enforcement action. It is unlikely, however, that that scheme would have proved more cost-effective than the one Pensacola actually used.

A car rental firm operating on a nationwide scale would also have more to lose than a less broadly based rival if it were caught providing substandard service or otherwise acting opportunistically.[7] Therefore, it would tend to exhibit such behavior less often. Thus, Pensacola's managers could have reasonably expected that by limiting franchises to such firms, they could secure the service that they desired without engaging in as much monitoring and enforcement (and incurring the associated costs) as they otherwise would.

Following the award of the franchises, Greyhound sued Pensacola as well as Dollar. It claimed that by purchasing at-the-terminal car rental service on the basis of the specifications in the solicitation, the city had committed an antitrust offense. In particular, it argued that the city, along with Dollar, had engaged in a "conspir[acy] to exclude it from being awarded a car rental concession at the airport, . . . a boycott within the pattern of *Klor's, Inc. v. Broadway Hale Stores, Inc.*, 359 U.S. 207 . . . (1959). . . ."[8] After a trial on the merits, the district court judge submitted Greyhound's claim to the jury under the "Rule of Reason." The jury gave a verdict for Pensacola and Dollar, and judgment was entered accordingly. On appeal, the Eleventh Circuit affirmed, ruling that Greyhound had introduced "insufficient evidence to establish any contract, combination, or conspiracy between Dollar and the [c]ity within the meaning of § 1 of the Sherman Act."[9]

Pensacola and Dollar were thrice blessed during this litigation. Their first blessing was the district court's "Rule of Reason" instruction. Greyhound had asked the judge to instruct the jury that the conduct of which it complained was illegal *per se*, illegal without regard to its actual or likely effect. Some powerful precedent militated in favor of granting that request. In its *Klor's* opinion the Supreme Court had suggested that a refusal to deal with one retailer at the request, or upon the complaint, of another was illegal *per se*,[10] and in decisions like *Cernuto, Inc. v. United Cabinet Corp.*,[11] several lower courts had so held. Had the judge bowed to this precedent and given the instruction requested by Greyhound, the jury would have been called upon to decide only whether Pensacola and Dollar had engaged in the behavior that Greyhound alleged they had. Since, for the most part, they had not denied those allegations, the jury would have been bound to find against them.

That the judge gave a "Rule of Reason" instruction, however, hardly guaranteed that the jury would find for them. Only a statement that the legality of their conduct turned on its actual or likely impact on consumer welfare might have done so.[12] His instruction contained no such statement.[13] In fact, it provided little, if any, meaningful guidance about the standard the jury was to use in assessing the "reasonableness" of what Pensacola and Dollar had done. "Rule of Reason" instructions rarely, if ever, do. They usually consist of some introductory words of art, which are not identified as such, and a laundry list of factors that the jury might wish to consider while it deliberates. Many, including the one given in this case, do no more than paraphrase an oft-quoted portion of Justice Brandeis's opinion for the Supreme Court in *Board of Trade of the City of Chicago v. United States*:

> The true test of legality is whether the restraint imposed is such as merely regulates and perhaps thereby promotes competition or whether it is such as may suppress or even destroy competition. To determine that question the [jury] must ordinarily consider the facts peculiar to the business to which the restraint is applied, its condition before and after the restraint is imposed; the nature of the restraint and its effect, actual or probable. The history of the restraint, the evil believed to exist, the reason for adopting the particular remedy, the purpose or end sought to be attained, are all relevant facts.[14]

Such instructions do little more than invite jurors to decide whether, in terms of the personal codes of conduct that they profess, an antitrust defendant's behavior under the circumstances was "acceptable." There is little reason to believe that refusals to deal with one retailer at the request, or on the complaint, of another would fare well when so evaluated.[15] For that matter, it seems a safe bet that many jurors would disapprove of the fifth practice, whatever form it took—it would offend their sense of egalitarianism.[16] Thus, Pensacola's and Dollar's second blessing was the jury verdict in their favor.

Their third blessing was the Eleventh Circuit's ruling that Greyhound had failed to prove that they had acted in concert. As a matter of sound antitrust policy, that ruling was correct.[17] It was seemingly inconsistent, however, with *United States v. Parke, Davis & Co.*[18] and *Albrecht v. The Herald Co.*,[19] in which the Supreme Court found concerted activity on the basis of far less evidence than Greyhound presented.

Pensacola was also lucky that the Eleventh Circuit's ruling

insulated it from liability. That ruling would not have done so had Greyhound claimed that Pensacola had "misused," or "abused," the "monopoly" it enjoyed by virtue of holding title to what was probably the only commercial airport in the immediately surrounding area. Many of those aggrieved by a local government's use of the fifth practice make analogous claims. To prevail, of course, they need not prove concerted activity.

Local governments using the fifth practice could not count on enjoying similar blessings. In that sense Pensacola was fortunate. In another sense, however, it was unfortunate. It had to bear the costs of mounting a full-scale antitrust defense to a claim that should not have even survived long enough to be tried. The function of the practice challenged by Greyhound, helping to secure the desired kind of at-the-terminal car renting service at the lowest obtainable price, was unobjectionable on consumer welfare grounds. In fact, it would have probably been unobjectionable on populist wealth-distribution preference grounds had they been applicable. It is difficult to believe that even the most die-hard populist would have required that Greyhound be favored at the expense of Pensacola and its taxpayers.

There are, of course, some atypical cases in which a casual observer might have some difficulty ascertaining what functions the fifth practice was supposed to serve. Consider two examples, one drawn from *Allegheny Uniforms v. Howard Uniform Co.*,[20] and the other from *Almeda Mall, Inc. v. Houston Lighting & Power Co.*[21]

The Port Authority of Allegheny County (Pennsylvania) required that its employee bus drivers, while performing their jobs, wear uniforms that conformed to particular specifications. The drivers bore sole responsibility for obtaining their uniforms, but not necessarily for paying for them. The Port Authority offered to make part-payment if the drivers purchased uniforms that it had approved and if they did so at the Gimbel Brothers, Inc., retail store in Pittsburgh. The Port Authority had approved only those uniforms made by the Howard Uniform Company. The Allegheny Uniform Company had attempted to secure approval for its uniforms but was unsuccessful even though they allegedly conformed with the relevant specifications and were, "for all practical purposes," identical with Howard's.[22] Thus, the Port Authority used the fifth practice. It bought uniforms on such terms that Howard was more successful than Allegheny. Allegheny claimed that by so doing, the Port Authority had committed an antitrust offense.

The Port Authority moved to dismiss the suit for failure to state a claim upon which relief could be based. Its grounds were that its conduct was exempt from the Sherman and Clayton Acts under *Parker v. Brown*. Presciently anticipating *Boulder I*, the district court denied the motion, observing that no state statute authorized the Port Authority's use of the fifth practice, even implicitly.

The district court never reached the merits of Allegheny's claims, but we can. Although the Port Authority used the fifth practice in the same context as did the City of Pensacola, that of making a purchase, it is not obvious that it was supposed to serve the same function, that of helping the local government secure desired goods at the lowest obtainable price. After all, it is difficult to believe that only Howard could have made uniforms that conformed to the Port Authority's specifications. Indeed, Allegheny alleged that it was doing so. And, it is unlikely that by using the fifth practice, the Port Authority could have induced Howard to quote a price per uniform significantly lower than the one that rivalry with other clothing makers would have prompted it to quote.[23]

The last point may call for an explanation. Assume that Howard was a price-taker. It is reasonable to make that assumption because the apparel industry was, and is, relatively atomistic, and nothing in the court's opinion even hints that Howard enjoyed any market power, that is, that it was a price-searcher. As a price-taker, Howard would have responded to everyday rivalry in the market by quoting a price per uniform approximately equal to the marginal uniform-maker's marginal cost of production and distribution. Howard would not have even considered quoting a lower price in connection with any particular supply arrangement unless the terms of that arrangement had held out the prospect of a substantial cost savings. No such prospect was held out by the practice challenged by Allegheny which was the key term of the supply arrangement proposed by the Port Authority. To see why, simply consider what a firm like Howard could have stood to gain by virtue of that practice. At most, it could have gained "exclusive approval"—approval for the firm's uniforms plus assurance that the Port Authority would refrain from approving uniforms made by anyone else.[24] Of course, a firm like Howard would have rather gained that than not, everything else being equal.

"Exclusive approval" might have reduced the risk of non-sale, which, presumably, the successful uniform-maker would have borne, and it might have served as a substitute for a marketing program aimed at the Port Authority's employee drivers. Thus, it might have permitted a firm to avoid some expenditures—but they probably would not have been significant ones. They would not have been significant because the size of both the reduction in risk and the marketing program foregone would have been proportional to the ratio between the number of drivers in the employ of the Port Authority and the number of potential purchasers of similar uniforms—and that ratio would have been quite small. Yet, as insignificant as these avoided expenditures would have been, we can be certain that cost savings would have been even less significant. We can be so sure because we know that the successful uniformmaker would have had to make expenditures in order to obtain "exclusive approval" for its uniforms. Thus, cost savings, if any, would have amounted to no more than the difference between the expenditures avoided and the expenditures made, a sum that probably would not have induced Howard, or any of its rivals, to quote a lower price per uniform.

Although it may not be obvious what the challenged practice could have done for the Port Authority, it is plain enough what it would have done to the Port Authority's employee drivers. There can be little doubt that it would have caused them to stock their work wardrobes with uniforms made by Howard and retailed by Gimbel's at their Pittsburgh store. In fact, it was presumably that behavior which prompted Allegheny to bring suit. The reason that a casual observer might have some difficulty in ascertaining the function of the practice is that it is not at all clear how the Port Authority could have profited from that behavior.[25]

Two interrelated preliminary observations should help unlock this "mystery." The first is that although the Port Authority managers must have known that several firms *could* have made the uniforms that they desired, they could not have known, *a priori,* which ones *would* actually do so. Thus, if they wanted their drivers to be "properly" attired, and they clearly did, they were almost bound to have done more than merely specify the kind of uniforms that they desired. They would have to have monitored and enforced compliance with their specifications. The second observation is that by limiting, as a practical matter, the number of vendors from whom their drivers obtained uniforms to one maker and one retailer, they would have economized on both of those activities. To see why that is so, we must deduce the likely nature of each.

Consider monitoring. It is perhaps obvious that this activity would have taken the form of inspections. It may not be as obvious, however, that the managers of the Port Authority would have probably conducted some of those inspections while the uniforms were still in the possession of the vendors. Indeed, one could easily construct a superficially appealing argument to the contrary. After all, a driver could render a uniform nonconforming just as well as a vendor could, and in order to search for offending features caused by drivers, the managers of the Port Authority would plainly have to have conducted some inspections after the uniforms had passed into their hands. Since the people conducting those inspections could have simultaneously searched, at little or no additional cost, for the other kind of offending features, those caused by vendors, one might jump to the conclusion that the managers would have conducted only post-vending inspections. Careful scrutiny reveals, however, that this conclusion would necessarily follow from the reasoning that precedes it only if post-vending inspections were fairly good substitutes for pre-vending ones—and that is rather doubtful. In fact, in terms of searching for vendor-caused offending features and securing remedial action from vendors, it is likely that pre-vending inspections would have offered some substantial advantages. They would have made searching easier because, unlike post-vending inspections, they would not have been subject to severe privacy constraints. They could have made securing remedial action from vendors easier because, again unlike post-vending inspections, pre-vending inspections could not have given rise to claims that drivers caused some or all of the offending features detected. And since pre-vending inspections lend themselves to sampling techniques (which post-vending inspections do not), Port Authority managers could have had these advantages on the cheap. Thus, the managers of the Port Authority would have probably found it cost-effective to conduct some pre-vending inspections. They could have economized on this kind of monitoring by limiting the number of vendors from whom their drivers obtained uniforms to one maker and one retailer. By so limiting the number of vendors, they would have limited the number of sites at which they would have had to conduct pre-vending inspections.[26] Both the number of pre-vending inspections required to achieve any given level of monitoring effectiveness and some of the costs of conducting those inspections, like the cost of transporting inspectors, would have varied directly with the number of sites at which those inspections would have to have been conducted.

Now consider enforcement, without which all of this monitoring would have been less than worthless. As a routine matter, enforcement would have surely taken the form of demands to alter or replace non-conforming uniforms. At times, the managers of the Port Authority would have directed such demands to the party being inspected, but on many occasions to some other party, one farther back in the chain of distribution—even though that might have involved compiling documentary or other evidence to substantiate the link between that other party and the non-conforming feature. For example, upon the discovery of an improperly stitched uniform being worn by a driver, they would almost certainly have directed their alter-or-replace demand to the maker of the uniform. To do otherwise would have been far too costly. Here's why. The Port Authority would have had to compensate whoever was subject to these demands for bearing the risk that uniforms would be non-conforming. It would have had to provide the least compensation to the party who could bear that risk most efficiently, and with respect to many offending features, that party would not have been the one being inspected. Using the example just given, the Port Authority would have had to compensate its employees far more than it would have had to compensate uniform-makers for bearing the risk that uniforms would suffer from improper stitching because the former could not have borne that risk nearly as efficiently as could the latter. The managers of the Port Authority would have economized on this kind of enforcement by limiting the number of vendors from whom their drivers obtained uniforms to one maker and one retailer. With the number of vendors so limited, there would have been no need to substantiate the link between a party that had not been inspected and a non-conforming uniform before demanding that that party alter or replace it.[27]

If it was not obvious how the Port Authority could have profited from the behavior of its employee drivers that was caused by the challenged practice, it should be now. It would have incurred fewer costs in monitoring and enforcing compliance with its specifications. Those costs would have been part of the total price paid by the Port Authority for what it wanted, having each driver "properly" attired. So, it should now also be obvious that the function that that practice was supposed to serve was, in the final analysis, the same as the one served by Pensacola's, securing a desired good at the lowest obtainable price. In fact, it is likely that this is the function that all "approved source" purchasing is supposed to serve.[28]

Now consider the other example, drawn from *Almeda Mall, Inc.* The owners of the Almeda Mall shopping center wished to purchase electric power service from Houston Lighting & Power (HL&P) at the rate charged to high-volume users rather than at the higher rate charged to ordinary commercial users. They argued that they qualified as high-volume users because they planned to purchase all of the service demanded by their tenants and then resell it to them, profitably, at the rate for ordinary commercial users. HL&P refused to grant the owners their wish just as a local government holding title to an electric power distribution company could well have done. Since HL&P was the only readily available source of "wholesale" electric service and since it would sell that service only at the rate for ordinary commercial users, the owners were unable to economically enter the market for the "retail" distribution of that service. Thus, HL&P used the fifth practice, but it did so in connection with selling rather than buying. When so used, the functions that the practice is supposed to serve are especially likely to elude the casual observer.

The careful analyst, however, would have had little trouble determining what it was. Observe that the owners of the Almeda Mall shopping center were trying to engage in a form of arbitrage. The possibility of arbitrage was created by virtue of HL&P's sale of electric power service at different rates to different customers. The difference in rates may have reflected, in part, a difference in the costs of providing service, but, no doubt, it primarily reflected a difference in demand elasticities.[29] HL&P was engaged in price discrimination, a rate-setting strategy used by almost all distributors of electric power. Arbitrage would have threatened that strategy. By selling service to the owners only at the rate for ordinary commercial users, HL&P prevented that threat from materializing. Thus, the fifth practice facilitated price discrimination.[30] It also largely eliminated the need to determine, perhaps at considerable expense, whether the responsibility for remedying any electric-power problems experienced by tenants at the shopping center laid with HL&P or the owners.[31]

Those functions were unobjectionable on the principle of consumer welfare maximization. The reduction in the cost of affixing responsibility for repair was, of course, efficient. HL&P's price discrimination probably resulted in a greater output at average prices no higher than those that would otherwise have prevailed.[32] Had it not, HL&P's rates would have been "unreasonably discriminatory,"[33] and the owners of the Almeda Mall would have been entitled to relief under the Texas statutes governing utilities.[34] Those functions may not have been objectionable on the principle of populist wealth distribution preference either since, market dynamics aside, it is not at all clear that they favored "larger" or "more advantaged" firms over "smaller" or "less advantaged" ones. Had HL&P been municipally owned, that principle would not have even been applicable.

Of course, helping to secure a desired good at the lowest obtainable price, whether by reducing the cost of monitoring and enforcement, as in *Allegheny Uniforms*, or more straightforwardly, as in *Greyhound Rent-A-Car, Inc. v. City of Pensacola*, is similarly unobjectionable. Some courts have implicitly suggested otherwise, but only because they misapplied the principle of populist wealth-distribution preference. For example, consider *Duke & Company, Inc. v. Foerster.*[35] Duke brewed beer, while Foerster and the other defendants operated the Pittsburgh Civic Arena, Three Rivers Stadium, and the Pittsburgh International Airport. Duke claimed that the defendants' refusal to purchase its beer for resale in those three public facilities constituted an antitrust offense. The district court dismissed the claim on *Parker v. Brown* state action grounds, but the Third Circuit reversed. It held that since no state statute had authorized the defendants to "discriminat[e] against certain suppliers," they could not avail themselves of state action "immunity."[36] Such "discrimination" is, of course, the essence of contracting. The court's implicit suggestion that it might be objectionable can be rationalized only on the principle that it is good to prefer Duke to the taxpayers of the Pittsburgh area, who collectively owned the facilities that the defendants operated. Surely, no populist would subscribe to that principle or any kindred one.

Although there can be no doubt that the function that the fifth practice was supposed to serve in *Duke v. Foerster* and other typical cases is unobjectionable, there can be considerable doubt about whether that function was well served or, for that matter, served at all.[37] The exchange to which the practice was related may appear to have been a "bad deal," but that should not prompt a court to rule that the practice constituted an antitrust offense. Such second-guessing would tend to minimize consumer welfare, particularly if exchanges made by private enterprises were subject to it.[38] That is so because, contrary to the presumption mandated by the Supreme Court, private enterprises are more likely than local governments to act like wealth-maximizers, and it is when entities so act that resources tend to be put to their highest-value uses. Moreover, appearances may be quite deceiving. Doubt about how well the practice served its function could reflect a failure to appreciate either the dynamics of the market or the significance of transactions costs.[39]

Of course, that doubt could also reflect an accurate perception that local government officials acted opportunistically, perhaps engaging in malfeasance or even crime,[40] or that they failed to ascertain what a court believes was the citizens' demand schedule for the good involved.[41] In other words, the exchange involved may appear to have been a "bad deal" because of corruption, bias, or stupidity.[42] Even so, the court should not rule that the practice constituted an antitrust offense. The fact that government officials did not act in a manner that was consistent with their responsibilities to the citizens is of no consequence under the Sherman or Clayton Acts.[43] It is easier to see that that must be so where the practice is unrelated to an exchange. *Highfield Water Co. v. Public Service Comm'n [of Maryland]*[44] and *Schiessle v. Stephens*[45] provide good illustrations of that situation. *Highfield Water* grew out of an alleged expropriation of a water utility by government officials who acted in contravention of state regulatory law. *Schiessle* grew out of an alleged misuse of eminent domain powers by government officials who planned to transfer property from one real estate developer to a group of others. In both cases, local government officials allegedly acted in violation of non-antitrust law, which surely would have been inconsistent with their responsibilities to the citizens, and, by so doing, injured some private enterprise. Such conduct would certainly be objectionable,[46] but clearly not on any principle embodied in the antitrust statutes.[47] The same is true of similar conduct that happens to be related to an exchange. The exchange is incidental.

The failure of local government officials to act in a manner that is consistent with their responsibilities to their constituent citizens is a special case of a common phenomenon: agents do not always do what their principals want them to do. It is difficult for any principal to control absolutely the behavior of his agent. Admittedly, it is particularly difficult for citizens to control the behavior of their agents. That is so because it is usually quite costly for those citizens to give directions, to ascertain whether their directions are being followed, and, if not, to revoke the authority granted to act on their behalf. These problems, however, no matter how acute, raise none of the efficiency concerns that are the domain of antitrust law. The Sherman and Clayton Acts do not speak to it or any aspect of the principal-agent relationship. A contrary interpretation would likely have an extraordinarily wide-ranging, and surely unintended, impact on ordinary business activities. For example, it would probably convert any breach by an executive of the fiduciary duty owed to his corporation's shareholders into an antitrust offense. Moreover, given the Supreme Court's decision in *American Society of Mechanical Engineers, Inc. v. Hydrolevel Corp.*,[48] a contrary interpretation would likely yield perverse results in litigated cases. In *Hydrolevel* the Court held that a principal could be held liable for an antitrust offense committed by his agents if they acted with apparent authority. Thus, if a failure to do a principal's bidding constituted an antitrust offense, the principal, who was victimized by that failure, could be held liable for it.

If the fifth practice is generally legal when engaged in by a local government, then, under the Supreme Court's "same treatment" teaching, it should also be generally legal when engaged in by a private enterprise. That would mean that *Klor's*-type boycotts would be legal. So, too, would the conduct of firms with market power that appeared to a court to be less-than-egalitarian, unseemly, or even tort-like, unless that conduct were clearly a strategic move. Similar conduct by firms without market power would always be legal.

NOTES

1. *See, e.g.*, Grason Electric Co. v. Sacramento Municipal Utility Dist., 526 F. Supp. 276 (E.D. Cal. 1981).

2. "Boycott" could be substituted for almost any other label commonly affixed to alleged antitrust offenses. *See generally* R. Posner, Antitrust Law: An Economic Perspective pp. 207-11 (1976).

3. *See, e.g.*, Greyhound Rent-A-Car, Inc. v. City of Pensacola, 676 F.2d 1380 (11th Cir. 1982), *cert. denied*, 459 U.S. 1171 (1983).

4. The good may be desired by residents or others for whom the local government is acting.

5. 676 F.2d 1380 (11th Cir. 1982), *cert. denied*, 459 U.S. 1171 (1983).

6. Other typical cases include: Famous Make Communications Co. v. Suffolk County Water Authority, 1982-1 Trade Cases ¶ 64,453 (E.D.N.Y. 1981); Kendrick v. City Council of Augusta, Ga., 516 F. Supp. 1134 (S.D. Ga. 1981); Crocker v. Padnos, 483 F. Supp. 229 (D. Mass. 1980); Cedar Riverside Associates, Inc. v. United States, 459 F. Supp. 1290 (D. Minn. 1979), *aff'd*, 606 F.2d 254 (8th Cir. 1979); George R. Whitten, Jr., Inc. v. Paddock Pool Builders, Inc., 424 F.2d 25 (1st Cir. 1970), *cert. denied*, 400 U.S. 850 (1970), *on remand*, 376 F. Supp. 125 (D.C. Mass. 1974), *aff'd*, 508 F.2d 547 (1st Cir. 1974), *cert. denied*, 421 U.S. 1004

(1975); Azzaro v. The Town of Branford, Conn., 1974 Trade Cases ¶ 75,337 (D. Conn. 1974).

7. *See generally* Klein, Crawford & Allen, *Vertical Integration, Appropriable Rents, and the Competitive Contracting Process*, 21 J. Law & Econ. 297 (1978).

8. 676 F.2d at 1382.

9. *Id.* at 1383.

10. Klor's, Inc. v. Broadway-Hale Stores, Inc., 359 U.S. 207, 213 (1959).

11. 595 F.2d 164 (3d Cir. 1979).

12. Of course, even an easily understood statement to that effect could not prevent members of a jury from misapprehending the likely impact of the practice on consumer welfare or from confusing it, either willfully or inadvertently, with the likely impact of the practice on the plaintiff.

13. In pertinent part, the judge instructed the jury as follows:

In this case Greyhound Rent-A-Car, Inc. claims that the defendants, The City of Pensacola and Dollar Rent-A-Car, Inc., violated Title 15, United States Code, Section 1, commonly known as Section 1 of the Sherman Act, which is a part of the antitrust laws of the United States.

Section 1 of the Sherman Act provides in pertinent part: "Every contract, combination in the form of trust or otherwise, or conspiracy in restraint of trade or commerce among the several states is declared illegal."

The general objectives of the antitrust laws, including the Sherman Act, are to preserve and advance our system of free and open competition, and to secure to everyone an equal opportunity to engage in the business, trade and commerce of this country—a policy which is the primary feature of our private enterprise system. The law promotes the concept that free competition yields the best allocation of economic resources, but it also recognizes that in the natural operation of our economic system some competitors are going to lose business while others prosper. Acts become unlawful only when they constitute an unreasonable restraint on interstate commerce.

The specific conduct which plaintiff claims violated Section 1 of the Sherman Act is an alleged contract, combination or conspiracy between the City of Pensacola and Dollar Rent-A-Car System, Inc. to exclude Greyhound Rent-A-Car, Inc. from the rental car market at the Pensacola Regional Airport.

There are four essential elements which the plaintiff must prove by a preponderance of the evidence in order to establish its claim under the Sherman Act, as follows:

First: That there was a contract, combination or conspiracy between the defendants, Dollar and City of Pensacola, to exclude Greyhound from the rental car market at the Pensacola Regional Airport;

Second: That such contract, combination or conspiracy constituted an unreasonable restraint on interstate commerce as hereafter defined;

Third: That such contract, combination or conspiracy constituted a restraint in interstate commerce; and

Fourth: That the plaintiff suffered injury in its business or property as a proximate result of the alleged contract, and combination or conspiracy.

. . .

The second element which the plaintiff must prove in order to establish its claim is that the alleged contract, combination or conspiracy resulted in an unreasonable restraint on interstate commerce. Not all restraints on interstate commerce are unreasonable restraints. All business affects commerce in some way. Therefore, in determining whether a restraint of interstate commerce exists, you must decide whether the conduct which you have found tends to restrict or otherwise control free and open competition. And in determining whether or not such an unreasonable restraint exists, you need not find a specific public injury but you must find that the conduct tends or is reasonably calculated to prejudice the public interest.

The law does not define which restraints are reasonable and which are not. It is for you to decide whether the evidence in this case shows an unreasonable restraint, and the plaintiff may recover unless you find an unreasonable restraint by a preponderance of the evidence as defined in these instructions.

The question of whether an alleged contract, combination or conspiracy constituted an unreasonable restraint on interstate commerce must be determined on the basis of full consideration of all the facts and circumstances disclosed by the evidence, including the nature of the particular industry or the product or service involved; the market area involved; any facts which you may find to be peculiar to that industry, product, service, or market area; the nature of the alleged restraint and its effect, actual and probable; the history of the circumstances surrounding the alleged restraint and the reasons for adopting the particular practice which is alleged to constitute the restraint.

. . .

The City of Pensacola has a right to reject any bid if the bid does not comply with the bid specifications, and it may do so even though the bid was in fact the highest bid made, so long as it does not act arbitrarily in so doing. However, it does not have the right to reject a bid for any reason whatsoever if the rejection of the bid is found to be a violation of the antitrust laws as charged in this suit.

14. 246 U.S. 231, 238 (1918).

15. *See, e.g.*, Beech Cinema, Inc. v. Twentieth Century-Fox Film Corp., 622 F.2d 1106 (2d Cir. 1980).

16. In the aggregate, resolving disputes on the basis of egalitarianism would tend to impoverish jurors, as well as others. In any particular case, however, a juror might indulge his taste for egalitarianism since he could share the cost of doing so with everyone else.

17. Note, 82 Harv. L. Rev. 254, 257-60 (1968) (Albrecht v. Herald Co.).

18. 362 U.S. 29 (1960).

19. 390 U.S. 145 (1968).

20. 384 F. Supp. 460 (W.D. Penn. 1974).

21. 615 F.2d 343 (5th Cir. 1980), *cert. denied*, 449 U.S. 870 (1981).

22. 384 F. Supp. 460, 461 (W.D. Penn. 1974).

23. It is implausible that the Port Authority, a co-purchaser, was trying to restrict the output and raise the price of uniforms.

24. I am not suggesting that the Port Authority, in fact, offered any such assurance. The court certainly did not mention it.

25. Although the Port Authority could have paid a fixed sum uniform allowance, it would still have wished for the lowest price per uniform, *ceteris paribus*, because it would likely have to compensate its employee drivers for the remaining price in the form of wages.

26. The total cost of acquiring information about the procedures and personnel employed by vendors (information likely to be critical to the effectiveness of pre-vending inspections) would vary directly, it is clear, with the number of vendors. Other such "economies of scale" might also be associated with pre-vending inspections.

27. Of course, even limiting the number of vendors to one maker and one retailer would not guarantee a favorable response to an alter-or-replace demand. The vendor to whom the demand was directed could still claim that the uniform in question conformed to the Port Authority's specifications or that the driver who wore it caused it to be non-conforming. The challenged practice would only reduce, not eliminate, enforcement costs.

28. When purchasers avoid open auctions, they do so almost invariably in order to reduce transactions costs of some kind. Designating "approved sources" is one way of avoiding them. Selecting a supplier on a rotating basis is another. *See* Goodner v. Bachofner, 1977-1 Trade Cases ¶ 61,369 (Wash. Superior Ct., Spokane County, 1977); Rose, *Municipal Activities and the Antitrust Laws after City of Lafayette*, 57 U. Det. J. Urb. L. 489, 500-01, 503-04 (1979).

The residents of southeastern Michigan, acting through the Comprehensive Health Planning Council of Southeastern Michigan, the City of Pontiac, and a number of other governmental units, used a more elaborate method when purchasing hospital care—a method that gave rise to Huron Valley Hospital, Inc. v. City of Pontiac, Mich., 466 F. Supp. 1301 (E.D. Mich. 1979), *vacated and remanded*, 666 F.2d 1029 (6th Cir. 1981). Huron Valley planned to build a new hospital in the Pontiac area. Its plans went awry, however, when the Health Planning Council refused to grant it a "certificate of need." Huron Valley responded to this refusal with an antitrust suit against the Council, the city, other units of government involved in the "certificate of need" process, and a group of area hospitals who opposed its planned construction. Huron Valley claimed, *inter alia*, that the defendants had "conspired to restrain [it] from entering the market." 466 F. Supp. at 1306.

The "certificate of need" process is part and parcel of the purchase of health care. Consider the rationale for requiring a certificate: (a) third-party payers can compensate health-care providers most cost-effectively when they use a formula based on costs (*see* Goldberg, *Regulation and Administered Contracts*, 7 Bell J. Econ. 426 [1976]), *provided* that the incentive effects of such compensation are disregarded; (b) in fact, such compensation tends to induce hospitals to supply more than an otherwise optimal number of beds (*see* Joskow, *The Effects of Competition and Regulation on Hospital Bed Supply and the Reservation Quality of the Hospital*, 11 Bell J. Econ. 421 (1980); *see generally* Averch & Johnson, *Behavior of the Firm Under Regulatory Constraint*, 52 Am. Econ. Rev. 1052 [1962]); (c) users and potential users of hospitals have an interest in limiting the hospitals' response to this inducement since they ultimately bear the costs of those "extra" beds; and (d) the most cost-effective method of effectuating that interest is to regulate the building of new hospitals and additions to old ones. Thus, when purchasers use the "certificate of need" process, they do so in order to reduce the costs of monitoring the behavior of hospital-care suppliers. *See generally* Williamson, *The Vertical Integration of Production: Market Failure Considerations*, 61 Am. Econ. Rev. 112, 116-17 (1971) ("In contrast therefore to a fixed-price contract, where it is sufficient to evaluate end-product performance, cost-plus contracts, because they expose the buyer to risks of inefficient [high cost] contract execution, require that *both* input and output be evaluated.")

29. The difference in demand elasticities might be attributable to mobility, capacity for self-generation, or other customer characteristics.

30. *See* Williamson, *supra* note 28, at 118-19.

31. 615 F.2d at 347 n.6 and accompanying text.

32. *See* Chapter 6, n.8 and accompanying text.

33. 2 A. Kahn, The Economics of Regulation: Principles and Institutions pp. 142-45 (1970).

34. Tex. Rev. Civ. Stat. Ann. art. 1446c, § 42 (Vernon 1980).

35. 521 F.2d 1277 (3d Cir. 1975).

36. *Id.* at 1281.

37. *See, e.g.*, Affiliated Capital Corp. v. City of Houston, 519 F. Supp. 991 (S.D. Tex. 1981), *rev'd*, 700 F.2d 226 (5th Cir. 1983), *vacated*, 714 F.2d 25 (5th Cir.), *rev'd on reh'g* (en banc), 735 F.2d 1555 (5th Cir. 1984); Huron Valley Hospital, Inc. v. City of Pontiac, 466 F. Supp. 1301 (E.D. Mich. 1979), *vacated and remanded*, 666 F.2d 1029 (6th Cir. 1981). *See generally* Rose, *supra* note 28, at 489-94.

38. The prospect of such second-guessing would render transactions riskier. As a result, prudent managers of private enterprises would tend to avoid some into which they would have otherwise entered. Since those avoided transactions would tend, on balance, to create wealth (although some might have been mistakes), consumer welfare would suffer.

39. *See* Williamson, *Assessing Vertical Market Restrictions: Antitrust Ramifications of the Transaction Cost Approach,* 127 U. Pa. L. Rev. 953 (1979).

40. *See, e.g.,* Affiliated Capital Corp. v. City of Houston, 519 F. Supp. 991 (S.D. Tex. 1981), *rev'd,* 700 F.2d 226 (5th Cir. 1983), *vacated,* 714 F.2d 25 (5th Cir. 1984), *rev'd on reh'g* (en banc), 735 F.2d 1555 (5th Cir. 1984).

41. Failing to ascertain what the court believes was the citizens' demand schedule for the good involved could reflect either the prohibitive cost of ascertaining it or an honest disagreement.

42. Rose, *supra* note 28, at 490-94. Here again we encounter the fundamental problem of principals controlling their agents' behavior, which is interesting but beyond the scope of antitrust law. *See* Chapter 4 n.84.

43. Huron Valley Hospital, Inc. v. City of Pontiac, 466 F. Supp. 1301, 1315 (E.D. Mich. 1979), *vacated and remanded on other grounds,* 666 F.2d 1029 (6th Cir. 1981); Sun Valley Disposal Co. v. Silver State Disposal Co., 420 F.2d 341, 342 (9th Cir. 1969). *Contra* Cirace, *An Economic Analysis of the "State-Municipal Action" Antitrust Cases,* 61 Tex. L. Rev. 481, 485-86 (1982).

44. 488 F. Supp. 1176 (D. Md. 1980). The district court dismissed Highfield's antitrust claim on *Parker v. Brown* grounds.

45. 525 F. Supp. 763 (N.D. Ill. 1981). The district court refused to dismiss Schiessle's claim on state action grounds.

46. That conduct might expose the actors to suit for failure to abide by state civil statutes or city ordinances, tort actions, or even criminal prosecution. Moreover, it might prompt either their firing or loss at the next election.

47. The same observation holds for zoning decisions allegedly undertaken for the benefit of the officials making them. *See* Stauffer v. The Town of Grand Lake, Colo., 1981-1 Trade Cases ¶ 64,029 (D.C. Colo. 1980); Miller & Son Paving, Inc. v. Wrightstown Township Civic Ass'n, 443 F. Supp. 1268 (E.D. Pa. 1978), *aff'd mem.,* 595 F.2d 1213 (3d Cir.), *cert. denied,* 444 U.S. 843 (1979); Whitworth v. Perkins, 559 F.2d 378 (5th Cir. 1977), *vacated,* Impact v. Whitworth, 435 U.S. 992 (1978), *on remand,* Whitworth v. Perkins, 576 F.2d 696 (5th Cir. 1978), *cert. denied,* 440 U.S. 911 (1979); Nelson v. Utah Co., 1978-1 Trade Cases ¶ 62,128 (D. Utah 1977). *But cf.* Dabney, *Antitrust Aspects of Anticompetitive Zoning,* 24 Antitrust Bulletin 435 (1979) (Dabney argues that a zoning decision should be deemed an antitrust offense if it was made for the purpose of restricting competition *or,* even if made for some other purpose, an alternative means less restrictive of competition was available. Dabney does not reveal how a court would go about ascertaining the purpose of a zoning decision. That could be problematic since all denials of zoning changes requested by the owner of the affected prop-

erty suppress competition in a sense. *See* Chapter 4, n.13. Nor does Dabney explain how a court should take into account efficacy and cost in evaluating alternative means.

48. 456 U.S. 556 (1983).

PART III

RETRENCHMENT TO REFORM

9

THE DEMISE OF POPULISM?

The major retrenchment suggested in Part II[1] would cause antitrust's war with itself to intensify. Practices often used by local governments would be almost *per se* legal because they would rarely, if ever, function to reduce consumer welfare—to restrict output and raise prices.[2] But other practices, like making a vertical acquisition or licensing the use of a patented input solely on the basis of an end-product royalty,[3] which are no more likely to function in that manner, would still be subject to expensive scrutiny and frequently condemnation since they would seldom, if ever, be used by local governments. Such inconsistency would be difficult to justify and so could easily create discomfort for judges. They would probably respond to it as they would respond to the discomfort created by the threat to local government posed by the antitrust statutes as they are now interpreted. A sizeable number might very well try to avoid the discomfort by employing intellectually suspect methods. Perhaps some would even disregard the Supreme Court's "same treatment" lesson. A few, however, would surely try to put an end to it by eliminating the cause of the inconsistency. The cause would be the use of two quite different, and often conflicting, principles to determine the legality of practices under the same statutes—the antitrust statutes. Judges who wished to eliminate it in an intellectually respectable way would simply choose to use only one, either (1) the principle of maximizing consumer welfare or (2) the principle of distributing wealth in populist-preferred ways. To avert truly calamitous results, if for no other reason, they would likely choose to use the former. They would likely discard the latter, and populism generally, as inapplicable to the resolution of antitrust suits against private enterprises as well as local governments. If they so chose, non-strategic conduct that had an exclusionary effect, like the conduct challenged in the famous *Alcoa* case,[4] would be *per se* legal.[5] Franchisor-franchisee disputes would be relegated to the realm of ordinary contract law.[6] Horizontal mergers of the kind that were the subject of *Von's Grocery*[7] and *Rome Cable*[8] would be free from challenges that could survive a motion for summary judgment based on minimal discovery.[9] And refusals by joint venturers to share the rewards of their enterprise with their rivals[10] would be free from challenges that could even survive a motion to dismiss for failure to state a claim upon which relief could be based. Moreover, the focus of the inquiry in antitrust cases would shift to the economic function served by a challenged practice rather than the status of the plaintiffs and the defendants, and that would prompt even more changes. In short, the common law of antitrust would be completely reformed and turned into an engine for promoting economic efficiency.

A reformed antitrust law would have little impact on local government. That is not to say that city councils and their kin will refrain from engaging in conduct that might restrict output and raise prices. They have done so in the past, and there is no reason to believe that they will cease doing so in the future. For example, officials of the City of Phoenix apparently agreed with officials of the City of Scottsdale to divide the water supply market territorially.[11] The managers of other units of local government have allegedly acquired their units' only rivals,[12] made purchases as a buying cartel,[13] used litigation to prevent competitive entry,[14] and served as the cat's paw for the members of a private cartel.[15] But such conduct is likely to be rare in comparison to the practices analyzed in this book; when local governments engage in it, it may tend, in fact, to promote consumer welfare;[16] and, if it does the reverse, it will usually be exempt from scrutiny under the antitrust statutes as state action[17] or as otherwise protected activity.[18]

Thus, the implications of the Supreme Court's opinions in the city-immunity cases are perhaps startling, and certainly counterintuitive.[19] Permitting antitrust attacks on a populist-preferred institution might, and certainly should, prompt courts to shed the populist trappings with which they have mistakenly, and injuriously, adorned the law. They would do so in order to protect the institution of local government, but in the process they would change antitrust law profoundly, embracing consumer welfare as the sole concern of the Sherman and Clayton Acts.

NOTES

1. This retrenchment would be largely consistent with Williamson's position on vertical restraints. Williamson, *Assessing Vertical Market Restrictions: Antitrust Ramifications of the Transaction Cost Approach,* 127 U. Pa. L. Rev. 953, 993 (1979).

2. Of course, they may be barred as inconsistent with some other federal statute under the Supremacy Clause, unreasonably burdensome on interstate commerce, or even contrary to the First Amendment as incorporated in the Fourteenth (*see* Bates v. State Bar of Arizona, 433 U.S. 350 (1977)). Generally, those aggrieved by the practices of local government may pursue a host of federal, as well as state, judicial remedies.

3. The Supreme Court condemned this practice in Zenith Radio Corp. v. Hazeltine Research, Inc., 395 U.S. 100 (1969), apparently pinning the "patent misuse" label on it.

4. United States v. Aluminum Co. of America, 148 F.2d 416 (2d Cir. 1945).

5. For example, the refusal by a sugar-beet processor to purchase beets from any grower who did not plant the processor's seeds would be legal, even though that conduct might exclude other seed sellers from the market, because it economized on transactions costs. *See* Betaseed, Inc. v. U & I, Inc., 681 F.2d 1203 (9th Cir. 1982).

6. Presumably, cases like Midwestern Waffles, Inc. v. Waffle House, Inc., 734 F.2d 705 (8th Cir. 1984), *aff'g* 1983-2 Trade Cases ¶ 65,567 [N.D. Ga. 1983]), would generally not even reach the summary judgment stage, as *Waffle House* did, and those that did would be promptly resolved in favor of the franchisor, as *Waffle House* was not.

7. United States v. Von's Grocery Co., 384 U.S. 270 (1966).

8. United States v. Aluminum Co. of America, 377 U.S. 271 (1964).

9. It appears from the 1982 Merger Guidelines of the Department of Justice that the Antitrust Division does not plan to challenge such merg-

ers in any event. Corporate executives contemplating a horizontal acquisition, however, must be concerned about not only the Antitrust Division but also private plaintiffs. *See* Marathon Oil Co. v. Mobil Corp., 669 F.2d 378 (6th Cir. 1981), *later pro.*, 669 F.2d 384 (6th Cir. 1982), *cert. denied*, 455 U.S. 982 (1982). After the reformation suggested in the text, presumably, companies like Marathon would be unable to invoke the antitrust statutes to block their acquisition by companies like Mobil.

10. *See, e.g.*, Associated Press v. United States, 326 U.S. 1 (1945).

11. *See* Community Builders, Inc. v. The City of Phoenix [Ariz.], 652 F.2d 823 (9th Cir. 1981).

12. *See* City of Fairfax v. Fairfax Hospital Ass'n, 562 F.2d 280 (4th Cir. 1977), *vacated and remanded*, 435 U.S. 992 (1978) (for reconsideration in light of *City of Lafayette*), *on remand*, 598 F.2d 835 (4th Cir. 1978).

13. *See* State of New Mexico v. American Petrofina, Inc., 501 F.2d 363 (9th Cir. 1974).

14. *See* City of Gainesville [Fla.] v. Florida Power & Light Co., 488 F. Supp. 1258 (S.D. Fla. 1980); Miracle Mile Associates v. City of Rochester [N.Y.], 1979-2 Trade Cases ¶ 62,735 (W.D.N.Y. 1979), *aff'd in part and rev'd in part*, 617 F.2d 18 (2d Cir. 1980) (antitrust judgment affirmed).

15. *See In re* The City of Minneapolis & The City of New Orleans, 1984-1 Trade Cases ¶ 22,149 (FTC Complaint 1984); Affiliated Capital Corp. v. City of Houston, 519 F. Supp. 991 (S.D. Tex. 1981), *rev'd*, 700 F.2d 226 (5th Cir. 1983), *vacated*, 714 F.2d 25 (5th Cir. 1984), *rev'd on reh'g*, 735 F.2d 1555 (5th Cir. 1984); Gibson Distributing Co., Inc. v. Downtown Development Ass'n of El Paso, Inc., 572 S.W.2d 334 (Tex. 1978), *appeal dismissed*, 439 U.S. 1000 (1978); A & H Transport, Inc. v. Mayor & City Council of Baltimore, 240 A.2d 601 (Md. 1968).

16. That was probably the case in State of New Mexico v. American Petrofina, 501 F.2d 363 (9th Cir. 1974).

17. *See, e.g.*, Community Builders, Inc. v. The City of Phoenix [Ariz.], 652 F.2d 823 (9th Cir. 1981).

18. *See, e.g.*, City of Gainesville [Fla.] v. Florida Power & Light Co., 488 F. Supp. 1258 (S.D. Fla. 1980); Miracle Mile Associates v. City of Rochester [N.Y.], 1979-2 Trade Cases ¶ 62,735 (W.D.N.Y. 1979), *aff'd in part and rev'd in part*, 617 F.2d 18 (2d Cir. 1980) (antitrust judgment affirmed).

19. Indeed, in the plurality's opinion in *Lafayette*, the discussion of the possible effects of Plaquemine's alleged tying may reflect a populist concern about the fate of "disadvantaged" Louisiana Power & Light and its shareholders. 435 U.S. at 404-05.

APPENDIX

This appendix is an annotated list of reported federal cases not discussed in the text, all of which involved an allegation that a local government committed a federal antitrust offense. The cases are classified according to the kind of practice in which the accused local government allegedly engaged. Where the accused local government allegedly engaged in more than one kind of practice, the name of the case (but not the annotation) appears under more than one classification. The annotations do not purport to be thorough analyses.

PRACTICE 1: Agreements with suppliers, or purchasers, pursuant to which a local government declines to buy from, or sell to, some or all of their rivals.

1. *All American Cab Co. v. Metropolitan Knoxville Airport Authority*, 547 F. Supp. 509 (E.D. Tenn. 1982), *aff'd mem.*, 723 F.2d 908 (6th Cir. 1982).

The Knoxville Airport Authority arranged for the availability of limousine service at its McGhee-Tyson Airport by entering into a requirements contract with Creative International Management, Inc. The contract provided that Creative would have the right to dispatch not only its limousines but also all taxicabs demanded by airport patrons. Creative probably insisted on this provision so that it could use dispatching as a self-help device for securing the revenues it reasonably expected to derive from its limousine business. Thus, the contract was quite similar in form, and identical in function, to the alleged agreement between the governing board of an airport and a fixed base operator (fbo) that was the focus of *Pinehurst Airlines, Inc. v. Resort Air Service, Inc.* Like that agreement, this contract was challenged in an antitrust suit. All American Cab Co., along with its employee drivers, alleged that the contract "restrain[ed] trade in the provision of ground transportation services from [the] [a]irport." Apparently, the plaintiffs were especially aggrieved by the way in which Creative exercised its right to dispatch, for they also alleged that "Creative [had] us[ed] its dispatching power to discriminate against taxicab service and to monopolize ground transportation." The Authority moved to dismiss the suit on the ground that its conduct was exempt from the Sherman Act as state action, and the trial court, mistakenly, granted that motion. A principled analysis of the antitrust merits of the contract would have paralleled the analysis of the *Pinehurst* agreement that is contained in Chapter 4, and it would have led to the dismissal of the suit.

2. *Alphin v. Henson*, 392 F. Supp. 813 (D. Md. 1975), *aff'd*, 538 F.2d 85 (4th Cir. 1976), *cert. denied*, 429 U.S. 960 (1976), *amended*, 552 F.2d 1003 (4th Cir. 1976), *cert. denied*, 434 U.S. 823 (1977). (The dispute between the parties resulted in still more litigation later. *See Alphin Aircraft, Inc. v. Henson*, 1984-2 Trade Case ¶ 66,161 [D. Md. 1984].)

The Hagerstown (Maryland) City Council had arranged for Henson to provide fbo service at its Hagerstown Regional Airport by leasing a portion of the airport to him in return for his promise to conduct a "full" fixed based operation (and, of course, to pay rent). In turn, Henson had arranged for Alphin to do all of the fbo's aircraft maintenance and repair work by simply promising to send all of his customers requiring such work to Alphin in return for Alphin's promise to see to their demands promptly. Initially, Alphin labored in the fbo hangar, part of which he subleased from Henson, but in the years immediately preceding the litigation, he labored in his own buildings which were adjacent to the airport's field and linked to its runways by airplane taxi paths. All of these arrangements were of long standing when Alphin decided to expand his business, and to do so in part by offering some additional services which were then available at the airport only from Henson. One of Alphin's first moves was to ask the city council to lease a portion of the airport to him for that purpose, but the airport manager, acting with the authority of the council, denied his request. (The manager did express a willingness to lease a portion of the airport to Alphin for another "full" fixed base operation, but Alphin did not pursue that possibility—a course of action that the manager no doubt anticipated—apparently because he did not believe that such an operation would be sufficiently lucrative.) Thus, the parties came to occupy virtually the same positions as did the parties in *Pinehurst Air Lines, Inc. v. Resort Air Service, Inc.* (analyzed in Chapter 4), with Alphin taking the part of Pinehurst and Henson that of Resort Air.

Like Pinehurst, Alphin attacked the denial of his request as, among other things, an antitrust offense. Unlike Pinehurst, he attributed the denial not so much to an explicit agreement to protect the in-place fixed base operator from ongoing rivalry, but to the fact that Henson served as that operator as well as the airport manager—but that should not have materially affected the antitrust analysis.

After a bench trial, the court ruled that by virtue of the city council's status as a unit of local government, its conduct was exempt from the Sherman Act as state action—a ruling that can be explained, in part, by the fact that it pre-dated *Lafayette* and *Boulder*. The court also ruled, however, that Henson's conduct in his dual role amounted to an antitrust offense, and so it enjoined him, in effect, from serving as airport manager in dealings with those who wished to, or did, compete with his fixed based operation. For all practical purposes, the court may as well have directed this injunction to the city council, and, in fact it did pursuant to its "general equitable jurisdiction" and article 41 of the Maryland constitution's Declaration of Rights, which the court interpreted, rather questionably, as a prohibition against monopoly.

The denial of Alphin's request served the same function, of course, as did the denial of Pinehurst's. The dual relationship between the city council and Henson, which is typical of smaller airports, merely served to further economize on transaction costs. Neither that relationship nor any opportunism on Henson's part would have altered the conclusion of a principled analysis on the merits that the city council's conduct did not transgress the antitrust laws.

3. *Azzaro v. Town of Branford* [Conn.], 1974-2 Trade Cases ¶ 75,337 (D. Conn. 1974).

The Town of Branford allegedly promised to purchase its requirements of fire and casualty insurance from members of the Branford Association of Independent Insurance Agents. That promise probably induced the members of the Association to provide advice and information to the Town for "free," a service which they would have been loathe to perform had the Town been contractually free to purchase insurance from others. Thus, unless the Town's management was acting opportunistically, its alleged promise probably helped secure a desired good, a package of insurance along with related advice and information, at the lowest obtainable price.

A group of agents and brokers working for national insurance companies, who were not members of the Association, challenged the arrangements between the Town and the Association as a "boycott" violative of the Sherman Act. On the Town's motion to dismiss, the court correctly held, *inter alia*, that the Town's conduct was not state action exempt from scrutiny under the antitrust laws.

4. *Campbell v. City of Chicago*, 577 F. Supp. 1166 (N.D. Ill. 1983).

In 1963 the Chicago city council enacted an ordinance that (1) reauthorized the 4,600 taxicab licenses then extant, and (2) provided for the issuance of new licenses, if any were ever authorized, to then current license-holders. A group of would-be license-holders claimed that by so doing the council had committed an antitrust offense. (In a subsequent proceeding, the court denied the group class certification. *See* 47 Antitrust & Trade Reg. Rep. 443 [N.D. Ill. 1984].)

The council enacted this ordinance in order to settle a suit for damages that had been brought against it by the Yellow and Checker taxicab companies, affiliated firms then holding more than 90 per cent of Chicago's licenses. The suit arose out of the council's tangled efforts to limit entry into the taxicab business, efforts that began in 1934. In that year, the council authorized the issuance of about 4,100 taxicab licenses. Yellow and Checker obtained almost 90 per cent of them. Three years later, the council sought the surrender of about 1,100 of the licenses it had just authorized. It secured them by enacting an ordinance purporting to vest preference rights to any licenses issued in the future in those holders surrendering their licenses. Yellow and Checker surrendered almost all of the licenses that the council sought. In 1946, when the council proposed to issue some new licenses in contravention of these rights, Yellow and Checker brought suit and secured an injunction. When city officials subsequently violated the injunction, Yellow and Checker brought their suit for damages. They offered to withdraw their suit if the council enacted the challenged ordinance, and the council accepted their offer.

In doing so, the council probably acted opportunistically. It is likely that Chicagoans would have been better off if the council had simply paid up and then authorized the issuance of so many licenses that Yellow and Checker would have declined to exercise their preference rights. The members of the council may well have thought, however, that avoiding the publicity connected with a trial and a cash payment to powerful firms was politically expedient, and, if so, they were probably correct.

5. *Catalina Cablevision Assoc. v. City of Tucson*, 1984-2 Trade Cases ¶ 66,249 (9th Cir. 1984).

6. *Central Iowa Refuse Systems, Inc. v. Des Moines Metropolitan Solid Waste Agency*, 557 F. Supp. 131 (S.D. Iowa 1982), *aff'd*, 715 F.2d 419 (8th Cir. 1983), *petition for cert. filed*, No. 83-825 (U.S.L.W. Nov. 18, 1983).

In the late 1960's the managers of Des Moines, fifteen smaller municipalities in the surrounding metropolitan area, and the county in which Des Moines is located agreed to develop a solid waste landfill capable of meeting the disposal demands of all of their constituents. They decided to do so under the auspices of a cooperative agency, the Des Moines Metropolitan Solid Waste Agency (Metro), with which each municipality entered into a service contract.

Iowa statutes obligated Metro to finance the landfill with revenue bonds, but its financial consultants despaired of marketing them unless steps were taken to ensure the deposit of all solid waste generated with the municipalities at the landfill and, thus, the landfill's revenues. The municipalities readily agreed to take such steps. The most important municipality, Des Moines, prohibited solid waste hauling without a permit and directed that all permits require haulers to make their deposits at either Metro's landfill or at a city-licensed transfer station from where the solid wastes would be taken to the landfill. Thus, these municipalities did together just what Akron did by itself (see the discussion of *Glenwillow Landfill* in Chapter 4), and, like Akron, were rewarded with an antitrust suit brought by the owners of a private landfill (which was located outside of Metro's jurisdiction).

7. *Central Telecommunications, Inc. v. City of Jefferson City, Mo.*, No. 83-4068, slip op. (W.D. Mo. Feb. 29, 1984).

8. *Cincinnati Riverfront Coliseum, Inc. v. City of Cincinnati*, 556 F. Supp. 664 (S.D. Ohio, 1983).

Cincinnati leased its stadium and associated parking facilities to the Cincinnati Reds baseball team, agreeing to make all the spaces in those facilities available to attending fans during the game. There can be little doubt that this arrangement served to maximize the city's capture of quasi-rents. The city also leased the stadium parking facilities to the owners of the Cincinnati Riverfront Coliseum. It did so, however, on the express condition that they would not schedule events in the Coliseum which would conflict with Reds' games if those events would require substantial parking. After profiting from the lease for some time, the owners claimed that the arrangement between the city and the Reds constituted a boycott. On cross motions for summary judgment, the court held, correctly, that Cincinnati's conduct.was not immune state action and, incorrectly, that the owners had stated a claim upon which relief could be based.

9. *Continental Bus System, Inc. v. The City of Dallas*, 386 F. Supp. 359 (N.D. Tex. 1974).

Surtran, the joint venture of Dallas and Fort Worth, not only made the arrangements for taxi service at D/FW Airport which were challenged in *Woolen*, (discussed in Chapter 4), but also provided bus service there. And just as the cities ensured that the firm with whom Surtran made its arrangements would be the exclusive supplier of taxi service, they also ensured that Surtran itself would be the exclusive supplier of bus service. They enacted ordinances that forbade other bus companies, like Continental, from picking up or discharging passengers at the airport. These ordinances served the same function as the ones attacked in *Woolen*. Continental claimed that by enacting them, the cities had run afoul of the Sherman Act, but in this pre-*Lafayette* opinion the court held that the cities' conduct was immune under *Parker v. Brown*.

10. *Crocker v. Padnos*, 483 F. Supp. 229 (D. Mass. 1980).

The Brockton (Massachusetts) Transit Authority had contracted with Crocker to run its bus system when its own bus drivers went on strike, but when that agreement expired, it contracted with one of Crocker's rivals for the same service. Alleging that the Authority had conspired with the drivers' union and others to end its franchise, Crocker claimed that the Authority's conduct constituted an antitrust offense. The court dismissed the claim, holding, incorrectly, that it was state action, exempt from scrutiny under the antitrust laws.

11. *Daley v. Town of New Durham, N.H.*, 733 F.2d 4 (1st Cir. 1984).

12. *Englert v. City of McKeesport*, 564 F. Supp. 375 (W.D. Penn. 1983), *rev'd and remanded*, 736 F.2d 96 (3d Cir. 1984).

By ordinance, the McKeesport City Council designated the city's own inspection agency as the exclusive inspector of electrical systems contained in buildings located in McKeesport. Assuming that the council was seeking to maximize the wealth of the city's residents, it is likely that the ordinance was designed to limit monitoring costs. Understandably aggrieved, however, a private inspector of electrical systems claimed that the ordinance ran afoul of the antitrust laws. The court dismissed this claim on the ground that the private inspector had not, and could not have, alleged that the ordinance would have the requisite impact on interstate commerce. The court did not address the question of whether the council's conduct was immune under *Parker v. Brown*, the other ground for dismissal urged by the city. On appeal, the Third Circuit reversed and remanded.

13. *Flip Side Productions v. Jam Productions, Ltd.* [and the Village of Rosemont, Ill.], No. 82-3684, slip op. (N.D. Ill. June 12, 1984).

14. *Hopkinsville Cable TV, Inc. v. Pennyroyal Cablevision, Inc.* [and the City of Hopkinsville, Ky.], 562 F. Supp. 543 (W.D. Ky. 1982).

After holding an auction, Hopkinsville awarded a cable television franchise to Pennyroyal Cablevision, which, in its bid, had expressed its understanding that the franchise would be exclusive unless the holder substantially failed to perform. The promise of an exclusive franchise would have probably helped the city to capture more quasi-rents and perhaps to secure cable television service at the lowest obtainable price. Of course, fulfilling that promise would have done nothing for the unsuccessful participants in the auction, and one of them, Hopkinsville Cable TV, objected to it as a "refusal to deal" violating section 1 of the Sherman Act and a "conspiracy to monopolize the cable television market in Hopkinsville" in violation of section 2. The court ruled, incorrectly, that the city's conduct was exempt from antitrust scrutiny under *Parker v. Brown*.

15. *Hudson & Assoc. v. City of Chula Vista*, 1984-2 Trade Cases ¶ 66,251 (9th Cir. 1984).

16. *Jonnet Development Corp. v. Caliguiri*, 558 F. Supp. 62 (W.D. Penn. 1983).

In accordance with its redevelopment scheme for a portion of Pittsburgh, the city's Urban Redevelopment Authority (URA) purchased Conrail's downtown Penn Station. To do so, it outbid Jonnet Development Corporation for the property. Jonnet had allegedly planned to erect a hotel there, a hotel that would have competed with the one called for by the URA's scheme. Jonnet attributed its failure to obtain the property to a conspiracy among Conrail, the URA, and other agencies and officers of the City of Pittsburgh. Its antitrust suit, however, did not survive a motion for summary judgment. The court ruled (a) that Jonnet had failed to show that the defendants had acted in concert, and (b) that the defendants' conduct was state action, exempt from scrutiny under *Parker v. Brown*.

17. *Mays v. Hosp. Auth. of Henry County*, 582 F. Supp. 425 (N.D. Ga. 1984).

18. *Mercy-Peninsula Ambulance, Inc. v. County of San Mateo*, 1984-2 Trade Cases ¶ 66,264 (N.D. Cal. 1984).

19. *Midway Airlines, Inc. v. County of Westchester*, 584 F. Supp. 436 (S.D.N.Y. 1984).

20. *Murdock v. City of Jacksonville, Fla.*, 361 F. Supp. 1083 (M.D. Fla. 1973).

Jacksonville entered into a multiyear lease of its municipal auditorium with a promoter of wrestling matches. The lease provided that the city would not permit anyone else to hold wrestling matches there. The city was manifestly attempting to maximize its capture of quasi-rents. That was small comfort, however, to the one rival promoter who had actively competed for the lease, and he claimed, *inter alia*, that the city had violated the antitrust laws. The court, however, entered summary judgment against him, ruling, correctly, that as a matter of law, the exclusive lease did not constitute an antitrust offense and, incorrectly, that the city was entitled to state action immunity.

21. *Omega Satellite Products Co. v. City of Indianapolis*, 694 F.2d 119 (7th Cir. 1982).

Chapter 8½ of the Code of Indianapolis and Marion County requires that before using Indianapolis's public ways, a cable television system first obtain a franchise from the city. Two firms have obtained franchises. Those franchises do not overlap at all, and, together, they cover the entire area that is subject to the ordinance. Nominally they are non-exclusive, but the city has turned down all other applicants.

Omega, an operator of cable television systems in Indianapolis, has never applied for a franchise. It does not operate conventional systems. Rather, it installs small satellite earth stations on the roof of apartment complexes and connects them to the television sets of its subscribers who live in the complexes. Until 1981 Omega ran all of its connecting cables over private property so it could safely ignore Chapter 8½. In that year, however, it decided to run a connecting cable through a drainage culvert in order to connect the earth station on the roof of one complex to the television sets of subscribers who lived in a neighboring complex. Since a drainage culvert is a public way, Omega had to concern itself with the ordinance. Its chairman wrote to the city council inquiring whether Omega might obtain a franchise, but, receiving no encouragement, he did not pursue the matter. Nevertheless, Omega went ahead and ran the connecting cable through the drainage culvert.

When Indianapolis inspectors discovered the cable, the city demanded that Omega remove it. Omega responded with a lawsuit similar to the ones brought by Community Cable Communications against Boulder. Omega claimed, *inter alia,* that the city's demand was no more than a device to effectuate a tacit agreement between the city and its franchisees to exclude competition from their areas. Omega sought a preliminary injunction against the enforcement of Chapter 8½, but the district court refused to grant it. On appeal, the Seventh Circuit upheld that decision. In the course of discussing the likelihood that Omega would prevail on the merits at trial, Judge Posner, for the Seventh Circuit, suggested that the city's conduct might very well be subject to scrutiny under the antitrust laws, but that it probably did not constitute an antitrust offense. His analysis is akin to the analysis of *Boulder I* and *Boulder II* in Chapter 5.

22. *Padgett v. Louisville & Jefferson County Air Board,* 492 F.2d 1258 (6th Cir. 1974).

The governing board of the Louisville airport arranged for taxicab service there in precisely the same way as did the governing board of D/FW (the subject of *Woolen v. Surtrans,* which is analyzed in Chapter 4), and it did so for the same reasons. The antitrust attack on those arrangements was turned aside in a pre-*Lafayette* holding that the board, by virtue of its status as a unit of local government, was immune.

23. *Scott v. The City of Sioux City, Iowa,* 1982-3 Trade Cases ¶ 65,203 (N.D. Iowa 1982); 1983-1 Trade Cases ¶ 65,352 (N.D. Iowa 1983); 1983-2 Trade Cases ¶ 65,589 (N.D. Iowa 1983), *aff'd,* 736 F.2d 1207 (8th Cir. 1984).

In arranging for the redevelopment of downtown Sioux City, the city's managers allegedly did precisely that which Mason

City's managers did: agree to use their zoning powers to prevent the development of regional shopping centers in outlying areas (the conduct of Mason City's managers is the subject of *Mason City Center Associates v. The City of Mason City, Iowa,* which is analyzed in Chapter 4). Developers claimed that the agreement constituted an antitrust offense, but the court, in the end, entered summary judgment against them, ruling, incorrectly, that Sioux City was entitled to state action immunity. The Eighth Circuit affirmed.

24. *Schrader v. Horton,* 471 F. Supp. 1236 (W.D. Va. 1979), *aff'd,* 626 F.2d 1163 (4th Cir. 1980).

By ordinance, the Tazewell County (Virginia) Board of Supervisors required owners of land abutting any part of a newly built public water system to connect with it and pay the appropriate fees. The Board probably adopted the ordinance in lieu of an improvements' tax which, at the time, Virginia forbade. A number of affected owners, all of whom had built their own water supply systems, claimed, *inter alia,* that the mandatory connection ordinance amounted to "monopolization," violative of the antitrust laws. Since a Virginia statute authorized precisely the ordinance that the Board had adopted, however, the district court quite properly dismissed the claim as barred by the state action doctrine, and the Fourth Circuit affirmed.

25. *Shurtleff v. City of San Jose,* 9th Cir. Dkt. 82-4064 (Jan. 3, 1983) (unpublished).

26. *Springs Ambulance Service, Inc. v. City of Rancho Mirage, Cal.,* 1983-2 Trade Cases ¶ 65,646 (C.D. Cal. 1983); 1984-1 Trade Cases ¶ 66,014 (C.D. Cal.), *rev'd in part and remanded in part,* 1984-2 Trade Cases ¶ 66,261 (9th Cir. 1984).

For annotation see Practice 5.

27. *Tulsa County Public Health Nursing Service, Inc. v. Tulsa City-County Health Dep't,* 475 F. Supp. 152 (N.D. Okla. 1979).

Tulsa, through its health department, hired the Tulsa County Public Health Nursing Service to provide various residents with home nursing and therapy. Payments for this service, most of them from third-party payors, were made to the Nursing Service, and the Nursing Service turned them over to Tulsa's treasurer, who placed them in a separate account. When the Nursing Service tried to appropriate the funds that had accumulated in this account in order to establish a hospice program, which, not incidentally, it planned to run, Tulsa objected and soon after refused to rehire the Nursing Service. The Nursing Service claimed, *inter alia*, that this refusal to rehire it evidenced a conspiracy "to monopolize the provision of Medicare certified home health care services in Tulsa County . . . and . . . to exclude [it] from the home health care service market in Tulsa County." The court dismissed this antitrust claim, but the grounds for doing so are not readily decipherable from its opinion.

28. *Walker County Wrecker & Storage Ass'n, Inc. v. Walker County*, 47 Antitrust & Trade Reg. Rep. 1186 (S.D. Tex. 1984).

29. *E. W. Wiggins Airways, Inc. v. Mass. Port Authority*, 362 F.2d 52 (1st Cir. 1966).

Following a competition, the Massachusetts Port Authority selected Butler Aviation as the exclusive fixed base operator for its Logan Airport. Wiggins, one of the unsuccessful competitors, brought an antitrust suit to challenge this arrangement. The Port Authority moved to dismiss the claim against it on the ground that it was immune by virtue of its status as a unit of local government, and the court granted its motion. The case is on all fours with *Pinehurst Airlines, Inc. v. Resort Air Service, Inc.*, which is analyzed in Chapter 4.

See also: *Datillo v. Tucson Gen. Hosp.*, 23 Ariz. App. 392, 533 P.2d 700 (1975).

Harvey & Corkey Corp. v. County of Erie [N.Y.], 1977-2 Trade Cases ¶ 61,627 (N.Y. S. Ct. App. Div. 1977).

Metro Cable Co. v. CATV of Rockford, Inc., 516 F.2d 220 (7th Cir. 1975).

Trinity Ambulance Service, Inc. v. G & L Ambulance Services, Inc. [and the City of Hartford, Ct.], 578 F. Supp. 1280 (D. Conn. 1984).

Winters v. Indiana & Michigan Electric Co., 1979-2 Trade Cases ¶ 62,797 (N.D. Ind. 1979).

PRACTICE 2: Constraining the market behavior of the provider.

1. *Century Federal, Inc. v. City of Palo Alto, Cal.*, 579 F. Supp. 1553 (N.D. Cal. 1984).

2. *Golden State Transit Corp. v. City of Los Angeles*, 563 F. Supp. 169 (C.D. Cal. 1983), *aff'd*, 726 F.2d 1430 (9th Cir.), *cert. denied*, 103 S. Ct. 729 (1984).

For annotation see Practice 5.

3. *Miami Int'l Realty Co. v. Town of Mt. Crested Butte, Colo.*, 579 F. Supp. 68 (D. Colo. 1984).

4. *Springs Ambulance Service, Inc. v. City of Rancho Mirage, Cal.*, 1983-2 Trade Cases ¶ 65,646 (C.D. Cal. 1983), *rev'd in part and remanded in part*, 1984-2 Trade Cases ¶ 66,261 (9th Cir. 1984).

For annotation see Practice 5.

PRACTICE 3: Selling a good on the condition that the purchaser buy another one.

1. *Town of Hallie v. City of Eau Claire* [Wis.], 700 F.2d 376 (7th Cir. 1983), *cert. granted*, 104 S. Ct. 3508 (1984).

Eau Claire, which owned the only sewage treatment facility in its vicinity, refused to provide sewage treatment services to residents of nearby towns unless they agreed to annexation. Annexation would have reduced the likely costs of collecting payments since it would have rendered those residents subject to Eau Claire's taxes. It would have also rendered them eligible for various other services, including sewage collection and transportation. The nearby towns claimed, *inter alia*, that the city was using its "monopoly" in sewage treatment to obtain a "monopoly" in sewage collection and transportation, that it was "tying" the services, and that it was illegally refusing to deal. Since Wisconsin statutes authorized cities within the state to do precisely what Eau Claire did, however, the district court dismissed the towns' claim as barred by the state action doctrine. On appeal, the Seventh Circuit affirmed the dismissal.

2. *Howland Township Board of Trustees v. City of Warren, Ohio*, 1983-2 Trade Cases ¶ 65,642 (N.D. Ohio 1983).

The City of Warren refused to sell water to the residents of nearby Howland Township unless they agreed to annexation. As in *Town of Hallie v. City of Eau Claire*, annexation would have reduced the likely costs of collecting payments. The Township's

Board of Trustees challenged the city's conduct as "tying," accusing Warren of an attempt to "monopolize the receipt of tax revenues." The court dismissed this claim on the grounds that (a) the receipt of tax revenues is not trade or commerce within the meaning of the Sherman Act, and that (b) the Township failed to allege sufficient facts to show that Warren's conduct affected interstate commerce.

3. *Mays v. Hosp. Authority of Henry County,* 582 F. Supp. 425 (N.D. Ga. 1984).

4. *City of Mishawaka, Ind. v. American Electric Power Co., Inc.,* 465 F. Supp. 1320 (N.D. Ind. 1979), *aff'd in part and vacated in part,* 616 F.2d 976 (7th Cir. 1980), *cert. denied,* 449 U.S. 1096 (1981).

Gas City, Indiana, annexed land adjacent to its boundaries and then required those living there to purchase their electricity requirements from its own distribution company. It thereby displaced Indiana & Michigan Electric Company (I&M), an investor-owned fully integrated electric company. I&M claimed that Gas City's conduct amounted to the tying of water and sewage service to electric service. On this claim the court entered judgment for Gas City, ruling (a) that I&M had "really" objected to the city's annexation practices which were not "goods, wares, merchandise, machinery, supplies, or other commodit[ies]" within the purview of the Clayton Act and (b) that, in any event, Gas City's tying was exempt state action.

See also: *Amalgamated Trust & Savings Bank v. Village of Glenview,* 98 Ill. App. 3d 254, 423 N.E.2d 1230 (1st Dist. 1981).

PRACTICE 4: "Predatory" Pricing.

1. *C.E. Middlebrooks v. City of Eustis* [Fla.], 563 F. Supp. 1060 (M.D. Fla. 1983).

2. *City of North Olmstead, Ohio v. Greater Cleveland Regional Transit Authority,* 722 F.2d 1284 (6th Cir. 1983), *cert. denied,* 104 S. Ct. 2387 (1984).

For annotation see Practice 5.

3. *Springs Ambulance Service, Inc. v. City of Rancho Mirage, Cal.,* 1983-2 Trade Cases ¶ 65,646 (C.D. Cal. 1983), *rev'd in part and remanded in part,* 1984-2 Trade Cases ¶ 66,261 (9th Cir. 1984).

For annotation see Practice 5.

PRACTICE 5: Selling or buying goods on such terms and under such conditions that (a) some potential competitors, purchasers, or suppliers find that they are unable to economically enter their respective markets, or (b) some existing ones are more successful than others.

1. *Brontel, Ltd. v. City of New York,* 45 Antitrust & Trade Reg. Rep. 620 (S.D.N.Y. 1983) (Dkt. Nos. 82 Civ. 2664 & 82 Civ. 2666).

Owners of residential buildings claimed that New York had transgressed the antitrust laws by subjecting their buildings but not the city's to rent control and related regulations. The court dismissed the claim as barred by the state action doctrine.

2. *Campbell v. City of Phoenix,* 1983-2 Trade Cases ¶ 65,753 (D. Ariz. 1983).

Phoenix allegedly granted waivers from its zoning density laws for land situated within the Hillside Development area unless that land was also within a special section of that area called the Phoenix Mountain Preserve. An owner of land situated in the Preserve claimed *inter alia* that this practice constituted an antitrust offense, but that was dismissed on state action grounds.

3. *Capital Telephone Co., Inc. v. City of Schenectady, N.Y.,* 560 F. Supp. 207 (N.D.N.Y. 1983).

Capital Telephone claimed that Schenectady's refusal to grant it a franchise for a "second landline telephone company" was, *inter alia,* a Sherman Act offense. The court dismissed the claim, holding, correctly, that Schenectady's conduct could not be subject to scrutiny under the antitrust laws.

4. *Cedar-Riverside Associates, Inc. v. United States,* 459 F. Supp. 1290 (D. Minn. 1978), *aff'd on other grounds sub nom. Cedar-Riverside Associates, Inc. v. City of Minneapolis,* 606 F.2d 254 (8th Cir. 1979).

5. *Central Telecommunications, Inc. v. City of Jefferson City, Mo.,* No. 83-4068, slip op. (W.D. Mo. Feb. 29, 1984).

6. *Coombs v. The Town of Ogunquit* [Maine], No. 83-0465, slip op. (D. Me. Jan. 26, 1984).

7. *Corey v. Look,* 641 F.2d 32 (1st Cir. 1981).

A parking lot operator claimed that the Town of Falmouth, Massachusetts, had violated the antitrust laws by leasing a parking lot to the Woods Hole, Martha's Vineyard and Nantucket Steamship Authority rather than to him and by imposing restrictions upon his lot that were not imposed upon the Authority's lots. (He also alleged that the Town failed to provide him with law enforcement assistance when the Authority used his lot without his permission to park cars its own lots could not accommodate.)

The district court dismissed the claim, holding, incorrectly, that Falmouth's conduct was exempt under *Parker v. Brown* and, correctly, that its alleged conduct could not constitute an antitrust offense. The First Circuit, apparently mesmerized by the "boycott" label pinned on that conduct by the operator, reversed and remanded.

8. *Famous Make Communications Co., Inc. v. Suffolk County Water Authority*, 1982-1 Trade Cases ¶ 64,453 (E.D.N.Y. 1981).

The Suffolk County Water Authority invited bids for a contract to maintain its radio system. It had purchased the system from Motorola. Since Motorola's warranty was conditioned on maintenance by authorized repairmen, the Authority limited the bidding to them. Famous Make, which was in the business of maintaining radio systems, wished to bid for the Authority's contract, but it could not do so because it had not obtained authorization to work on Motorola's products. Unhappy with this outcome, it brought suit charging the Authority with violating the antitrust laws. After a trial, the court entered judgment against Famous Make, ruling that it had shown neither concerted action, "anticompetitive effect on the market as a whole," or "monopoly power or abuse thereof."

9. *Flip Side Productions v. Jam Productions, Ltd.* [and the Village of Rosemont, Ill.], No. 82-3684, slip op. (N.D. Ill. June 12, 1984).

10. *Gibson v. Greater Park City Co.* [and Park City, Utah], 1984-1 Trade Cases ¶ 65,978 (D. Utah 1984).

11. *Golden State Transit Corp. v. City of Los Angeles*, 563 F. Supp. 169 (C.D. Cal. 1983), *aff'd*, 726 F.2d 1430 (9th Cir.), *cert. denied*, 103 S. Ct. 729 (1984).

Upon the expiration of all the taxicab franchises issued by Los Angeles, the holders applied for renewal. The city's Board of Public Utilities and Transportation recommended that the city council grant all of the applications, but before the council acted, the Teamsters struck Golden State Transit and lobbied for the denial of Golden State Transit's application pending a new collective bargaining agreement. The Teamsters were successful; the city council granted all of the renewal applications except Golden State Transit's.

The city council provided additional help for the Teamsters in the ensuing several months, during which, pursuant to interim court orders, Golden State operated without a franchise. It denied Golden State Transit's request for a fare increase while granting similar requests made by other franchise holders.

Golden State Transit claimed *inter alia* that Los Angeles had transgressed the antitrust laws by treating it so poorly, but, on the basis of the state action doctrine, the court entered summary judgment against it on that claim.

12. *Grason Electric Co. v. Sacramento Municipal Utility Dist.*, 526 F. Supp. 276 (E.D. Cal. 1981); 571 F. Supp. 1504 (E.D. Cal. 1983).

The Sacramento Municipal Utility District (SMUD) distributes virtually all of the electricity consumed in greater Sacramento. Its distribution network includes the power lines and equipment required to transport electricity across the boundary lines of its customers' property. In fact, in the case of detached dwellings, the network does not end until it reaches the meter boxes on the outside walls. A group of electrical contractors wished to compete with SMUD in the installation and maintenance of this cross-boundary lines equipment, but they were frustrated by SMUD's refusal to provide electricity except over its own network. They brought an antitrust suit in which they claimed, *inter alia*, that this refusal constituted an "abuse" of SMUD's electric distribution "monopoly." (They similarly objected to two more of SMUD's practices. One, SMUD installs street lights for developers and public entities without charging them an initial fee—instead it charges them higher monthly fees than it otherwise would. The electrical contractors apparently found it difficult to compete with this financing scheme. Two, SMUD will not permit anyone, except one of its employees, to place security lamps on its poles. No doubt this created problems for the electrical contractors when they tried to sell these devices.) SMUD moved to dismiss this claim on *Parker v. Brown* grounds, but the district court denied its motion. Subsequently, the electrical contractors moved for summary judgment on this claim, but the district court denied their motion as well.

13. *Grendel's Den, Inc. v. Goodwin*, 495 F. Supp. 761 (D.C. Mass. 1980), *rev'd*, 662 F.2d 88 (1st Cir. 1981), *reh'g en banc* 662 F.2d 102 (1st Cir. 1981), *aff'd*, 459 U.S. 116 (1982), *later proc.* 582 F. Supp. 1220 (D. Mass. 1984).

14. *Richard Hoffman Corp. v. Integrated Building Systems, Inc.* [and Village of Glendale Heights, Ill.], 581 F. Supp. 367 (N.D. Ill. 1984).

15. *Kendrick v. City Council of Atlanta, Ga.*, 516 F. Supp. 1134 (S.D. Ga. 1981).

Augusta invited sealed bids for a contract to remove wrecked and abandoned vehicles from its public ways. The invitation provided that the contract would not be awarded until the low bidder had satisfied the city's inspectors that he would have the personnel, facilities, and equipment to perform the required towing services. Kendrick made the low bid, but failed to satisfy the inspectors. As a result, the City Council awarded the contract to one of Kendrick's rivals. Kendrick claimed, *inter alia*, that the city council had committed an antitrust offense. On this claim the court entered summary judgment against him, ruling that he had failed to show that the City's conduct had affected interstate commerce and that the city had acted in concert with the successful bidder.

16. *Koston v. State of New York*, 1974 Trade Cases ¶ 74,970 (S.D.N.Y. 1974).

17. *LaSalle Nat'l Bank of Chicago v. The County of DuPage* (Illinois), No. 82-6517, slip op. (N.D. Ill. Jan. 16, 1984).

18. *LaSalle Nat'l Bank v. County of Lake, Illinois*, 579 F. Supp. 8 (N.D. Ill. 1984).

The owners of certain land in the Village of Round Lake Park, Illinois, alleged that Lake County, in which Round Lake Park is located, and the Village of Grayslake, a neighboring community, concertedly denied their request for connection to the Lake County sewer system. In particular they alleged that Lake County had ceded to Grayslake the county's power to approve sewer connections, and that Grayslake had exercised that power against them in order to prevent the develoment of their land (despite the fact that they had granted the county easements over their land for the sewer system and had done so with the understanding that the system would serve them). The owners claimed, *inter alia,* that this conduct ran afoul of the antitrust laws. The defendants moved to dismiss this claim on state action grounds, but the court denied the motion.

19. *Lockary v. Kayfetz,* 1983-2 Trade Cases ¶ 65,594 (N.D. Cal. 1983); 1984-1 Trade Cases ¶ 65,839 (N.D. Cal. 1984).

Owners of undeveloped land claimed, *inter alia,* that the Bolinas (California) Community Public Utility's moratorium on water hook-ups transgressed the antitrust laws. The court dismissed the claim as barred by the state action doctrine.

20. *Mercy-Peninsula Ambulance, Inc. v. County of San Mateo,* 1984-2 Trade Cases ¶ 66,264 (N.D. Cal. 1984).

21. *Miami Int'l Realty Co. v. Town of Mt. Crested Butte, Colorado,* 579 F. Supp. 68 (D. Colo. 1984).

22. *Miller & Son Paving, Inc. v. Wrightstown Township Civic Ass'n,* 443 F. Supp. 1268 (E.D. Penn. 1978), *aff'd mem.* 595 F.2d 1213 (3d Cir.), *cert. denied,* 444 U.S. 843 (1979).

23. *Nelson v. Utah County* (Utah), 1978-1 Trade Cases ¶ 62,128 (D. Utah 1978).

Landowners claimed that Utah County officials had violated the antitrust laws by adopting an "unlawful" zoning ordinance and denying them building permits pursuant to a conspiracy with at least one rival in the real estate business. The County moved to dismiss the claim on the grounds that its conduct was exempt state action and did not have the jurisdictionally requisite connection with interstate commerce. The court denied the motion.

24. *City of North Olmstead, Ohio v. Greater Cleveland Regional Transit Authority,* 722 F.2d 1284 (6th Cir. 1983), *cert. denied,* 104 S. Ct. 2387 (1984).

In 1975 North Olmstead and the Greater Cleveland Regional Transit Authority (GCRTA) entered into an agreement whereby

North Olmstead promised to provide transit services within its boundaries and the GCRTA promised to provide funds to subsidize those services. When the agreement finally expired in 1980, the GCRTA began offering rival service and refused to make any more funds available to North Olmstead. North Olmstead claimed, *inter alia,* that by so doing the GCRTA was monopolizing bus service in the area in violation of section 2 of the Sherman Act. (North Olmstead similarly challenged GCRTA's allegedly "sham negotiations" regarding the renewal of the agreement and its allegedly "anti-competitive fare rates.") The GCRTA moved for summary judgment on this claim, asserting that its conduct was exempt from scrutiny under the antitrust laws. The district court granted its motion, and, on appeal, the Sixth Circuit affirmed.

25. *Omni Outdoor Advertising, Inc. v. Columbia Outdoor Advertising, Inc.* [and the City of Columbia, S.C.], 566 F. Supp. 1444 (D.S.C. 1983).

Columbia ordinances severely limited or banned the erection of billboards. Omni and Columbia Outdoor Advertising (COA) were both erectors and lessors of billboards, but Omni was a new entrant and COA already owned 95 percent of the billboards in the Columbia area. Omni claimed that the Columbia city council had passed these ordinances pursuant to a conspiracy with COA, and that it had thereby committed an antitrust offense. Columbia moved to dismiss this claim on *Parker v. Brown* grounds, but the court denied the motion.

26. *Ossler v. Village of Norridge,* 557 F. Supp. 219 (N.D. Ill. 1983).

The would-be developer of a condominium complex claimed, *inter alia,* that the Village of Norridge violated the antitrust laws by denying his request for rezoning (from single-family residences to multiple family units) while granting identical requests from the developers of "substantially similar developments . . . at substantially similar locations." The court dismissed this claim on the grounds that the developer failed to allege "anticompetitive motivations or consequences attending upon the conspiracy," and that the complaint itself foreclosed any such contention.

27. *Parks v. Dorey, Inc.,* 47 Antitrust & Trade Reg. Rep. 857 (W.D. Ark. 1984).

28. *Parks v. Watson*, 716 F.2d 646 (9th Cir. 1983).

Klamath Valley Co., co-owned by Parks, acquired land situated in Klamath Falls, Oregon, that contained geothermal wells. Klamath Valley planned to build apartment houses on this land, houses whose heat would come from the wells. Before Klamath Valley could implement its plan, however, it had to purchase the city's rights to certain platted streets. As part of the purchase price, the city, whose manager was Watson, demanded the dedication of a twenty-foot strip of property near the main road serving Klamath Valley's land. Dedication would have given the city rights to some of the geothermal wells. Klamath Valley refused the city's demands, and, of course, the city refused to vacate the platted streets. (Klamath Valley also considered selling some of the heat from its wells to those residing on nearby land. To do that, it had to obtain a utility franchise from the city, but the city refused it an application.) Klamath Valley brought suit claiming that the city had combined with others to unreasonably restrain the marketing of residential heating in violation of section 1 of the Sherman Act and that it had attempted to monopolize the "geothermal heating market" in violation of section 2. The city moved to dismiss these claims on the ground that Klamath Valley lacked standing to sue, and the district court granted the motion. On appeal, the Ninth Circuit reversed, rejecting the city's argument that the dismissal should be affirmed on the ground that its conduct was exempt from scrutiny.

29. *Security Fire Door Co. v. County of Los Angeles*, 484 F.2d 1028 (9th Cir. 1973).

In connection with the construction of a hospital, Los Angeles County invited bids for the supply of a dumbwaiter system. In an antitrust suit, Security Fire Door alleged that the county had drawn up the specifications for the system in concert with one of Security Fire Door's rivals so that only the rival would qualify to bid. The district court dismissed the suit on *Parker v. Brown* grounds. On appeal, the Ninth Circuit pointedly did not consider these grounds. Rather, it held that as a matter of law the challenged conduct did not constitute an antitrust offense. The Ninth Circuit's opinion is remarkably free of the analytical errors that have appeared all too frequently in the opinions of other courts faced with similar disputes.

30. *Springs Ambulance Service, Inc. v. City of Rancho Mirage, Cal.*, 1983-2 Trade Cases ¶ 65,646 (C.D. Cal. 1983); 1984-1 Trade Cases ¶ 66,014 (C.D. Cal.), *rev'd in part and remanded in part*, 1984-2 Trade Cases ¶ 66,261 (9th Cir. 1984).

In 1982, the County of Riverside (California), three cities within the county, and the cities' fire commission began operating an emergency ambulance service. According to Springs Ambulance, a privately owned provider of ambulance service that had been operating in Riverside County since 1967, these local governments (a) directed as many emergency calls as they could to their own provider; (b) required Springs Ambulance to post and adhere to a schedule of maximum rates for its services, and (c) set rates for their own provider's services at levels that were "below actual cost." On the basis of these allegations, Springs Ambulance brought suit against these local governments. The local governments moved to dismiss the suit on the grounds that their conduct was (1) immune under *Parker v. Brown* and (2) did not have the jurisdictionally requisite nexus with interstate commerce. The court, correctly, denied the motion. Subsequently it, incorrectly, ordered interim equitable relief for Springs Ambulance.

31. *Stauffer v. The Town of Grand Lake, Colo.*, 1981-1 Trade Cases ¶ 64,029 (D. Colo. 1980).

The owner of some Grand Lake property alleged that the members of the town's Planning Commission and Board of Trustees had rezoned his property single-family residential from multifamily in order to insulate their businesses from the competition of rivals who would have located there. He claimed, *inter alia*, that this conduct constituted an antitrust offense. The town moved to dismiss the claim on the grounds that its conduct was exempt state action, did not have the requisite connection with interstate commerce for the exercise of federal jurisdiction, and did not constitute an antitrust offense. The court denied the motion.

32. *Pete Thoesen Tractor & Equip. Repair Co. v. City of Chicago*, No. 83-8549, slip op. (N.D. Ill. April 27, 1984).

33. *Unity Ventures v. County of Lake, Illinois*, 1984-1 Trade Cases ¶ 65,883 (N.D. Ill. 1983).

As in *LaSalle Nat'l Bank v. County of Lake*, which is annotated in this section of the Appendix, a group of landowners challenged as an antitrust offense the refusal of Lake County and the Village of Grayslake to permit interconnection with the Lake County sewer system. (These landowners similarly challenged three lawsuits brought by the local governments against them which were designed to block the development of their land.) The county and the village moved to dismiss the landowners' suit on four grounds: (1) that their conduct did not have the jurisdictionally requisite connection with interstate commerce; (2) that the landowners lacked standing; (3) that their conduct was exempt from antitrust scrutiny under *Parker v. Brown*, and (4) as a matter of law, that their conduct did not constitute an antitrust offense. The court denied the motion. Subsequently, the jury found in favor of the landowners and the court entered a judgment accordingly for $28.5 million on the antitrust claim. 46 Antitrust & Trade Reg. Rep 595 (N.D. Ill. 1984).

34. *Vickery Manor Service Corp. v. Village of Mundelein* (Ill.), 575 F. Supp. 996 (N.D. Ill. 1983).

Owners of land situated in the Village of Mundelein offered to sell it to a housing developer. Before accepting their offer, the developer inquired of Village officials whether he could obtain the required permits to proceed with his plan. The officials made it clear that sewage treatment would be a problem. Vickery Manor Service Corp., a privately owned utility in the business of treating sewage, stood ready to provide the necessary service. Village officials, however, refused to issue the required permits unless the developer promised to take over the operation of Vickery Manor, invest substantial sums in its facilities, and pay for its eventual displacement by the Village's own sewer system (except for high-cost service areas outside the village—village officials demanded that the developer promise that he would provide sewage treatment for the residents of those areas even after the remainder of Vickery Manor had been displaced). The developer declined to make these promises so he was unable to obtain the permits that he needed. He therefore rejected the landowners' offer. The landowners and Vickery Manor then brought suit against the Village, claiming that it was attempting to monopolize sewage treatment service in violation of the antitrust laws. The Village moved to dismiss the suit on state action grounds, but the court denied the motion.

35. *Westborough Mall, Inc. v. City of Cape Girardeau, Mo.*, 532 F. Supp. 284 (E.D. Mo. 1981), *rev'd and remanded*, 693 F.2d 733 (8th Cir. 1982), *cert. denied*, 103 S. Ct. 2122 (1983).

In 1974 the would-be developers of the Westborough Mall persuaded Cape Girardeau to rezone their land C-4, which they needed to do before they could begin building. Unfortunately for them, they were not nearly as successful in taking the other steps they had to take. In fact, by 1979 they had made no progress toward bringing the mall into being. In that year Cape Girardeau's City Manager directed that the zoning maps be changed to reflect his mistaken belief that their C-4 classification had lapsed and instructed the City Engineer to refrain from issuing building permits for their land.

The would-be developers subsequently claimed, *inter alia*, that the City Manager gave these orders pursuant to a conspiracy between Cape Girardeau and the successful developers of another mall, which was built during the same period in the same metropolitan area, to "monopolize the regional shopping center market" in greater Cape Girardeau. On this claim, the district court entered summary judgment for the defendants, ruling that the City Manager's conduct was exempt state action, that it was not taken pursuant to any conspiracy, and that it had had no effect on the would-be developer's proposed mall. On appeal, the Eighth Circuit reversed and remanded.

36. *Whitworth v. Perkins*, 559 F.2d 378 (5th Cir. 1977), *vacated* (for reconsideration in light of *Lafayette*), 435 U.S. 992, *aff'd on reh'g per curiam*, 576 F.2d 696, *reh'g denied*, 580 F.2d 1052 (5th Cir. 1978), *cert. denied*, 440 U.S. 911 (1979).

Perkins incorporated the City of Impact, Texas, near Abilene, in Taylor County. Abilene and Taylor banned the selling of alcoholic beverages, but Impact permitted it. That was Impact's *raison d'etre*. Impact did ban such selling, however, from lots that had been zoned residential. Whitworth purchased such a lot and requested Impact's permission to sell alcohol from it. Impact denied his request, and he brought suit claiming, *inter alia*, that that denial constituted an antitrust offense. Impact moved to dismiss the claim as barred by the state action doctrine. The district court granted the motion, but the Fifth Circuit reversed and remanded. The Supreme Court vacated that decision for reconsideration in light of *Lafayette* and, on remand, the Fifth Circuit reaffirmed it.

See also: *City of Auburn, Indiana v. Mavis*, 1984-2 Trade Cases ¶ 66,219 (Indiana Court of Appeals 1984).

Goodner v. Bachofner, 1977-1 Trade Cases ¶ 61,369 (Wash. Super. Ct. 1977).

Jeffrey v. Southwestern Bell, 518 F.2d 1129 (5th Cir. 1975).

George R. Whitten, Jr., Inc. v. Paddock Pool Builders, Inc., 424 F.2d 25 (1st Cir. 1970), *cert. denied*, 400 U.S. 850 (1970), *on remand*, 376 F. Supp. 125 (D. Mass.), *aff'd*, 508 F.2d 547 (1st Cir. 1974), *cert. denied*, 421 U.S. 1004 (1975).

Meetinghouse Associates v. Warwick Township [Penn.], 1984-1 Trade Cases ¶ 66,045 (E.D. Penn. 1984).

BIBLIOGRAPHY

ARTICLES

Alchian & Demsetz. *Production, Information Costs, and Economic Organization*, 62 Am. Econ. Rev. 777 (1972).

Areeda. *Antitrust Immunity for "State Action" after Lafayette*, 95 Harv. L. Rev. 435 (1981).

Areeda & Turner. *Predatory Pricing and Related Practices under Section 2 of the Sherman Act*, 88 Harv. L. Rev. 697 (1975).

Averch & Johnson. *Behavior of the Firm under Regulatory Constraint*, 52 Am. Econ. Rev. 1052 (1962).

Bangasser. *Exposure of Municipal Corporations to Liability for Violations of the Antitrust Laws: Antitrust Immunity after the City of Lafayette Decision*, 11 Urb. L. Rev. vii (1979).

Baumol. *Quasi-Permanence of Price Reductions: A Policy for Prevention of Predatory Pricing*, 29 Yale L.J. 1 (1979).

Bosselman and Bonder. *Potential Immunity of Land Use Control Systems from Civil Rights and Antitrust Liability*, 8 Hastings Const. L.Q. 453 (1981).

Brennan. *Local Government Action and Antitrust Policy: An Economic Analysis*, 12 Fordham Urb. L.J. 405 (1984).

Butler & Baysinger. *Vertical Restraints of Trade as Contractual Integration: A Synthesis of Relational Contracting Theory, Transaction-Cost Economics, and Organization Theory*, 32 Emory L. J. 1009 (1983).

Carrel. *Annual Survey of Antitrust Developments (1977-1978)*, 36 Wash. & Lee L. Rev. 36 (1979).

Center for Economic and Management Research, University of Oklahoma. "A Process for Setting Community and State Policies Regarding EMS System Performance Capabilities" (unpublished paper 1974).

Cirace. *An Economic Analysis of the "State-Municipal Action" Antitrust Cases*, 61 Tex. L. Rev. 481 (1982).

Civiletti. *The Fallout from Community Communications Co. v. City of Boulder: Prospects for a Legislative Solution*, 32 Cath. U.L. Rev. 379 (1983).

Coase. *The Nature of the Firm*, 4 Economica 386 (1937).

———. *The Problem of Social Cost*, 3 J. Law & Econ. 1 (1960).

Curtin. *Antitrust Comes to the Cities—Analysis of City of Lafayette v. Louisiana Power and Light Co. and Its Effect on Municipal Antitrust Liability*, 5 U. Dayton L. Rev. 7 (1980).

Dabney. *Antitrust Aspects of Anticompetitive Zoning*, 24 Antitrust Bulletin 435 (1979).

Dale. *Boulder's Far Reaching Impact: An Impediment to Home Rule?* 4 Nat'l L.J., Mar. 29, 1982, at 32, col. 1.

Demsetz. *Some Aspects of Property Rights*, 9 J. Law & Econ. 61 (1966).

———. *Why Regulate Utilities?*, 11 J. Law & Econ. 55 (1968).

Deutsch. *Antitrust Challenges to Local Land Use Control*, 60 Chi.-Kent L. Rev. 63 (1984).

Driker & Shore. *Community Communications v. Boulder—New Problems for Municipalities, Antitrust Liability*, 61 Mich. B.J. 426 (1982).

Easterbrook. *Predatory Strategies and Counterstrategies*, 48 U. Chi. L. Rev. 263 (1981).

Elzinga. *Predatory Pricing: The Case of the Gunpowder Trust*, 13 J. Law & Econ. 223 (1970).

Fama. *Agency Problems and the Theory of the Firm*, 88 J. Pol. Econ. 288 (1980).

Freilich & Donovan. *Antitrust Liability and Preemption of Authority: Trends and Developments in Urban, State and Local Government Law*, 15 Urb. Law. 705 (1983).

Goldberg. *Regulation and Administered Contracts*, 7 Bell J. Econ. 426 (1976).

Goodrich. *The Limits of Municipal Power*, 4 Cal. Law. 26 (1984).

Henderson. *Municipal Ownership of Cable Television: Some Issues and Problems*, 3 J. Com. & Entertainment L. 667 (1981).

Hermann. *Airports and the Applicability of the Antitrust Laws*, 45 Albany L. Rev. 351 (1981).

Hirshleifer. *Economics from a Biological Standpoint*, 20 J. Law & Econ. 1 (1977).

Hoskins. *Boulder Revolution in Municipal Antitrust Law*, 70 Ill. B.J. 684 (1982).

Jacobs. *Antitrust and the Public Defendant: Application of the Antitrust Laws to Governmental Entities*, 9 U. Dayton L. Rev. 451 (1984).

James. *Municipal Defenses to Antitrust Liability*, 6 U. Ark. Little Rock L.J. 273 (1983).

Jenson & Meckling. *Theory of the Firm: Managerial Behavior, Agency Costs and Ownership Structure*, 3 J. Fin. Econ. 35 (1976).

Joskow. *The Effects of Competition and Regulation on Hospital Bed Supply and the Reservation Quality of the Hospital*, 11 Bell J. Econ. 421 (1980).

Joskow & Klevorick. *A Framework for Analyzing Predatory Pricing Policy*, 89 Yale L.J. 213 (1979).

Kelty. *Antitrust Do's and Don'ts*, 19 Ill. St. B.A. Sec. on Local Gov't L., Aug. 1982, at 1.

Klein, Crawford & Allen. *Vertical Integration Appropriable Rents, and the Competitive Contracting Process*, 21 J. Law & Econ. 297 (1978).

Klitzke. *Antitrust Liability of Municipal Corporations: The Per Se Rule vs. The Rule of Reason—A Reasonable Compromise*, 1980 Ariz. St. L.J. 253 (1980).

Lee. *Antitrust: A Collage of Vertical Territorial Restraints, Tying and Monopoloy "Misuse," Arbitrability, and the General Dynamics Defense*, 55 Chi.-Kent L. Rev. 1 (1979).

———. *Economic Regulation of Business: The Seventh Circuit's Non-Economic Approach*, 56 Chi.-Kent L. Rev. 205 (1980).

———. *Antitrust: Market Definition, the Section Two Offenses and Literalism*, 57 Chi.-Kent L. Rev. 25 (1981).

Lerner. *Community Communications Co. v. City of Boulder: Forcing a Reorganization of the State-Municipality Relationship Through the Antitrust Laws*, 60 U. Det. J. Urb. L. 241 (1983).

Lester. *Municipal Antitrust Liability after Boulder*, 36 Okla. L. Rev. 827 (1983).

Levin. *The Antitrust Challenge to Local Government Protection of the Central Business District*. 55 Colo. L. Rev. 21 (1983).

Malciauskas & Rasnak. *Local Government Exposure to Antitrust Liability and Treble Damage Awards in the Wake of City of Lafayette and City of Boulder*, 15 Loy. U. Chi. L.J. 645 (1984).

Marvel. *Exclusive Dealing*, 25 J. Law & Econ. 1 (1982).

McMahon. *Recent Significant Developments in "State Action" and Noerr-Pennington Exemptions: From Boulder to the "Sham" Exception*, 14 U. Tol. L. Rev. 531 (1983).

McGee. *Predatory Price Cutting: The Standard Oil (N.J.) Case*, 1 J. Law & Econ. 137 (1958).

———. *Predatory Pricing Revisited*, 23 J. Law & Econ. 289 (1980).

Melton. *The State Action Antitrust Defense for Local Governments: A State Authorization Approach*, 12 Urb. Law. 315 (1980).

P. Posner. *The Proper Relationship Between State Regulations and the Federal Antitrust Laws*, 49 N.Y.U.L. Rev. 728-32 (1974).

R. Posner. *The Rule of Reason and the Economic Approach: Reflections on the Sylvania Decision*, 45 U. Chi. L. Rev. 1 (1977).

———. *The Chicago School of Antitrust Analysis*, 127 U. Pa. L. Rev. 925, 939-44 (1979).

———. *The Next Step in the Antitrust Treatment of Restricted Distribution: Per Se Legality*, 48 U. Chi. L. Rev. 6 (1981).

Rose. *Municipal Activities and the Antitrust Laws after City of Lafayette*, 57 Univ. Det. J. Urb. L. 483 (1979).

Rubin. *Theory of the Firm and the Structure of the Franchise Contract* 21 J. Law & Econ. 223 (1978).

Schenefield. *The Parker v. Brown State Action Doctrine and the New Federalism of Antitrust*, 51 Antitrust L.J. vii (1983).

Scherer. *Predatory Pricing and the Sherman Act: A Comment*, 89 Harv. L. Rev. 869 (1976).

———. *Some Last Words on Predatory Pricing*, 89 Harv. L. Rev. 901 (1976).

Simon. *Rationality as Process and as Product of Thought*, 68 Am. Econ. Rev. 1 (1978).

Sims. *Antitrust Comes to City Hall*, 3 Regulation 35 (1979).

Slater. *Antitrust and Government Action: A Formula for Narrowing Parker v. Brown*, 69 Nw. U.L. Rev. 71 (1974).

———. *Local Government and State Action Immunity after City of Lafayette and City of Boulder*, 51 Antitrust L.J. 349 (1983).

Smith. *Antitrust Immunity for State Action: A Functional Approach*, 31 Baylor L. Rev. 563 (1979).

Spiegel. *Local Governments and the Terror of Antitrust*, 69 A.B.A. J. 163 (1983).

Strauss & Stegman. *Moderate-Cost Housing after Lafayette: A Proposal*, 11 Urb. Law. 209 (1979).

Symposium. 32 Cath. U. L. Rev. 371 (1982).

Taurman. *Reflection on City of Lafayette v. Louisiana Power and Light Co.: Applying the Antitrust "State Action" Exemption to Local Governments*, 13 Urb. Law. 159 (1981).

Venderstar. *Liability of Municipalities under the Antitrust Laws: Litigation Strategies*, 32 Cath. U.L. Rev. 395 (1983).

Wiley. *Boulder Unanswered Questions: The Future of Cable Franchising*, 4 Nat'l L.J., Mar. 29, 1982, at 33, col. 1.

O. Williamson. *The Vertical Integration of Production: Market Failure Considerations*, 61 Am. Econ. Rev. 112 (1971).

———. *The Economics of Antitrust: Transaction Cost Considerations*, 122 U. Pa. L. Rev. 1439 (1974).

———. *Franchise Bidding for Natural Monopolies—In General and with Respect to CATV*, 7 Bell J. Econ. 73 (1976).

———. *Predatory Pricing: A Strategic and Welfare Analysis*, 87 Yale L.J. 284 (1978).

———. *Assessing Vertical Market Restrictions: Antitrust Ramifications of the Transaction Cost Approach*, 127 U. Pa. L. Rev. 953 (1979).

——— . *Predatory Pricing II*, 88 Yale L.J. 1183 (1979).

———. *The Modern Corporation: Origins, Evolution, Attributes*, 29 J. Econ. Lit. 1537 (1981).

R. Williamson. *The Reagan Administration's Position on Antitrust Liability of Municipalities*, 32 Cath. U.L. Rev. 371 (1982).

Witt. *Antitrust Law and the Boulder Case: New Threat to the Planning and Zoning Process*, 1983 Inst. on Planning, Zoning and Eminent Domain 75 (1983).

BOOKS

A. Alchian & W. Allen. Exchange and Production: Competition, Coordination, and Control. Belmont, California: Wadsworth Publishing Co., 1977.

P. Areeda & D. Turner. Antitrust Law: An Analysis of Antitrust Principles and Their Application. Boston: Little, Brown & Co., 1978.

R. Bork. The Antitrust Paradox: A Policy at War with Itself. New York: Basic Books, 1978.

W. Bowman. Patents and Antitrust Law: A Legal and Economic Appraisal. Chicago: University of Chicago Press, 1973.

J. Buchanan & G. Tullock. The Calculus of Consent. Ann Arbor: University of Michigan Press, 1962.

E. Goffman. Strategic Interaction. Philadelphia: University of Philadelphia Press, 1969.

A. Kahn. The Economics of Regulation: Principles and Institutions. New York: John Wiley & Sons, 1970.

C. Kaysen & D. Turner. Antitrust Policy: An Economic and Legal Analysis. Cambridge: Harvard University Press, 1965.

D. Mueller. Public Choice. New York: Cambridge University Press, 1979.

National Commission for the Review of Antitrust Laws and Procedures. Report to the President and the Attorney General. 1979.

A. Neale. The Antitrust Laws of the United States, 3rd ed. New York: Cambridge University Press, 1980.

M. Olson, Jr.. The Logic of Collective Action. Cambridge: Harvard University Press, 1965.

A. Polinsky. An Introduction to Law and Economics. Boston: Little, Brown & Co., 1983.

R. Posner. Antitrust Law: An Economic Perspective. Chicago: University of Chicago Press, 1976.

T. Schelling. The Strategy of Conflict. Cambridge: Harvard University Press, 1960.

G. Stigler. The Organization of Industry. Homewood, Ill.: R.D. Irwin, 1968.

L. Sullivan. Handbook of the Law of Antitrust. St. Paul: West Publishing Co., 1977.

G. Tullock. The Logic of Law. New York: Basic Books, 1971.

O. Williamson. Markets and Hierarchies: Analysis and Antitrust Implications. New York: Free Press, Macmillan Co., 1975.

NOTES AND COMMENTS: *Lafayette, Boulder,* and the Liability of Local Governments

Comment. *The Antitrust Liability of Municipalities Under the Parker Doctrine,* 57 Boston U.L. Rev. 368 (1977).

Comment. *The Airport Car Rental Concession: The Role of City of Lafayette v. Louisiana Power & Light Co. in Restricting Threats to Free Competition,* 14 Cal. Western L. Rev. 325 (1978).

Comment. *Alternative Approaches to Municipal Antitrust Liability,* 11 Fordham Urb. L.J. 51 (1982).

Comment. *The Preemption Alternative to Municipal Antitrust Liability,* 51 Geo. Wash. L. Rev. 145 (1982).

Comment. *Municipal Liability to Antitrust Suits: A Proposal for a "Governmental Action" Defense,* 21 Hous. L. Rev. 209 (1984).

Comment. *Antitrust Liability for Municipal Airport Operations: Will it Fly?* 49 J. Air L. & Com. 245 (1983).

Comment. *The State Action Doctrine and State Antitrust Laws—Thirty-five Years of Struggle,* 30 Mercer L. Rev. 1039 (1979).

Comment. *State Action Antitrust Immunity: The Parker Doctrine's Application to Municipalities,* 8 Ohio North L. Rev. 513 (1981).

Comment. *Federalism, Antitrust and Illinois Home Rule,* 1983 S. Ill. U.L.J. 31.

Comment. *Post Lafayette Municipal Liability for Refusing to Zone Outlying Development,* 59 Wash. U.L.Q. 485 (1981).

Note. 64 A.B.A.J. 742 (1978) (Lafayette).

Note. 68 A.B.A.J. 344 (1982) (Boulder).

Note. 69 A.B.A.J. 66 (1983) (Boulder).

Note. 17 Am. Bus. L.J. 386 (1979) (Lafayette).

Note. 1980 Ariz. St. L.J. 245 (1980) (Lafayette).

Note. 31 Baylor L. Rev. 563 (1979) (Lafayette).

Note. 35 Baylor L. Rev. 791 (1983) (Affiliated Capital Corp. v. City of Houston).

Note. 24 B.C.L. Rev. 1399 (1983) (Boulder).

Note. 45 Brooklyn L. Rev. 165 (1978) (Lafayette).

Note. 49 Brooklyn L. Rev. 259 (1983) (Boulder).

Note. 4 Cardozo L. Rev. 199 (1983) (Boulder).
Note. 34 Case W. Res. 303 (1984) (Boulder).
Note. 32 Cath. U.L. Rev. 413 (1983) (Boulder).
Note. 79 Colum. L. Rev. 518 (1979) (Lafayette).
Note. 5 Com. & L. 39 (1983) (Boulder).
Note. 11 Conn. L. Rev. 126 (1978) (Lafayette).
Note. 1979 Det. Coll. L. Rev. 299 (1979) (Lafayette).
Note. 28 Drake L. Rev. 513 (1978) (Lafayette).
Note. 21 Duq. L. Rev. 709 (1983) (Boulder).
Note. 30 Fed. Bar News & J. 227 (1983) (Boulder).
Note. 92 Harv. L. Rev. 277 (1978) (Lafayette).
Note. 96 Harv. L. Rev. 268 (1982) (Boulder).
Note. 28 Kan. L. Rev. 166 (1979) (Lafayette).
Note. 24 Loyola L. Rev. 804 (1978) (Lafayette).
Note. 61 Mich. B.J. 426 (1982) (Boulder).
Note. 3 Miss. C.L. Rev. 149 (1982) (Boulder).
Note. 49 Miss. L.J. 725 (1978) (Lafayette).
Note. 23 Nat. Resources J. 711 (1983) (Lafayette).
Note. 57 Neb. L. Rev. 1140 (1978) (Whitworth v. Perkins).
Note. 25 S.D.L. Rev. 314 (1980) (Lafayette).
Note. 12 Seton Hall L. Rev. 835 (1982) (Boulder).
Note. 16 Suffolk U.L. Rev. 821 (1982) (Boulder).
Note. 47 U. Cin. L. Rev. 469 (1978) (Lafayette).
Note. 57 U. Det. J. Urb. L. 483 (1980) (Lafayette).
Note. 5 U. Hawaii L. Rev. 327 (1983) (Boulder).
Note. 16 U. Rich. L. Rev. 705 (1982) (Boulder).
Note. 18 Urb. L. Ann. 265 (1980) (Lafayette).
Note. 11 Urb. Law. vii (1979) (Lafayette).
Note. 11 Urb. Law. 209 (1979) (Lafayette).
Note. 14 Urb. Law. v (1982) (Boulder).
Note. 1983 Utah L. Rev. 139 (Boulder).
Note. 35 Vand. L. Rev. 1041 (1982) (Boulder).
Note. 15 Wake Forest L. Rev. 89 (1979) (Lafayette).
Note. 36 Wash. & Lee L. Rev. 129 (1979) (Lafayette).
Note. 40 Wash. & Lee L. Rev. 143 (1983) (Boulder).
Note. 9 Wash. St. U.L. Rev. 113 (1982) (Boulder).
Note. 25 Wash. U.J. Urb. & Contemp. L. 297 (1983) (Boulder).
Note. 58 Wash. U.L.Q. 1026 (1980) (Boulder).
Note. 18 Washburn L.J. 129 (1978) (Lafayette).
Note. 1979 Wisc. L. Rev. 570 (1979) (Lafayette).

TABLE OF CASES

Cases in **boldface** are discussed in the text. Other cases are merely cited.

INDEX

About the Author

MARK R. LEE is Professor of Law at Southern Illinois University, Carbondale. He served as antitrust consultant to the prevailing defendant in *Kurek v. Pleasure Driveway and Park District*, the first antitrust claim against a local government to go to trial on the merits following the Supreme Court's landmark decision in *Lafayette* and as an attorney for the Antitrust Division of the United States Department of Justice. He is the author of a number of articles appearing in legal periodicals.